"Jennifer is passionate about both the art of writing and the science of forensics. This accessible overview of criminal investigation is a valuable tool for anyone trying to combine the two."
— Sheryl J. Anderson, writer, *Killer Heels, Charmed, Flash Gordon, Who Is Simon Miller?*

"I've been writing forensic procedurals for over seven years and I've read every forensic reference out there, so believe me when I say *Forensic Speak* is the only one you'll ever need. This book not only defines the current principles of forensic science, but also gives you the terminology to put in your characters' mouths and shows how to use them dramatically. After reading *Forensic Speak*, I have to admit I was mad ... where was Jennifer when I was starting out? This book would've saved me hours of research."
— Brian Davidson, writer/producer, *CSI: Miami*

"*Forensic Speak* is a great dictionary of death investigation. But Dornbush takes the extra step of showing writers how to employ the terminology, which serves as both inspiration and insurance that the language is expressed accurately. I only wish there were a way to download this directly into one's brain."
— Wendy West, executive producer, *Dexter*

"From crime scene investigation to toxicology to fingerprints to DNA, guns, and courtroom procedures, *Forensic Speak* gives writers a concise and easy-to-understand guide to making their stories more believable. The book covers important terms and . . . reduces the amount of research writers have to undertake in order to craft realistic crime stories. It's a great resource."
— Tom Farr, Tom Farr Reviews, *http://tom-farr.blogspot.com*

"I highly recommend this book to any crime writer. Very informative, useful, and best of all realistic and factual material. Definitely a must-have reference book."
— Cristina E. Fish, forensic specialist, Pasadena Police Department

"If you write TV or films about crime, this book is as i... cup of coffee. Rather than drop down the procrastination rabbit hole of Internet research, you can turn to *Forensic Speak* for the technical terms that make you sound savvy, those authentic details that make the end of your act sing. Dornbush writes about the intricate and specific details of forensics in a way you can understand well enough to make her genius your own. It's like cheating, without the guilt."
— Liz Garcia, executive producer/co-creator, *Memphis Beat*; writer/producer, *Cold Case*

"*Forensic Speak* should be in every crime writer's library. Jennifer Dornbush takes a grimly serious topic and makes it easy to understand, highly entertaining, and even fun."
— Tess Gerritsen, mystery/thriller novelist, *Harvest, Life Support, Bloodstream, The Surgeon*

"A writer's greatest aim is to sound honest and truthful in whatever they're writing. So I can only imagine that touching this book is like the literary equivalent of putting on Green Lantern's ring; use it, and instead of power, you feel yourself surging with enough knowledge to write authentic crime stories and characters."
— Chad Gervich, writer/producer, *Dog with a Blog, After Lately, Cupcake Wars*; author, *Small Screen, Big Picture: A Writer's Guide to the TV Business*

"Jennifer Dornbush takes you on an incredible journey of understanding the inner workings of a crime scene. I couldn't put the book down. She knows what she's talking about because she grew up in this world. You will be shocked by what she uncovers. When you finish the book, you will feel like an expert. This is a valuable tool and a secret weapon for any writer that wants to write a crime drama and have it come across in an authentic way. I highly recommend it."
— Jen Grisanti, story consultant, Jen Grisanti Consultancy, Inc.; writing instructor, Writers on the Verge, NBC; former studio executive and author, *Story Line: Finding Gold in Your Life Story, TV Writing Tool Kit*, and *Change Your Story, Change Your Life: A Path To Your Success* (forthcoming)

"This is an excellent, quick reference book I wish I had had when I first started writing crime stories. It has all the gory details."
— Aaron Guzikowski, writer, *Contraband*, *Prisoners* (forthcoming)

"Those of us who toil in the career field always appreciate writers who are able to write about the forensic sciences with authenticity and truth. Jennifer Dornbush has written a terrific guide for writers at all levels."
— Craig R. Harvey, F-ABMDI, chief coroner investigator and chief of operations, Department of Coroner, County of Los Angeles

"Where has this book been for the past ten years? Like a machete in the jungle, *Forensic Speak* cuts through the technical complexities of forensic science to carve a clear path for procedural writers, whether aspiring or experienced. Fusing encyclopedic knowledge to a common-sense approach, this book is a must-have for anyone who spends their days writing dead people.
— Chris Levinson, writer/executive producer, *Touch*, *Lone Star*, *Law & Order*, *Charmed*

"*Forensic Speak* is the perfect crime procedural writer's companion! From the layout to the table of contents to chapter examples, Jen Dornbush makes the material accessible, engaging, and intriguing. I found the various sections (especially on Electronic Crime Scene Investigation, Fabrication, and the different types of evidence) loaded with bite-size, digestible nuggets of great information that are invaluable to writers both aspiring and professional. *Forensic Speak* is a must for those that want to take their crime scene writing to the next level!"
— Monica Macer, writer/producer, *Lost*, *Prison Break*, *Teen Wolf*, *The Playboy Club*, *Deception*

"Jennifer Dornbush›s *Forensic Speak* would have saved me days, even weeks, of research while writing *Déjà Vu*. For the screenwriter who aspires to authenticity, this book is invaluable. For the screenwriter who does not, please quit now."
— Bill Marsilii, screenwriter, *Déjà Vu*, *Blood of the Innocent*

"The daughter of a medical examiner, Jennifer Dornbush grew up in a household where death was neither feared nor shunned but simply a fact of everyday life. This background gives her a unique perspective from which to denote the ABCs of CSI. Engrossing but not gross, Dornbush's book is an invaluable overview for readers who want to separate fact from fiction in this burgeoning field. I highly recommend *Forensic Speak* for writers, students, viewers, or anyone else who seeks to expand their knowledge base."
— Thomas Parham, Ph.D., professor, co-chair, Department of Theater, Film, and Television, Azusa Pacific University

"It's my job to come up with intriguing forensic clues in my scripts, but man, has Jennifer Dornbush made it easier. *Forensic Speak* has it all: practical explanations, anecdotes, and exhaustive research in an easy-to-digest book. A great resource written by a generous and intelligent writer."
— Janet Tamaro, creator, writer, executive producer, TNT's *Rizzoli & Isles*

"Whether you are writing the next blockbuster feature crime thriller, mystery novel, or procedural TV or Web series, don't submit it until you've had a chance to get *Forensic Speak*. Author Jennifer Dornbush lays bare the facts and jargon needed to give your project the authenticity to set it apart. And to make things a snap, she's organized it in chapters that will make it easy for you to look things up by subject. In addition, she's provided exercises and a handy reference/resource section to make even the most tongue-tied writer sound like he's right at home in the crime lab!"
— Kathie Fong Yoneda, consultant, workshop leader, and author of *The Script-Selling Game: A Hollywood Insider's Look at Getting Your Script Sold and Produced*

4/20/13

Harry —
Thank you for all
your service and
years of protecting
Los Angeles!

JDornbush

HOW TO WRITE REALISTIC CRIME DRAMAS JENNIFER DORNBUSH

FORENSIC SPEAK

MICHAEL WIESE PRODUCTIONS

Published by Michael Wiese Productions

12400 Ventura Blvd. #1111

Studio City, CA 91604

(818) 379-8799, (818) 986-3408 (FAX)

mw@mwp.com

www.mwp.com

Cover design by Johnny Ink. www.johnnyink.com

Interior design by William Morosi

Printed by McNaughton & Gunn

Manufactured in the United States of America

Copyright 2013 by Jennifer Dornbush

Library of Congress Cataloging-in-Publication Data

Dornbush, Jennifer, 1971-

Forensic speak : how to write realistic crime dramas / Jennifer Dornbush.

   p. cm.

ISBN 978-1-61593-131-6

1. Television authorship. 2. Television authorship--Handbooks, manuals, etc. 3. Detective and mystery television programs. I. Title.

PN1996.D65 2013

808'.066791--dc23

2012028049

Printed on Recycled Stock

MIX
Paper from responsible sources
FSC® C011935

FSC
www.fsc.org

DEDICATION

For Dad, Mom, Melanie, and Amy — where it all began

In memory of Jack Gilbert, my friend and writing mentor

"Keep death always before your eyes."
— The Holy Rule of St. Benedict

TABLE OF CONTENTS

Special Thanks and Acknowledgments

Dr. Ronald E. Graeser, D.O., Medical Examiner, Retired

Gail Graeser, Office Manager, Newaygo County Medical Examiner's Office, Retired

Dr. Janis Cavanaugh, Professor, East Los Angeles College, Founder of the Forensic Science Academy, and Retired Police Chief of Rowland Unified School District

Diana Castro, Principal Forensic Prints Specialist, Los Angeles Police Department, Retired

Cristina Fish, Forensic Specialist, Pasadena, California

Margaret Bernal, Judge of the Los Angeles Superior Court

Helen Wolcott, M.S. Criminalistics, California State University Los Angeles

T. Prince, Forensic Chemist/Toxicologist, San Luis Obispo County Sheriff's Office

Terry Armenta, Husbandry Services Supervisor, City of Hope/Beckman Research Institute

Melissa Gonzalez, Coroner Intern, Los Angeles County Department of the Coroner

The Forensic Science Academy, *www.forensicscienceacademy.org*

Lieutenant Brian Elias, Los Angeles County Department of the Coroner

Chief Craig Harvey, Los Angeles County Department of the Coroner

Martin Gostanian, The Paley Center for Media, Museum of Radio and Television

Dr. Karen Crabb for being my blood spatter guinea pig and photographer. I certify that no human or animal blood was used in the creation of this manuscript.

My TV Writers Group: Anthony, Mollie, Ben, Kari, Melissa, Jessica, Monica, and Amy, for supporting me as I wrote this book and being awesome sounding boards.

Zoila for strongly suggesting I write this book and pointing me to MWP.

Amy Graeser for her keen editing eye, patience, attention to detail, and awesome scones.

Michael Wiese Publishing, especially: Michael Wiese, Ken Lee, Manny Otto, Pamela Grieman, John Brenner, and William Morosi.

And finally, thank you to my husband, Ryan, for putting up with me and my forensic family with humor and grace.

Introduction

Long before American television was saturated with *CSI*, *Forensic Files*, *Bones*, *Criminal Minds*, and multitudes of similar shows, I was living my own weekly CSI adventure with my family in rural, northern Michigan. My father began his medical examiner career in 1973 and my mother assisted as office manager, accountant, and counselor. They ran the office out of our home because the county was too poor to provide him with a proper office and storage.

Dad performed autopsies at the small county hospital morgue, and all the records, paperwork, and photographs were kept in our family office. Samples of blood and tissue were stored in a basement freezer, right under the pork chops and frozen beans like some B-rated horror flick. Dinnertime conversations often revolved around the case of the week. "Let me tell you about an interesting suicide I saw today. Oh, and pass the corn, please."

Dad investigated an average of one hundred deaths a year. Accidents, suicides, natural deaths, and scores of drunk-driving fatalities filled Dad's days and nights and kept food in the cupboards. During the twenty-three years Dad worked in forensics, I had a one-on-one education about how people died, why they died, why they were murdered (sex, drugs, money), and how to prove a person's death. Being around death investigation was as natural as brushing my teeth.

Our family's existence appeared strange if you were looking in from the outside. One Sunday after church, when I was about ten, my father toted us all to the local airstrip. A single-engine plane had crashed the night before and Dad wanted to return to the scene in daylight to scour the area for any remaining body pieces. My younger sister and I paired up to help him. Outfitted in our Sunday best, we roamed the damp field beyond the runway that early spring morning in search of brain matter and skullcap. And, yes, we found some.

Until my twenties, I felt the need to hide what my father did for a living from my friends. We were living in a pre-CSI generation before TV glamorized forensics. I didn't know a single other person my age whose father kept body bags in his truck and smelled like formaldehyde when he came home from work. It was weird and icky to me. And, as a young teenage girl, I already felt grossly out of place in my own skin. Dad's work was a constant reminder of just how strange my family was and how strangely my peers might perceive me. Ironically, my friends found the family business intriguing, and, to this day, I can't remember a single time I was teased about what my father did for a living — at least not in front of me.

One of the first times I remember my home life intersecting with my social life was in third grade. I had the new girl over to play in our fort in the barn loft. She became intrigued by a fifty-five-gallon barrel in the middle of our barn floor. She wanted to take a look inside despite my strong discouragement. Eventually, she weaseled the truth out of me. I told her, "There's a man's leg in that barrel." Dad was preserving it for a case he was working on. It thrilled her. She carefully slid the top off the barrel and peeked in. It was wrapped in thick plastic. I cowered back as the rank smell of decomp and formaldehyde wafted out. Would she uncover the leg? Silently I prayed that she would chicken out. Not a chance. She peeled back that plastic, and a cross section of thigh stared back at both of us. She took a good hard look and then, satisfied, wrapped it back up and put the lid on. I wanted to puke, but she didn't seem a bit fazed and climbed back up the ladder to play.

By my senior year in high school I was becoming a little more comfortable about letting people into the family business. My friends and I hosted a Halloween party for our senior class at my house. Our family home is fairly secluded and sits on twenty acres of land. My friends and I designed a haunted hunt through the fields and woods. The prize for making it through was a scary viewing of Sam, our family skeleton. Sam was a real human skeleton that a doctor friend of my Dad's bequeathed him. Sam lived in our barn and Dad stuck a cigarette between his teeth. He teased that Sam's demise was lung cancer. During college Sam and I formed a closer bond when I used him to help me learn my bones for anatomy class.

As I grew older, I allowed my most trusted friends into the family business. During my freshman year of college, my best friend, who was studying to be a nurse, would often assist my Dad with his autopsies. She considered her time in the morgue superb training for a nursing career. One weekend I came home from college to find my friend sitting on the front porch with several buckets of decaying human parts soaking in bleach. My Dad had employed her to scrape the bones clean of flesh for a case he was investigating. After the bones were clean, they laid the skeletal remains on the lawn and reconstructed the body to figure out what pieces were missing. I shriveled back in disgust. She was in anatomical heaven.

Shortly after I graduated from college, Dad retired from medical examiner work. Dinnertime conversations were tamed and body bags disappeared from the truck. I learned to embrace my childhood and the family business. In fact, I feel quite blessed to have had Quincy for a father and a doting, self-confident mother who put up with his homegrown experiments in forensic science. (Mom surely must have had a foreshadowing of their future on their first date when Dad took her to see a cadaver in medical school.)

When I started screenwriting, I discovered that I was drawn to mysteries, especially Hitchcock and dark and quirky Coen brothers' stories (*Blood Simple*, *Fargo*, *The Big Lebowski*). My tastes in television tended towards mysteries with levity like *Moonlighting*, *Monk*, *House*, *Pushing Daisies*, *Life*, or *Bones*.

Writing about crime challenged me in ways others genres could not. Writing a crime story gives both the left and right sides of your brain an intense workout. Enduring mysteries should not just stop at a series of plot points revealing chains of evidence. They can include dynamic and memorable plots. Complicated, quirky, troubled, or damaged characters. Investigators you fall in love with. Criminals that make the neck hairs stand at attention and your blood turn cold. Settings where you see things like you've never seen them before. And at the end of the story a certain satisfaction should arise that something that was amiss has now been restored and redeemed (*True Grit*). Or perhaps a dissatisfaction pricks at you that evil is always lurking and one needs to be constantly vigilant (*No Country for Old Men*).

The discovery that I loved this genre surprised me. Until this point, I was not a *CSI* fan and rarely read crime novels. I spent most of my teenage years trying to hide the pictures of dead bodies that littered our dining room table when my friends would come over after school. Now, suddenly, I wanted more. I wanted to know everything so I could write about it. I hounded Dad and Mom with phone calls, emails, and questions. I read books and articles. It wasn't enough. Like mystery writer Patricia Cornwell, I longed to get out there and get my hands dirty. Note that I said *dirty* and not *bloody* because my stomach is still a bit squeamish where live carnage is concerned. And believe me when I say I've had my fill of real dead bodies. Mine was a literary bloodlust.

To satiate it, I enrolled in the Forensic Science Academy in Southern California, founded by superstar Janis Cavanaugh, one of the first female police officers hired in El Monte, California. (Since then she and I have become friends.) I completed their six-month program, during which I received hands-on CSI experience under the guidance of dozens of Los Angeles forensic professionals. I gained more than 360 hours of forensic training.

Forensic Speak started as an independent-study project I proposed in order to fulfill a prerequisite requirement at the Forensic Science Academy. But when my TV writer friends got wind of it, they raved and encouraged me to go public. I was a little surprised by their intrigue. One friend emailed me a list of things she wanted to see from such a book and added, "I was starting to write my next TV spec script and I went in search of this type of book and didn't have much luck. I'll be waiting for your book to hit store shelves." Well, that was all the encouragement I needed. Why not write something I could share?

Forensic Speak evolved into its current form because I wanted to put all my forensic knowledge, training, and resources in one handy-dandy place where I could reference it as needed. This is the book I wish I had had when I started writing crime fiction: a north star to the world of forensic science.

With *Forensic Speak*, I am at home. The welcome mat is out. Take a seat around my dinner table and pass the corn. We've got a lot to talk about.

Warmly,
Jennifer Dornbush
http://www.jenniferdornbush.com

How to Get the Most Out of *Forensic Speak*

Forensic Speak is divided into eight chapters that cover the major fields of study in forensic science. At the end of the book is a large reference and resource section. These are resources that I've used in my own writing and researching. Forensics professionals have recommended them to me and I wanted to share them with you. I know that these resources will prove trustworthy and helpful. Some of the resources are serious scientific studies. Some are there simply because they are fun forensic facts.

Each chapter is divided into a series of the most used terms in each field. Each term is divided into three parts. What is it? Where do I see it? How can I use it?

What is it?

The first section of each chapter gives a clear definition of a given term. These terms and their definitions are compiled from more than twenty years of firsthand knowledge of the field combined with hundreds of years of experience and expertise from dozens of law enforcement officers, DNA scientists, fingerprinting specialists, judges, attorneys, criminalists, and other forensic professionals. Textbooks, reliable websites, journals, and articles also served as sources. The technology in the field of forensic science is in perpetual evolution, but the core terms that you'll find in this book remain tried and true since the field of study was first recognized as such in the 1960s.

Where do I see it?

Many of us are visual learners, myself included. This section provides a visual example of the term. Here I have cited either a TV or film scene, or in some cases I'll show an actual photograph to illustrate the term.

How can I use it?

This is the practical part of each term. Once you have the definition and you've seen an example, you'll probably be wondering, so what? How can I use that in my own writing? In this last section, I am talking specifically to people creating fictional crime stories. I have to preface this by saying, there are many, many ways you can use the terms found in *Forensic Speak*. It would be virtually impossible for anyone to cover them all. Besides, it's *your* job to come up with ways to use forensics in your fiction. View this section as a springboard to your creativity. As you go through the book, you'll notice that I've taken a lot of liberty in the way that I've answered: How can I use it?

- Sometimes, I'll address things you should or could have your characters do on the scene.
- Sometimes I give an additional tip or two about the term.
- Sometimes I give a real-life scenario.
- Sometimes I'll refer to a real-life criminal case.
- Sometimes I'll raise questions that I want writers to think about.
- Sometimes I talk about how things were done in the past as compared to how they are done now.
- Sometimes I point out myths or misconceptions to inform writers.
- Sometimes (as in the Toxicology chapter), I'm just plain ridiculous. Laughter is the best drug of all.
- Sometimes I've included a fun fact or unknown bit of information about the term being defined.

Who Needs to Speak Forensics?

Newbie crime writers. TV writers. Researchers. Writers' assistants. Any writer who wants to get that extra edge.

This book started with you in mind. My heart bleeds for writers longing for a thorough cross section of forensic science who don't have the time and resources to peruse forty-five forensic textbooks or take half a dozen classes at their local junior college. And most do not have the luxury of a forensic network, resources, researchers, staff, specialists, and consultants at their fingertips. This book is designed to be that touchstone for you.

Forensic Speak contains a lot of information to assimilate at one time. Choose your poison carefully. Chapters are written to stand alone. You don't have to take them in any particular order. Concentrate on one at a time, depending on what you need for the story you're writing. If you're working on a specific idea or aspect of forensics, you may want to jump to that chapter and read all you can. Also check the references at the back of the book, which will lead you to more resources.

Share a copy with your peers. Give a copy to your family and crime-show friends.

If you can't find what you're looking for in here, ask me. I love research. I love pointing people to helpful research. I love talking to forensic professionals. It is my personal writer's code to answer smart questions and to share them with the rest of our crime-writing community. Forensic science, like writing, is an imperfect and constantly changing art. We must live, breathe, and move with it. Sharing our insights, our information, is the best way to keep us all fresh.

Seasoned crime writers. TV and film writers. Producers. Show runners.

I imagine that your iPod, iPad, and Web bookmark histories are already loaded with files, contacts, and lists of forensics data, but I believe that this book will also become your one-stop guide to fictional crime fighting. And my hope is that you will find some nuggets in this book that will add to your toolbox. Even if you are familiar with every term in the book (in which case you need to go immediately to your local law enforcement and apply to be a CSI), you can continue to hone your forensic authenticity with the resources found at the end.

- You may find *Forensic Speak* useful in fact-checking your scripts and stories.
- If you are on a writing staff, a writing team, or running a writing staff, use *Forensic Speak* as a baseline so everyone is speaking the same language.
- Consider gifting this book to other crime writers in the biz.
- Want to add to the pool of forensic knowledge? Start a dialogue with me. Send in your facts and findings, and I will share them with others in my writing community.

- Have a question? I'll work with you to find a solution to the problem you are dealing with on your show or in your own writing.
- If you can't find what you're looking for in here, ask me.

Crime genre fans. College instructors. Writing teachers. Writing mentors.

If you are reading this, chances are you are part of the CSI generation or you are teaching them. You are a breed of fan or an instructor who is extremely curious and well-educated. My guess is that you're science-minded; you like gadgets, hands-on learning, and those volcano kits you can buy at toy stores. I have a hunch you'll find this book satisfying because it brings you behind the scenes, leagues and leagues under the sea where you can learn how things are done — forensics finally explained in lay people's terms.

Chapters are written to stand alone, so start anywhere you like, maybe with a topic you're most interested in. DNA? Death investigation? Ballistics? Courtroom forensics? You pick. Start there. Move around the book as needed.

The resources at the end of the book will to help you plumb deeper into the topic of your choice. Use the filmography to find a TV show or movie you haven't seen yet or to illustrate a point to your students. Feel free to suggest shows and films to be added to the list for the next edition by contacting me.

Ask me if you can't find what you're looking for in here.

I.
Chewing the Fat with CSIs

"There is only one honest witness to every murder – the victim."

– Forensic saying

Crime scene investigation on the airwaves did not start with CSI. It has a history as long as television has been broadcast.

When creating a crime story, start where investigators start, with the points of proof. There are three points of proof and they originate with the suspect. Suspects must have access to a weapon (or method of killing), access to the victim, and motivation for the crime. The investigator's main goal (real or fictional) is to find evidence that reveals something about each point of proof. In TV and film life, a single protagonist hero becomes the central force in solving these points of proof. In real life, an investigative team does this — CSIs, medical examiners, criminalists, toxicologists, DNA scientists, ballistics experts, fingerprint examiners.

Crime scene investigators enter the scene after first responders. They secure the scene if it hasn't already been done. Then they process the scene to get all the evidence to help other investigators prove weapons, victim's relationship, and motive. This chapter focuses on the equipment, techniques, and terms that CSIs use in their jobs. It begins by describing different types of evidence, then moves into general terms, and concludes with what you'll find in a CSI's toolkit.

There are six main types of evidence for which investigators look at a crime scene: biological, circumstantial, direct, impression, physical, and trace. On screen, it's possible to gather all six because writers are creating the crime. In real life, investigators may only get bits and pieces of a few types of evidence. This sheds some light on why it's often difficult to rely solely on forensic science to prove a criminal case.

TYPES OF EVIDENCE

Biological Evidence

What is it?

As its name suggests, biological evidence comes from a live source, meaning that it came from something once or still living. Blood. Urine. Saliva. Semen. Skin tissue. Organ tissue. Hair. Teeth. Bone. Feces. Vomit. It's the ooey-gooey stuff we're all made of and all produce. Biological ooze is teeming with our DNA and all sorts of clues as to our unique chemical makeup — diseases, deficiencies, excesses. It tells us if a certain person was at the crime scene or not.

Where do I see it?

In the first season of *CSI*, episode 110, Sara Sidle (Jorja Fox) examines a victim's hair strand under a microscope to find that it has trace elements of Teflon from the bullet that killed her. Sara uses this evidence to match the bullets from the suspect's personal ammo supply.

How can I use it?

Any investigator worth his or her weight will recognize the value of biological evidence in creating a link to the victim or suspect. Investigators should thoroughly scour the victim and the immediate surroundings for biological evidence, and then properly collect it and take it to a lab for testing. DNA testing seems to be the default test for bio evidence.

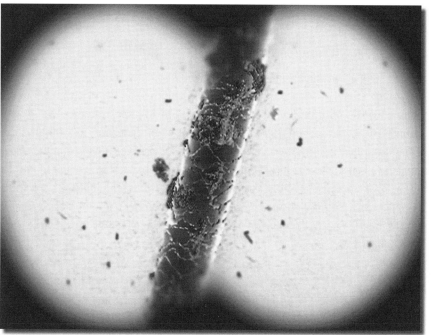

Hair strand of murder victim under microscope. Sara Sidle examines and compares it to bullet fire from suspect's gun. *CSI*, episode 110; Jerry Bruckheimer TV, 2000–present.

However, there are limitations to biological evidence. For instance, multiple-touch places like steering wheels and door handles have too many persons' DNA on them to be of much help. Also, public places like libraries, banks, stores, and schools carry hundreds of people's DNA. And then there are environmental factors like heat, evaporation, and rain that ruin biological DNA evidence. Another little-known fact is that acids in feces and urine kill DNA. And, contrary to TV forensics, DNA testing cannot determine the sex of a person. More on that in the DNA section.

Don't feel limited to using only bio evidence to make DNA matches. Use other clues from bio evidence to build the case: a victim who has contracted HIV postmortem. A suspect whose hair fiber shows lethal aluminum levels works in a canning factory. Vomit or feces is very helpful in identifying what foods a person last ate. Blood and urine can also tell us a great deal about what kind of environmental toxins, pesticides, or heavy metals are in a person's system. Diseases are also detected through bio evidence.

Circumstantial Evidence

What is it?

Circumstantial evidence suggests that a crime happened. It is indirect evidence. You arrive home and you notice a broken window, muddy shoe tracks on your carpet, and a hole ripped into a wall where your 60" TV used to hang. You infer that there was a burglary. You're walking down the street and hear a gunshot. You run towards the sound and find a body. You infer that a murder took place. Circumstantial evidence deals in claims, probabilities, assumptions, and appearances. It tries to show that a series of facts reasonably leads to the conclusions about how the crime was committed and if the person on trial for it is guilty. When trying to prove a crime, it's always best if circumstantial evidence can be accompanied by its siblings: physical and direct evidence.

Jeff Jeffries, Stella, and Lisa examine two pictures. *Rear Window*, Universal, 1954.

Where do I see it?

L. B. Jeff Jeffries (James Stewart), along with his nurse Stella (Thelma Ritter) and girlfriend Lisa (Grace Kelly), compare two photos that Jeff took as part of the circumstantial evidence he has been collecting to solve the alleged murder of a neighbor's wife in Hitchcock's *Rear Window*.

How can I use it?

We are used to seeing cases being proved based on very concrete lines of direct and physical evidence. We like that because there's something definitive we can grasp. DNA matches satisfy us. We don't like fuzzy lines. We squirm when we can't rely on science to prove it for us. Circumstantial evidence throws logic puzzles and ethical obstacle courses at us. Great, I say! What a fun place for a storyteller. Give your audience a rigorous hike through the switchbacks of What-Most-Likely-Happened Mountain. One note: Physical evidence (bullet casings, guns, victim's clothing) is considered circumstantial evidence.

Direct Evidence

What is it?

Direct evidence is a term meaning factual evidence recovered from a crime scene that cannot be disputed. You see a person hold up a convenience store and steal from the cash register. You see a shooter shoot his gun at a victim. A cop car surveillance video records a traffic violator attacking a police officer. Direct evidence arrives in the courtroom in the form of photographs, video, or witness testimony.

Where do I see it?

Monk (Tony Shalhoub), Sharona (Bitty Schram), Lt. Randall Disher (Jason Gray-Stanford), and Captain Leland Stottlemeyer (Ted Levine) view a video surveillance tape that proves which suspects were in an alley at the time of a murder they are investigating in the episode, "Mr. Monk and the Red-Headed Stranger," season 1 of *Monk*.

Monk, Sharona, Disher, and Stottlemeyer watch a video surveillance tape of a murder scene. *Monk*, "Mr. Monk and the Red-Headed Stranger"; USA Network, Universal, 2002–09.

How can I use it?

Use it when you really want to provide clear links between your suspect and the crime.

Direct evidence can be the trump card to solving your case. Introduce it early in the story to establish that indeed a crime has occurred or pull it out when you need to step up a case against a particular suspect. Uncover it later in the story to clinch the case. Or distort direct evidence and create a diversion by introducing a lying witness or video that has been altered.

Impression Evidence

What is it?

Impression evidence is another subcategory of physical evidence. Most commonly it includes impression marks made in soft and malleable material by shoes, tools, tires, or teeth. Soft or malleable material includes anything that can bear an impression: paper, fabric, drywall, metal, dirt, mud, snow, slush, carpet, skin, bone, wood.

Where do I see it?

CSIs Gil Grisson (William Petersen) and Catherine Willows (Marg Helgenberger) make molds of an impression in a victim's skull to try to match a murder weapon in *CSI* episode 121.

How can I use it?

Take your pick. There are infinite ways a criminal could leave impression evidence: a fist into drywall, a crowbar used to pry open a door, shoe tracks outside a window, bloody footprints, fabric in the grill of a truck, tire skid marks on pavement, bite marks in a piece of cheese from the fridge. Incidentally, delinquency works up quite an appetite.

Tool marks and bite marks are analyzed. *CSI* 121; Jerry Bruckheimer TV, 2000.

Physical Evidence

What is it?

Like its name suggests, physical evidence is anything touchable, tangible, or present collected from a crime scene that is related to the crime. This includes freestanding evidence like a firearm on the floor, a bullet casing on the ground, a wallet left behind, an article of clothing. Physical evidence can be adherent, meaning it's stuck to something else: a carpet fiber from the floor, grease or oil, soil. Bonded evidence is physical evidence that has been transferred from one force to another: a fingerprint impression on a soda can, blood leaking into a wooden doorframe, car paint rubbing off as it swipes another car. And last is integral evidence, which can't be easily removed from the crime scene because it's part of something else, like a bullet hole in a wall, a crowbar indentation, or a shoeprint in the mud.

Where do I see it?

In the *Law & Order: Criminal Intent* pilot, Detective Robert Goren (Vincent D'Onofrio) discovers copper wiring fragments on the gloved hand of a murder victim, which will lead him to his next clue.

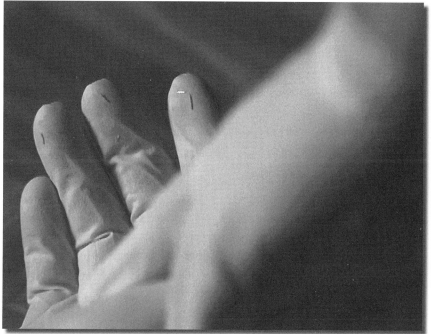

Copper wire fragments on gloved hand of murder victim. *Law & Order Criminal Intent* pilot; Wolf Films, Universal, 2001.

How can I use it?

Physical evidence is the butter to the bread of crime writing. Your criminal should leave some physical evidence behind for investigators to track. However, don't be tempted to use too many pieces of physical evidence. Select three to five key clues that your investigator will find to track down suspects. Some common ones include body fluids, broken glass, drugs, documents, bite marks in skin or food, bullet casings, hair (human or animal), fibers (clothing, furniture, carpet), fingerprints, shoeprints, serial numbers, tool marks, vehicle tire tread, bugs, or paint particles.

Trace Evidence

What is it?

Trace evidence is a subcategory of physical evidence. Often only very small quantities of physical evidence are left at a crime scene or on a victim. You may only get one strand of hair, a few skin cells, a thread from a fabric, a glass shard, a paint chip, or a few granules of soil — just traces that someone has been there.

Where do I see it?

CSI Warrick Brown (Gary Dourdan) examines a toenail in the pilot episode of *CSI*.

How can I use it?

Most physical evidence you plant in your stories is going to fall into the trace evidence category. Plus you want to give your investigators a challenge to make your criminals seem smart and dangerous. Have your criminal leave half a fingerprint. The tip of a shoe print. A smudge of gunshot residue as he tries to wipe off the gun barrel. One carpet fiber on a victim's eyelash. Less is more, like what real-life investigators have to go on.

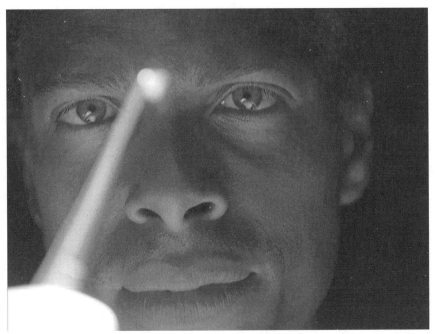

Warrick with toenail clipping. *CSI* pilot; Jerry Bruckheimer TV.

Consider this section your quick course on criminology. You probably won't hear characters in crime shows using the words *Locard Exchange Principle* or *individual characteristic*. But every crime show is built around them. Once you learn what they are, you'll recognize them in the shows you watch and use them in the stories you write.

GENERAL TERMS

Accelerant

What is it?

Accelerants are used intentionally to create instant, long-lasting fires. In other words, it indicates arson. An accelerant is anything used to sustain a fire. Common examples include gasoline, kerosene, acetone, alcohol, cleaning solution, camping stove fuel, diesel fuel, propane, lacquer, paint thinner, or turpentine. Accelerants are lit from ignition devices, which can be anything from a candle to a time-delay device.

Where do I see it?

Martin Blank's assistant, Marcella (Joan Cusack), pours accelerant over her office space in order to destroy evidence of her presence in *Grosse Pointe Blank*.

How can I use it?

Proving arson involves many things. Two of them are finding out where accelerant was used or whether an incendiary device was ignited. CSI investigators should take

Joan Cusack pours gasoline in her office. *Grosse Pointe Blank*, Buena Vista Pictures, 1997.

photos, observe smells, and look for matches, cigarette butts, and irregularly shaped patterns on the floor that contain ash, soot, or other burned residue. Test suspicious areas right away because accelerants have a short after-fire life, only a few hours to a few days. Cracks and crevices may have more remaining accelerants than flat surfaces. The water used to put out the fire will not impede testing for accelerants. Go high tech if need be and use a "sniffer," aka a portable hydrocarbon detector.

Chain of Custody

What is it?

Chain of custody is sometimes referred to as chain of evidence, which simply means keeping a specific record of physical evidence taken from the scene of the crime. From the time the investigator arrives on the scene until evidence is received in the lab and throughout the trial, items should be recorded by collector's name, location of the evidence, and date of collection. To be admissible in court it has to be collected and processed by people who have no personal interest in the crime at hand. Each time an evidence item is received, removed, tested, or observed, it is tracked. Evidence items (depending on the nature of the item) are collected in manila envelopes, sealable paper bags, metal tins, glass vials, or paper bindles.

Where do I see it?

An investigator in *CSI*, episode 120, scoops up dog poop from a suspect's home. The sealed and signed container he uses establishes chain of custody as this piece of evidence moves to the evidence locker and through the crime lab.

How can I use it?

We only have to take a jaunt into the recent past and look at the O. J. Simpson trial to see how important chain of evidence is in prosecuting a killer. O. J. was acquitted because the defense convinced the jury that evidence was planted, tampered with, or did not follow chain of custody. Evidence can quickly be dismissed from court if, let's say, a detective slips the evidence vial in his jacket pocket and accidentally forgets to bring it to the lab for processing until the next day. A corrupt detective or sly suspect

An investigator scoops dog poop for evidence in *CSI*, episode 120; Jerry Bruckheimer TV, 2001–present.

may plant evidence at a crime scene or add tainted evidence later. Property technicians could open an evidence bag incorrectly or fail to mark that they opened the bag. Another way to compromise evidence in your fictional case is to have a person related to the victim comb through the crime scene before the CSIs arrive.

Chemical Processing

What is it?

Spraying Luminol over a carpet to detect unseen blood. Dipping paper in a Ninhydrin bath to detect fingerprints. Applying a Hemadent test to confirm a suspected blood source. These are all uses of chemical processing on physical evidence from a crime scene. There are hundreds of ways and means and sources that facilitate testing evidence. Chemical processing is a complex and developing field. Simply stated, chemical processing occurs in a forensic crime lab. Evidence is delivered in person from the crime scene to the property lockers and recorded to keep the chain of custody pure. Unlike on TV, forensic labs don't just automatically check the evidence for every substance under the sun. It's usually the investigator's job to direct the lab technicians to test for a specific substance.

Some of the most commonly used chemical tests in the forensic lab are:

● Luminol, BlueStar, and HemaTrace to detect blood (see Presumptive Testing).

● Ninhydrin, iodine fuming, cyanoacrylate, silver nitrate, sticky side powder to detect fingerprints (see Fingerprinting).

● Gas chromatography, mass spectrometry, and microcrystalline to analyze alcohol, drugs, and poisons (see Toxicology).

● Static, passive, and dynamic headspace to test for accelerants in arson fires.

● Thermal cylinder and electrophoresis to determine biological makeup (see DNA).

Need more? Of course you do. Try *http://www.HowStuffWorks.com*. Or be a nerd and befriend a forensic chemist.

William Petersen collects bugs and pours coffee in the container to preserve them. *CSI* 110; Jerry Bruckheimer TV, 2000.

Where do I see it?

Gil Grissom (William Petersen) collects bugs and pours coffee in the container to preserve them in the first season of *CSI*, episode 110. This is a form of chemical processing to preserve the evidence. It's a little rustic and hard to believe that a sophisticated operation like the Vegas crime lab wouldn't have the proper chemical, formaldehyde, but it makes TV watching interesting.

How can I use it?

If it sounds overwhelming, it is. But you don't need a PhD in chemistry to write a procedural. It does help to understand the basics about what happens to evidence once it reaches the crime lab. This makes your characters look smarter and gives you more to play with during those musical montage scenes in the lab. It also helps your story to go somewhere. It's not just the discovery of evidence at a crime scene that's important, but it's finding out what's *in* that evidence that helps the investigator solve the crime and catch the criminal. Use your resources. Research. But, please, once you're outside the fictional world, have a little patience with forensic chemistry. Chemical processing can take weeks — months even. Cases are backlogged. Technicians are few. Lab equipment may be inadequate or outdated. Budget cuts prohibit lab expansion. That's a big reason why it can take years to determine the cause of death properly and prosecute criminals. Of course, in TV it happens in a brief forty-four minutes.

Class Characteristic

What is it?

Class characteristic is the opposite side of the coin to individual characteristic. Class refers to a restricted group, individual to a single source. When trying to identify a piece of evidence like a tire tread, you start with a broad class: a tire. Then narrow it down: a truck tire, a pickup truck tire, an all-weather pickup truck tire. Eventually, the forensic lab will be able to identify this tire as a Firestone Firehawk GT Performance tire with a 28.6" diameter. Coincidentally, this tire was specially designed for the police and fire department and tested by the LAPD. There are probably hundreds, maybe thousands of them out there. This is an example of a class characteristic.

Where do I see it?

Blood spatter specialist Dexter Morgan (Michael C. Hall) and Sgt. James Doakes (Erik King) find a severed foot in a soccer shoe next to a soccer ball in *Dexter*, season 1, "Let's Give the Boy a Hand." Both the ball and the shoe are part of a restricted class of shoes and balls. While Dexter and Doakes will be able to use the severed foot to draw some conclusions about the victims, they can also use the class characteristics from the ball and shoe to determine individual characteristics, such as manufacturer, lot, location shipped, store where they were sold, and purchaser.

How can I use it?

When writing about evidence in procedurals, always start from a class characteristic and work toward an individual characteristic. Take the example above. Start broad. Eventually, narrow it down to individual characteristics that are unique to one tire and one vehicle. If there are thousands of Firestone Firehawk GT Performance tires with 28.6" diameter out there, then how can your investigator narrow it down to a single vehicle? Here's how: Reveal an odd wear pattern that belongs to a retired cruiser out of alignment. Find out who owned that cruiser and when the tires were last changed. That should narrow it down very specifically to just a few suspects.

Dexter examines a severed foot. The shoe and the ball are class characteristics. *Dexter*, "Let's Give the Boy a Hand"; Showtime, 2006.

Consistent With

What is it?

Consistent with is a term investigators use when describing physical evidence and how it relates to the crime and the victim. It means compatible, in agreement with, or similar to. When, at a crime scene, you see a red fluid around the body of the victim, you cannot report that it is human blood because it hasn't yet been proved to be human blood. It could be animal blood or red food coloring and corn syrup, right? Instead, report that a red substance consistent with blood was observed near the body. Take a swab of the substance to have it tested later (see Presumptive Testing).

Where do I see it?

The red substance on the bumper of this BMW from *CSI*, episode 121, is a substance consistent with blood. But no one will know for sure until it's tested.

How can I use it?

Terms like *consistent with* get blown out of the water on crime shows. The investigator sails in and announces bloodstains on the carpet or semen stains on a mattress. How does he know? He doesn't. He wouldn't. Not until it's tested. But doing investigations this way is shorthand in storytelling. A forty-four-minute show doesn't always lend us enough time to illustrate proper science. So the detectives see it, declare it, and we buy it. However, you could use the concept of consistent with to create a red herring. What if the detective declares a substance human blood but when it's tested in the lab it turns out to be animal blood? Hmmm....

A red substance found on the back of a car bumper will be tested to see if it's human blood. *CSI* 120; Jerry Bruckheimer TV, 2000.

Conventional Processing

What is it?

Photographing a scene, dusting for fingerprints, swabbing a soda can for DNA, casting a shoeprint in dental stone. These are the basic and ordinary means of collecting evidence. It doesn't get any simpler. These conventional methods of processing a crime scene for physical evidence are *the* cornerstone of each case. Every piece of physical evidence that *can* be collected *must* be collected through conventional processing before it can move on to chemical processing in a lab setting.

Where do I see it?

In *Dexter*, season 1, "Let's Give the Boy a Hand," a fingerprint technician dusts a beach pail next to a severed hand.

How can I use it?

In real life, detectives don't get a second chance to revisit the crime scene and find

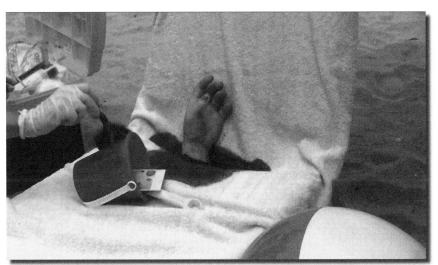

A fingerprint technician dusts a beach pail next to a severed hand. *Dexter*, "Let's Give the Boy a Hand"; Showtime, 2006.

more evidence. TV allows for more leeway, and we often see detectives returning to the scene of the crime several times, each time finding a new piece of evidence. If you want to write authentically, be thorough in your conventional processing on the first (and only) visit. Allow your investigator to find every piece of evidence she needs and use the rest of the script to unravel the mysteries that evidence provides. With all the evidence in hand, your investigator doesn't look sloppy and she can begin to connect evidence to other leads such as friends, coworkers, family, enemies, jobs, hobbies, financial records, places the victim frequented. The list goes on.

Corpus Delicti

What is it?

Corpus delicti is Latin for body of crime. Corpus delicti are all of the types of evidence (see Evidence Types) that help prove that a crime was committed. It's the testimony of the witnesses. It's alibis and motivations. It's videotape, photographs, email messages, faxes, journal entries. It's the weapon, clothes, footprints, blood, hair, or saliva, and anything else related to the crime.

Where do I see it?

Detective Goren (Vincent D'Onofrio) goes over the corpus delicti of a murder/jewel heist case in the second act of the pilot of *Law & Order: Criminal Intent*.

How can I use it?

When creating a crime story, you are creating the entire world of the crime. Therefore, you are creating a corpus delicti, a body of evidence and proof for the crime. One of the hardest things in creating a crime story isn't coming up with your corpus delicti; it's deciding what you can fit into a fifty-to-ninety minute story. Start by making a list of everything that might be related to the crime at hand. Then pare the list down to the top five to ten pieces.

Det. Goren goes over the corpus delicti of a murder/jewel heist case. *Law & Order: Criminal Intent* pilot; Jerry Bruckheimer TV, 2000.

Digital Algorithim

What is it?

For our purpose the digital algorithm (DA) refers to providing secure images of digital snapshots taken at the scene of a crime. This DA, or signature, includes a photo stamp of the date, the F-stop, shutter speed, camera ID, photo number. Why is this important? To maintain a chain of custody so that each picture can be admissible in a courtroom. But wait! Digital pics can be easily manipulated, right? How do you prevent that? A histogram or graphical representation of the exposure is made of the entire roll of film shot at a scene. A digital management program facilitates the chain of evidence. Each time a change is made to a photograph, this program will document that change to keep a record of the chain of custody. The entire photo log is kept on an archived server and a working server in the crime lab. So you can always go back to the archived server to see what the original pic looked like.

Veronica downloads pictures she's taken from an adultery case. *Veronica Mars* pilot; UPN Network, Warner Bros., 2004.

Where do I see it?

In the pilot episode of *Veronica Mars*, Veronica works on a cheating spouse case. She stakes the scene, captures photos of the cheating couple, and downloads the pics from her camera onto her computer so she can print the evidence. Each one of those photos will have a digital algorithim to show the history of it.

How can I use it?

Digital algorithm happens so far behind the curtain you might as well be in the janitor's closet. But you can bring it to front and center of your story. If applied and working correctly, DA gives all those involved in solving the crime very detailed and foolproof information to prosecute a case. But what if you want to throw a monkey wrench into your case? A conflict? A hurdle for your investigator to jump? Create a scenario in which the digital algorithm is not working correctly and the detective doesn't know it until it's too late. Let's say the F-stop stamp is off. Since the F-stop controls the amount of light that reaches the lens, lighting conditions could be interpreted based on what the incorrect F-stop stamp says in the signature algorithm. So if the stamp shows an F-stop of 4, but the picture was actually taken at an F-stop of 16, the argument could be made that the picture was overexposed and not truly representative of the conditions at the time the scene was being processed. A huge shadow of doubt has now been cast over your case. Or have your investigator walk away from his camera at the scene long enough to enable someone to tamper with it. A handful of people at the crime lab have access to the server. What if one of them overrode the algorithm? A shady detective, lab tech, or crafty criminal could manipulate the digital management program to delete or alter important crime scene photos without being detected.

Electronic Crime Scene Investigation (ECI)

What is it?

One of the hottest and fastest-growing forms of forensic investigation happens without ever involving a messy crime scene or a dead body. Electronic crime scene investigators fight crime in cyberspace. Criminals leave scads of electronic evidence behind in emails, hard drives, memory cards, iPods, digital cameras, and cell phones. ECIs recover digital data that links a crime to its crime maker.

Where do I see it?

In *The Fugitive*, Dr. Richard Kimble hacks into the hospital computer records to find the guy with the prosthetic arm in his pursuit to solve his own case.

How can I use it?

Unless your criminal has absolutely no access to technology he *will* leave an electronic trace. You can always track the bad guy through a cell phone or security camera, but those are a bit clichéd. Use sparingly. Answering machines are great on-screen devices and still crop up a lot in TV shows, although how many people do you know in real life who still have one? And, of course, your cyber cop could discover a criminal through good, old-fashioned hacking. Get more creative mileage by using Internet history, cookies, bookmarks, "favorites," Facebook, emails, chats, or IP addresses.

Dr. Richard Kimble hacks into the hospital records to try to solve his own case and prove his innocence. *The Fugitive*, Warner Bros., 1993.

Environmental Forensics

What is it?

Not all crimes of murder involve guns or knives. The water you drink or the air you breathe could be just as deadly. Environmental forensics is an emerging field in forensic science aimed at finding out who's liable for contaminating us and how to prosecute them more quickly. Environmental scientists gather data to show who, what, where, when, and why environmental violations or catastrophes are happening and whether attempts have been to cover them up. The ultimate goal is to compel the offender to take responsibility and make things right.

Karen checking files and gathering evidence x-rays to prove contamination. *Silkwood*, 20th Century Fox, 1983.

Where do I see it?

Karen Silkwood (Meryl Streep) sneaks into the lab at her metallurgy plant to find x-ray evidence that will prove she was intentionally contaminated in the 1983 film *Silkwood*.

How can I use it?

There are really so many ways to go with this. Whether it's slow-leaching lead poisoning or an oil spill in the Gulf of Mexico, you can build a very compelling story around deadly pollution. The effects could be localized or far-reaching. The culprits may be large oil companies or a small city businessman interested in personal wealth. The poison is up to you, but it had better be a personal story. We want to know how the contamination ruined someone's life (or a community's livelihood) and how Lady Justice prevailed at the end of the day.

Forensic Photography

What is it?

Forensic photography isn't about taking pretty, artistic pictures. It's about getting the facts on film. You get one shot to get your shots. Once a crime scene is cleared away you are never able to reproduce the exact evidence or victim again. Investigators use a three-tiered technique for photographing the scene. They start with overall shots. These are taken from the widest range to encompass the entire area of the crime scene; smaller pieces of evidence and scales will not be easily identifiable. Next, they circle in for medium format shots. These photographs are taken so that you can see the evidence in relation to each other and the victim. Finally, they home in on close-up shots with a scale or ruler. The scale and the piece of evidence must both be in the shot on a parallel plane to show a one-to-one ratio. A photo log is kept to list all the photographs taken at the scene of the crime. Types of cameras used on scene include 35mm SLR (film or digital), video, point and shoot, and Polaroid.

Catherine Willows photographs a crime scene. *CSI* pilot; Jerry Bruckheimer TV, 2000.

Where do I see it?

CSI Catherine Willows (Marg Helgenberger) photographs a crime scene in the pilot episode of *CSI*.

How can I use it?

Start by learning how crime scenes are photographed. Understand that you don't get a second chance to record the scene. Imagine how the scene looks through the eye of a camera. What details does it pick up that you don't see until you're looking at the picture later on screen?

Individual Characteristic

What is it?

Individual characteristic is probably not a term you're going to hear mentioned a whole lot in crime show dialogue. But it is a core principle of investigation that is so common it is often assumed. In this principle it is understood that specific things identify one particular person, place, or thing from another. Using the example from class characteristics, the individual characteristic comes down to how that tire tread was worn. Statistics dictate that only one person is going to drive a certain way, a certain number of miles, over certain territory to create that worn tread.

Where do I see it?

Tommy Lee Jones as Agent K deletes all of Will Smith's, Agent J's, individual characteristics — ID, fingerprints — in *Men in Black*, minute 37:50.

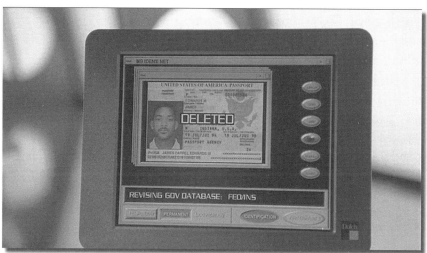

Will Smith's ID is deleted. *Men in Black*; Columbia Pictures 1997.

How can I use it?

How does this apply to forensic science? Let's say you need to identify a victim. You have to be able to prove certain individual characteristics about that person. Start with class characteristic: The victim was a female, five-eight, with brown hair and blue eyes. Certain features that belong only to this female will tell us that: her fingerprints, her DNA, a birthmark, her social security number, her dental records or driver's license. The same goes for nonhumans. Take a vehicle, for instance. A witness claims that the suspect drove away in a red 1998 Chrysler Concorde. We have to be able to link this specific Concorde to its criminal driver through specific identifiers; use the car's VIN number, plates, registration, repair records, or insurance cards.

Individual characteristics are helpful in narrowing down any clue. After you have compiled your corpus delicti, examine the items and people that need individual characteristics and list at least three specific things about each one that make them individual. Now you and your investigator have something to zero in on as you move through the case.

Locard Exchange Principle

What is it?

Two objects come into contact with one another. One transfers some of its material to the other. This is the Locard exchange, named for Edmond Locard who started the first criminalistics lab in Lyon, France, in 1910. What does it mean exactly? Locard believed that the exchange of one material to another could connect criminals to their crime scene, or victims to criminals, or crimes to victims. And he proved it by finding metallic particles from counterfeit coins on three suspects' clothing. The particles were tested and found to be of the same material as the coins. Busted!

Where do I see it?

In the pilot episode of *CSI*, Warrick Brown (Gary Dourdan) examines a tennis shoe. Inside the shoe he finds a piece of a toenail, evidence that one object came into contact with another. The toenail proves to be crime-solving evidence.

How can I use it?

Whatever the criminal comes into contact with can be later tested to link her to the scene of the crime. Think about where your crime takes place. What is in that place that a criminal might come into contact with? Dust from a chalkboard? Metal shavings from a welder's shop? Salt pellets from an icy sidewalk? Or vice versa. What does your criminal leave behind at the scene of a crime that identifies her as having been present? A dab of hair gel on a door handle? Ash from a cigarette butt? Fiber from a sweater? Skin cells? Or what if someone has entered the crime scene who shouldn't be there? He may have altered the evidence. He probably left some of his own at the scene.

Warrick looking at shoe in CSI evidence locker. *CSI* pilot; Jerry Bruckheimer TV, 2000.

Modus Operandi

What is it?

Modus operandi is Latin for mode of operation. It is the recurring techniques a criminal uses to enact a crime. He establishes an MO by employing a certain identifiable pattern or procedure to his delinquency: the tools he uses, the way he enters a location, the time of day he commits the crime, the type of person he attacks. The MO may change over time as the criminal becomes more experienced at committing crimes or gains better tools to make his job easier. The MO may also be affected by unplanned events during the crime.

Where do I see it?

In the first season of *Dexter*, the Ice Truck Killer has a predictable modus operandi. He drains the blood from his victims, severs their limbs, and then wraps them in packaging paper.

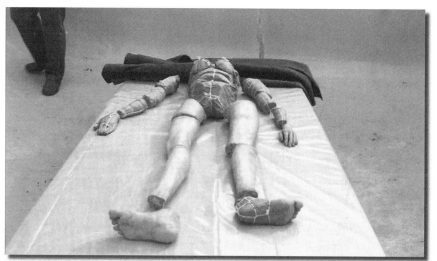

The Ice Truck Killer drains the blood from his victims and severs their limbs. *Dexter*, season 1; Showtime, 2006.

How can I use it?

Giving your criminal a modus operandi makes him eerily predictable and aids your investigator in identifying him. You might have fun linking MOs to a copycat crime. The more odd and creative your MO is, the more interesting your character and his situation. Ironic or humorous MOs are nicely suited to dark comedies. And remember, MOs can evolve and change as the criminal becomes smarter and more efficient at committing his crimes.

Non-Sworn Personnel

What is it?

Non-sworn personnel are not required to take an oath to protect and serve their communities and uphold the constitution of the United States. They are unarmed and cannot make arrests or enforce laws. Usually they are regular citizens who work closely with sworn officers. Non-sworn personnel in the field of forensics include criminalists, records officers, evidence technicians, public safety dispatchers, police specialists, and coroners.

Where do I see it?

Sharona Fleming (Bitty Schram), Monk's assistant, helps Monk (Tony Shahloub) solve cases but he is non-sworn, non-practicing personnel on psychiatric leave from the San Francisco Police Department, *Monk*, season 1, "Mr. Monk and the Red-Headed Stranger."

Sharona and Monk are non-sworn personnel. *Monk*, "Mr. Monk and the Red Headed Stranger"; USA, Universal, 2002–09.

How can I use it?

Understand the distinction between sworn and non-sworn personnel. Although TV loves to blur this line, you now know that it's not plausible for your coroner to be wielding a gun and chasing after the criminal. It's not her job. Instead, make her brilliant at what she does and pair her with a police detective. The sworn officer can do the heavy lifting when it comes to arrests. But what if the police aren't cooperative? What if they're downright dirty? Appeal to a higher authority. I'm not talking about God here (although your coroner probably could use some prayer at this point in the story). A state or federal officer will do just fine.

Point of Entry (POE)

What is it?

POE is the place or point at which the criminal entered the scene of the crime either illegally or with illegal intent. After securing the scene, this is the first thing investigators try to determine when processing a crime. What does POE tell you about a crime or a criminal? It tells you whether or not a crime actually happened. Was the window broken or the keyhole punched out? Was it a forced entry or not? Were any tools used to gain entry? Knowing the POE also tells you where to start processing the scene.

Where do I see it?

Adrian Monk (Tony Shalhoub) and Lt. Randall Disher (Jason Gray-Stanford) note the POE of a crime scene in *Monk*, episode, "Mr. Monk and the Captain's Wife."

How can I use it?

POEs may provide vital evidence for your case. The POE is the first place the perpetrator touched. Dust it for fingerprints. Let's say your perp broke a window to enter. Your investigators may be able to recover fabric fibers, soil, or even the suspect's blood. Suspects often exit the scene of a crime where they entered, thus doubling your chances that they left something behind. See Locard Exchange Principle.

Monk at fence. *Monk*, "Mr. Monk and the Captain's Wife"; USA, Universal 2002.

Powwow

What is it?

Powwow is investigator lingo for the time before the investigation begins when all the detectives, police, and CSIs gather to go over the known details of the crime.

Where do I see it?

Detectives Robert Goren (Vincent D'Onofrio) and Alexandra James (Kathryn Erbe) powwow on a case with the attending officer in the pilot episode of *Law & Order: Criminal Intent*.

How can I use it?

A powwow scene offers a chance for the writer to lay a lot of story pipe in just a page or two. As your main character investigators arrive on the scene, others can fill them in on the victim's identity, how they found her, if they've recovered a weapon, potential motives, who saw her last, or what witnesses have reported so far. You've cannonballed into the deep end of your case and now your investigators can fast-track it from there.

Goren and Eames powwow with the officer in charge. *Law & Order: Criminal Intent* pilot; NBC, Universal, Dick Wolf Films.

Prone

What is it?

Prone means face-down position. When a report lists a body being found prone, this indicates the body was positioned backside to the sky, nose to the ground. Does this mean the person died in a prone position? Not necessarily. The body could have been moved by people, animals, or forces of nature.

Where do I see it?

Detective Goren (Vincent D'Onofrio) examines a double homicide case in which the victims are lying in prone positions in the pilot of *Law & Order: Criminal Intent*.

How can I use it?

Know the difference between prone and supine so you can use them intelligently in your dialogue and descriptions.

Det. Goren examines two murder victims who are lying prone. *Law & Order: Criminal Intent* pilot; Jerry Bruckheimer TV 2000.

Scale
··········

What is it?

A scale is a ruler used in photographing small objects at the scene of a crime. Scales can be very short (2"), adhesive, magnetic, L-shaped, T-shaped, bi-fold, or round like thermometers to fit inside gun barrels. Scales create a point of reference and should be shot on a one-to-one ratio. This means that the camera lens needs to be parallel to the photographed object.

Where do I see it?

The investigators in *CSI* use a scale to photograph footprints in episode 121.

How can I use it?

First, a scale is an essential part of the CSI's toolkit. Second, photographs taken at the crime scene become reliable and protected documentation of the event. Most likely, they'll show up in court when it comes time to prosecute the offender. If your investigator hasn't used a scale, there is no empirical way for a judge or jury to interpret the exact size of the evidence in relation to other objects at the scene. It casts doubt on the investigation. And it's sloppy.

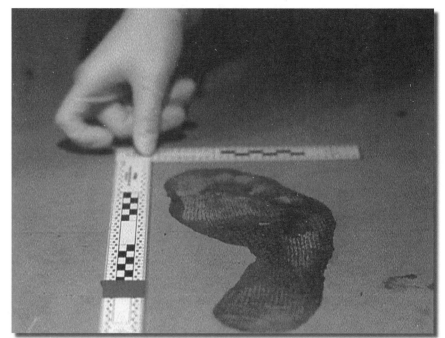

Footprint and ruler. *CSI*, episode 121; CBS, Jerry Bruckheimer TV, 2000.

Signature

What is it?

Just as your own handwritten signature says something about you emotionally, so too does a criminal's signature mark at the crime scene convey a message about the killer's psyche. A killer's signature goes beyond modus operandi and embodies the unusual or unique characteristics she repeats at her crime scenes or on her victims. The murderer's signature is her psychological calling card because the criminal is using the victim or the crime to fulfill a psychological need. For example, the Night Stalker, Richard Ramirez, liked to rape his victims before he killed them.

Where do I see it?

Charlie (Mike Meyers) falls in love with and marries Harriet (Nancy Travis), but shortly after, he finds evidence to suspect she's a serial killer. Charlie soon learns the truth when he is hunted by the real killer, Harriet's sister, Rose (Amanda Plummer), who is jealous that Harriet keeps getting married and leaving her. She kills a string of Harriet's husbands, making the deaths look like suicide. Rose's signature is the forged break-up notes she writes before killing Harriet's husbands in *So I Married an Axe Murderer*, Columbia TriStar Pictures, 1993.

How can I use it?

Signatures are useful when writing about a serial criminal who will eventually be identified by her signature marks. Signatures give investigators clues about criminal motivation and fantasy preferences, which can lead them to the offender. Signatures don't spring out of nothing. They are usually tied to very deeply seeded childhood trauma, loss, neglect, or lack. For instance, the Night Stalker was strongly influenced by his cousin who showed him pictures and gave lurid descriptions of the people he killed in Vietnam. What is the backstory of your criminal? What caused him to create a signature act? Use this to write multidimensional villains. Even the bad guy has an Achilles' heel somewhere in his life.

Supine

What is it?

Supine means face-up position. When a body is reported being found supine, it is positioned nose to the sky, backside to the ground. Does this mean the person died in a supine position? Not necessarily. The body could have been moved by people, animals, or forces of nature.

Where do I see it?

The bully in the 2005 film, *The Chumscrubber*, gets what's coming to him after a car hits him and he lands supine on the hood.

How can I use it?

Know the difference between supine and prone so you can use them intelligently in your dialogue and descriptions.

The bully lying supine on the car. *Chumscrubber*, Newmarket Films, 2005.

Sworn Personnel

What is it?

Sworn personnel are highly trained individuals who take an oath to uphold the constitution, and protect and serve their communities. They complete the police academy, carry a weapon, can make arrests, and are required to enforce the law. According to the constitution, sworn personnel work under the executive branch of government. The ranking of sworn police goes as follows from lowest to highest: police officer, corporal, sergeant, lieutenant, commander or captain, assistant chief or deputy chief, and chief.

Where do I see it?

Special Agent Jethro Gibbs (Mark Harmon) flashes his badge to prove he's a sworn personnel in *NCIS*, "The Good Samaritan."

How can I use it?

Gibbs flashes his badge. *NCIS*, "The Good Samaritan"; CBS, 2003.

Start by understanding the distinction between sworn and non-sworn personnel. The lines between the two often become blurred in crime shows. Now that you know the difference, you can be a savvier crime writer. In your story, lean on sworn personnel to sweep in to do the heavy enforcing and make the arrests. If your lead is a sworn personnel, she holds a lot of power. How does she use that power? How does that power get twisted as she goes through the investigation? Where does she rely on non-sworn forensic specialists to solve the case? Is she influenced or blackmailed by another sworn personnel? Great. The more hurdles for your protagonist, the better.

Tire Exemplar

What is it?

A tire exemplar is a fingerprint of a tire track. It is a known impression of the individual thing found or used at the crime scene. An actual is the thing from which the impression came or the actual piece of evidence. Once the tire tread is analyzed, it can be traced back to the exact tire and provide a clue to the vehicles present at the scene of the crime. Lifting the print is like making a photocopy of the tire track. Here's how it's done. Lay down a long sheet of butcher paper, about 10–12 feet so you get the entire rotation of the tire. Find the main wear marks on your tire — usually indicated by small arrows on the rim of the tire. Chalk a line down the side of the tire at each of about six wear marks and label each section numerically. Grease the tire with Vaseline. As you roll the vehicle forward onto the paper, you'll have to rub more jelly on the part underneath. Select someone to drive the vehicle slowly over the butcher paper. Another person marks each section as the print is laid with that corresponding section. As the tire rolls over the paper it leaves a nice, gooey trail. Dust the gooey trail with magnetic powder to "lift" and preserve the print. Like other physical evidence, tire exemplars are booked into property lockers. A tire impression specialist will examine it later.

Tire track photo. *My Cousin Vinny*, 20th Century Fox, 1992.

Where do I see it?

The prosecuting attorney shows his expert tire witness a set of tire treads leaving the Sac O' Suds in the trial during *My Cousin Vinny*.

How can I use it?

Armed with information about the tire tread from a crime scene, your investigator can analyze and interpret the results. From this information he can track down the vehicle and eventually the person driving that vehicle at the crime scene. Tire exemplars can also indicate the size and weight of the car and the direction in which it was heading.

What are all those little bottles, cotton swabs, and sprays they use at the scene of the crime? Find out in this section as we take a look into the CSI's toolkit.

CSI'S TOOLKIT

AIDS Wipe

What is it?

The AIDS wipe is a term formerly used in the CSI field for an antimicrobial wipe. Before antibacterial products flooded the market and before we knew exactly how HIV was contracted, investigators sanitized themselves with what they called AIDS wipes. This practice made investigators acutely aware of the biological and environmental dangers that often lurk at a crime scene. Today, investigators consider personal safety paramount at the scene of a crime.

Where do I see it?

Monk (Tony Shalhoub) was infamous for his use of antibacterial wipes both on and off the crime scene. In the *Monk* episode, "Missing Granny," Monk wipes his hands as his assistant, Sharona (Bitty Schram), endures the ritual.

Monk wipes his hands. *Monk*, "Missing Granny"; USA, Universal, 2002–09.

How can I use it?

This term is useful to know if you are writing about an investigation that took place in the 1980s. Today we would consider this term discriminatory. It would be like calling it the Bubonic Plague Wipe in the 1300s. But maybe you want to portray a character who has a nasty discriminatory streak. Here's one way to do it. The character totes around a red biohazard bag and makes sure that even the pens used to mark evidence are tossed after use. Or take this a step further to create a character who is obsessive about crime-scene safety. Or create the opposite type of character, one who has a complete lack of concern for it. He likes to live life dangerously and refuses to wear goggles and gets body fluid in his eyes. He leaves his gloves in his kit and picks up a drug user's needle with his bare hands.

Bindle

What is it?

You've run out of collection envelopes at the scene of the crime? No problem. Take a piece of notebook paper and create a bindle. Bindles are envelopes in which to store trace evidence. To make one, use a druggist fold or diamond fold. On the front write the case number, date and time collected, location, and collector's name. Bindles are just one collection device, but probably the most commonly used.

Where do I see it?

In the first season, episode 110 of *CSI*, investigator Sara Sidle (Jorja Fox) uses a bindle to extract a trace fiber that will prove that a young wife was murdered in the hallway of her home.

How can I use it?

Many times I'll be writing about evidence at a crime scene and wonder, how do they collect something like that — dried blood, teeth, or gunshot residue, for instance? All three are collected in a bindle using a cotton swab moistened with distilled water. It gives investigating a hands-on feel, doesn't it? To learn more about collection of evidence, check out the FBI's Guide to the Collection of Physical Evidence.

Sara Sidle picks uses a bindle to collect evidence. *CSI*, episode 110; Jerry Bruckheimer TV, 2000.

Buccal Swab

What is it?

A buccal swab is both a tool and a process used in DNA testing. A buccal swab is typically a wooden stick with a sterile cotton tip. Buccal swab also refers to the process of taking a sample of saliva and skin cells from those involved in a crime. It works best if the person being tested bites his cheek lightly first. This helps loosen skin cells. Roll the swab on the inside of the cheek for about ten seconds, like you're brushing your teeth. You'll need four samples from different areas. Let them air dry. Store and transport the swabs to the lab in a clean paper envelope or bindle. Food, tobacco, and the common cold virus do not affect buccal swabs. Of all the ways of obtaining DNA samples, buccal is the most straightforward, least invasive, and most common.

Where do I see it?

A forensic technician in the *CSI* pilot tests a buccal swab for the presence of blood.

How can I use it?

When your investigator finds evidence at the crime scene, she should swab it for DNA testing. But that's not the end. She'll also need to collect a reference or control swab. This swab is collected from the victim, suspect, or anyone else who might have come into contact with the crime and evidence. Later, the evidence swabs and control swabs will be tested to see if they match (see Presumptive Testing).

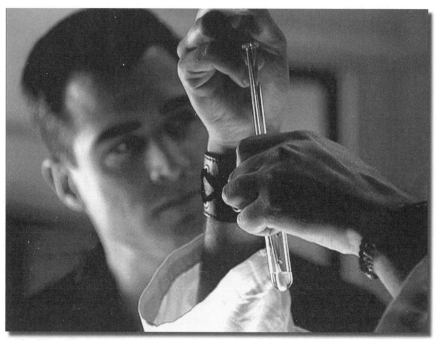

In the lab with a test tube. *CSI* pilot; Jerry Bruckheimer TV, 2000.

Bunny Suit

What is it?

It is not what Frank wore during those weird dream sequences in *Donnie Darko*. A bunny suit is the investigator's street name for the protective gear that CSIs wear when they are investigating a particularly messy situation. A fully suited CSI would wear a pair of coveralls with hood, gloves, disposable overboots or shoes, face mask, and face shield. Tyvek is one popular brand.

Where do I see it?

When sisters Rose (Amy Adams) and Norah (Emily Blunt) start a crime scene clean-up business, they have to learn the ropes of biohazard waste removal, which includes wearing protective bunny suits in the 2008 film *Sunshine Cleaning*.

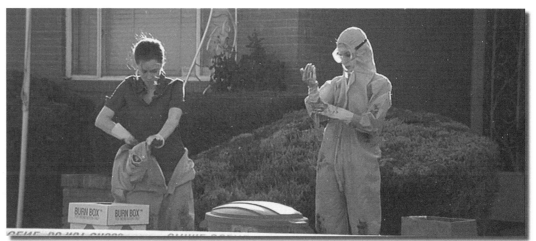

Girls suited up. *Sunshine Cleaning*, Overture Films, 2008.

How can I use it?

This will probably be the director's and wardrobe person's decision. But you can always write it in the script if you find a way to tie it into a character trait, probably a nerdy one.

Collection Kit

What is it?

The collection is the basic toolkit a CSI brings to investigate the scene of a crime. At minimum, it will include fingerprint dusting powders, brushes, tape, lift cards, tape measure, camera, extra batteries, dust mask, gloves, glasses, respirator, bags and containers, GSR (gunshot residue) kit, paper, pens, and dental stone mix.

Where do I see it?

The CSI's trusty collection kit can be seen in the pilot episode of *CSI*.

How can I use it?

The CSI collection kit is now part of your writing toolbox. When your character investigator reaches her fictional crime scene, she can show her CSI savvy by employing these real-life tools, which will prevent your script from being too vague. Instead of writing, "Detective Jane notes a shoeprint near the body," you can advance your description: "Detective Jane mixes dental stone with distilled water and carefully pours it into a shoeprint near the body." How the tools are used can also play a part in your investigation. If Jane's dental stone cracks while she's lifting it, she's compromised the evidence because the shoeprint in the soil is now gone and the shoeprint on the dental stone is unreadable.

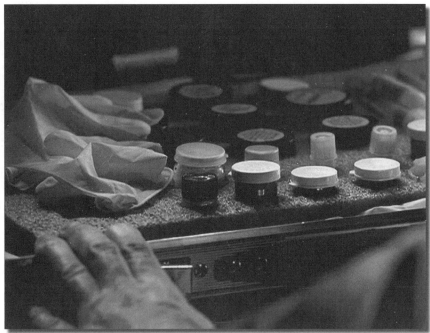

CSI collects dog poop in a jar to be analyzed later. *CSI* 120; Jerry Bruckheimer TV, 2000.

Dental Stone

What is it?

Dental stone starts as a mustard-colored powder. When mixed with distilled water to a pancake-like consistency, it can be very, very gently poured into shoe tracks to lift the impression so that an expert can match it later. Dental stone creates a cast of the imprint much like your dentist would make a mold of your teeth. Dental stone can be used in snowy conditions, too. But you have to add potassium sulfate so it cures faster and cooler. (Dental stone heats up when it cures!) When snow conditions are wet or slushy, snow print wax (which comes in an aerosol can) should be used. Spray the wax on the print first to set it so the dental stone won't melt or crush the print.

Where do I see it?

Adrian Monk (Tony Shalhoub) and Lt. Randall Disher (Jason Gray-Stanford) examine a set of a suspect's footprints at the crime scene in "Mr. Monk and the Captain's Wife." Good investigators would photograph them and then cast them in dental stone so they can examine the prints at the lab.

How can I use it?

Dental stone is one of those processes on crime shows that are usually assumed, not shown. And it is assumed that the cast always comes out perfectly readable. You could throw a wrench into your investigation if there's a screwup with the dental stone. Once a cast is made, the print is absorbed into the cast and is gone from the ground. If the cast breaks or the dental stone is applied too roughly, you'll lose the imprint and, therefore, your evidence.

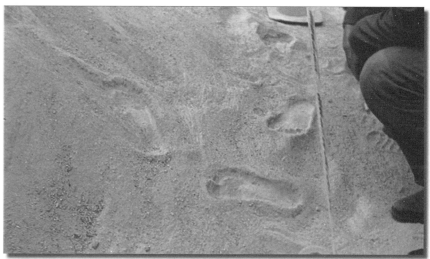

Footprints in the sand. *Monk*, "Mr. Monk and the Captain's Wife"; USA Network, Universal, 2002–09.

Luminol

What is it?

Luminol is investigative magic. Spray a little on what looks to be a clean surface and remaining bloodstains will luminesce like a neon sign. Luminol is a powder made up of nitrogen, carbon, oxygen, and hydrogen mixed with a hydroxide that reacts with the hemoglobin in the blood to produce a short-term blue glowing effect. Have you ever poured hydrogen peroxide on a bloodstain to try to remove it? It foams and fizzes, right? The same action happens when investigators use luminol, except the luminol compound creates the blue glow. If you're going to try this, make sure it's dark and have your camera ready. The reaction doesn't last long — less than a minute. As the peroxide reacts with the blood to make it fizz, it also breaks it down, thereby destroying evidence. So investigators use luminol as a last resort. However, there is a version of luminol called BlueStar that can be applied numerous times and still yield correct DNA typing. Many believe this is the most sensitive and long-lasting solution available.

Where do I see it?

In episode 110, or the first season of *CSI*, investigator Sara Sidle (Jorja Fox) sprays a suspect's clean wall with a substance to see if there is evidence of blood. In the scene, the substance turns pink on the wall and she indicates that this is where the victim had bled. She may have been using a phenolphthalein test. But a couple of

Sara sprays a substance on the walls and it turns pink. *CSI*, episode 110; Jerry Bruckheimer TV, 2000.

things are askew. First, in real CSI, luminol is more commonly used to detect blood on large surface areas. Second, when you conduct this test, you have your camera ready to photograph the evidence. Phenolphthalein and luminol don't last long before they fade and they cannot be repeated to yield the same results.

How can I use it?

Use luminol to find blood when the murderer tries to hide her crime, to find out the direction of a blood-spatter pattern, to find bloody footprints that show where the murderer walked, to determine how many victims were present. A murderer may think she's very thorough in cleaning up the blood at a crime scene, but tiny particles of blood cling to surfaces for years. Red herring tip: Household bleach, some metals, paints, fecal matter, dyes, Drano, and plant materials will also cause a blue glowing reaction if they come into contact with luminol. To be on the safe side, other tests will need to be run to determine if the glowing substance is actually blood.

■ *Exercise 1.*

Watch an episode from your favorite crime show or film. As you watch, make a running list of the types of evidence recovered from the crime: biological, circumstantial, direct, impression, physical, trace. As you watch, take notes on how investigators recover the evidence. Has it been collected and stored properly? What kind of protective gear are investigators wearing at the scene? Does the evidence follow a proper chain of custody? What kind of processing does the evidence undergo? Was the body found prone or supine? Was there an identifiable modus operandi or signature that the criminal used? How many items from the CSI's toolkit can you identify in this film or show? Based on what you learned in this chapter, how would you do things differently to apply real-life forensics?

■ *Exercise 2.*

Take the terms from this chapter and make flash cards. Blindly pick three and weave them into a scene you are working on. Now, put those cards aside and blindly pick three more from the pile. See if you can add another layer of investigative techniques into the same scene.

II.
Coroner Chat

"*Mortui vivos docent.* The dead teach the living."
— *Anonymous*

What you'll find in this chapter are the key terms used in the coroner's office, listed in alphabetical order so they are easy to find. Let me direct you to a few terms. Take note of the difference between coroners and medical examiners. Many people don't know that there is a difference. If you really want to know what's going on with our coroner and medical examiner systems, check out *Post Mortem: Death Investigation in America,* a PBS *Frontline* report from February 2011: *http://www.pbs. org/wgbh/pages/frontline/post-mortem/*. The program does a good job of examining the coroner versus medical examiner system and the flaws in our death investigation systems. If you want a better understanding of how a body decomposes and what that means to your investigation, check out the decomposition time line. And make sure to understand the four manners of death and how rigor mortis, algor mortis, and livor mortis play key roles in determining the time of death.

This chapter is like coming home for me. As the daughter of a medical examiner I was in coroner training from the time I could walk and talk. My father's business in rural northern Michigan was in our home and we often helped my dad with his cases. As an engineer and inventor it turns out he was ahead of his time, as he created infrared studies on decomposition and wrote procedures for mass disasters decades before school shootings and the attacks of 9/11/01. But, since most people don't have a medical examiner in the family, you can rely on this chapter. And if you need more, the definitive text on death investigation is Spitz & Fisher's *Medicolegal Death Investigation.* Warning: it's highly technical and graphic. You may want to supplement it with a call to your local coroner's office.

Abrasions

What is it?

Abrasions are light cuts and scrapes on the body. They usually aren't deeper than the first layer of skin (through the epidermis but not the dermis). Abrasions are sometimes referred to as grazing or brushing the skin. Abrasions on the skin may take on the imprint of the object with which it came into contact — such as tire treads, floor mats, escalator grates, carpet, gravel, or fabric.

Where do I see it?

A prostitute in the pilot episode of *CSI* sustains abrasions on her forehead during a minor car accident, which eventually leads the crime scene investigator to solving a theft case.

How can I use it?

The key thing an abrasion will tell you is where and how a person has been injured. The indentation of gravel on the side of a leg indicates that the leg was dragged across dirt. Tire treads across a person's back tell you that the victim was run over by a vehicle. A woven fabric pattern embedded into the forearm reveals where an object impacted the skin. You will see the imprint of the fabric and the tire on the skin, proving the fabric was covering the skin at the leg.

The woman in this car received an abrasion during a minor car accident in the pilot episode of *CSI*; Jerry Bruckheimer TV, 2000.

Algor Mortis

What is it?

Algor mortis is the temperature of the body after death. In the first few hours after death, the body slowly loses heat to match the ambient temperature. During the first twelve hours after death, the body loses two degrees per hour, as long as the air temperature is less than 98.6 degrees Fahrenheit. After twelve hours, it loses one degree per hour. Eventually, the body will cool to the ambient temperature. However, once the body starts to decompose (in normal conditions, about thirty-six hours after death), the temperature rises again.

Where do I see it?

The frozen victim in *Pushing Daisies*, "Corpsicle," will have a very, very low body temperature after being left out in the snow. It will be impossible to tell the time of death. When the body thaws, the tissue will contain "freeze artifact" — tiny bubbles throughout the tissue.

How can I use it?

The coroner takes the body temperature once he arrives at the scene, which can tell you how long the body was dead before the temperature was taken to give you a fairly reliable time of death.

Ned and Charlotte investigate deaths where the bodies are frozen and would have a very low algor mortis. *Pushing Daisies*, "Corpsicle"; ABC, 2007–09.

Asphyxiation

What is it?

Asphyxiation happens when the respiratory system shuts down and oxygen can no longer pass in and out of the lungs. Carbon monoxide has eaten up all the oxygen and none is replaced.

Where do I see it?

When the victim insults his friend about his blow-up girlfriend, the girlfriend and friend take matters into their own hands in *Pushing Daisies*, "Bitter Sweets."

How can I use it?

Asphyxiation takes many forms — some self-induced, some chemically induced, some pure accident. You can create a cause of death by asphyxiation via strangulation, smothering, something heavy falling on the chest, being placed in a posture that cuts off oxygen, pneumonia, CO^2 poisoning.

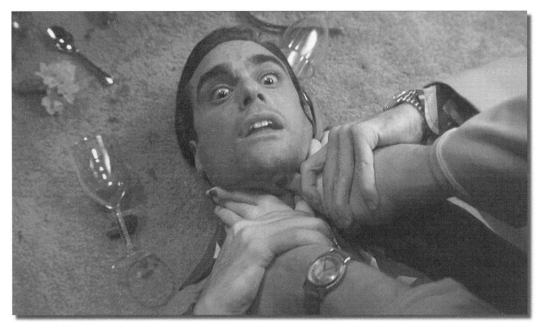

A killer murders his friend by strangulation with his blow-up doll. *Pushing Daisies*, "Bitter Sweets"; ABC, 2007–09.

Autopsy

What is it?

Autopsy refers to the medical-surgical procedure performed on a dead human body to discover the manner and cause of death.

Where do I see it?

This autopsy room as depicted in the 1993 film, *The Fugitive*, presents a fairly accurate picture of what a well-equipped autopsy room looked like then. Even today, many autopsy rooms in smaller communities and rural areas might still look like this.

How can I use it?

Not every dead body undergoes an autopsy. There are several key factors involved in determining if an autopsy should be conducted. Autopsies are performed for any one of these reasons:

- to help solve a crime
- to identify a person
- upon personal request of a family member or law enforcement
- upon the request of attorneys who need it for a case
- if there's a good chance it'll go to court
- if it was a medical misadventure (i.e., surgery gone bad)
- for public safety reasons (i.e., no guardrail on a busy road)

An autopsy room depicted in an early 1990s film. *The Fugitive*, Warner Bros., 1993.

Body Bag

What is it?

A body bag is literally a large, zippered, thick plastic bag with heavy straps used to lift or carry the body from the scene of death to the morgue. Body bags are not cheap. They run $25 to $50 per bag, which is why some large counties, like Los Angeles, use clear plastic sheets instead of body bags and burrito-wrap the corpse.

Where do I see it?

Nate Fisher (Peter Krause) sips on his coffee as he awaits instructions from his brother about what to do with a dismembered body in "The Foot," *Six Feet Under*.

How can I use it?

In TV and film, a body bag is used mostly as a prop piece or a line of dialogue: Tag 'em and bag 'em. Movie style body bags run their zippers down the middle, whereas industrial-use bags have side or middle zippers for easy access.

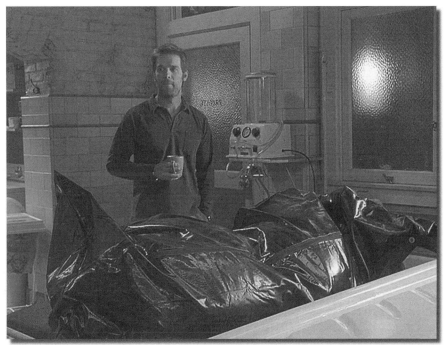

Peter stares at the bag. *Six Feet Under*; HBO, 2000–05.

Brain Death

What is it?

Over the years the medical field has defined brain death differently. Just forty years ago, a four-step test for brain death was repeated every twenty-four hours until the body reached a temperature below 90 degrees. Today, the medical field measures brain death as the stoppage of circulation and all activity of the brain and brain stem.

Where do I see it?

You don't see brain death; you witness the results — a dead body. Most of us can remember the first time we saw a dead person, probably the body of a loved one in a coffin at a funeral home. In the classic coming-of-age story, *Stand By Me* (1986), four young boys venture out to see their first dead body, Vern (Jerry O'Connell), Chris (River Phoenix), Gordie (Wil Wheaton), and Teddy (Corey Feldman).

How can I use it?

Classically, time of death occurred when the heart stopped beating, but it is becoming more and more accepted now that brain death determines time of death. In most cases, you need at least two independent declarations of death before organs can be harvested.

Four friends find the dead body they've been searching for. *Stand By Me*, Columbia Pictures, 1986.

Close Range Shot

What is it?

How close is a close range shot? If gunpowder residue and other metal fragments from the bullet are imbedded in the skin around the wound (see Stippling), then the weapon was fired at close range. Usually this means twelve to eighteen inches for handguns and rifles, but up to several feet for shotguns.

Where do I see it?

At close range, criminal Gaear Grimsrud (Peter Stormare) shoots the police officer, who has stopped them for speeding and now threatens their kidnapping as Carl Showalter (Steve Buscemi) watches in astonishment in *Fargo*.

How can I use it?

A coroner will closely examine the wound and determine how far the gun was from the victim. To find out exactly the distance between the gun's muzzle and the target or victim, a firearms criminalist will perform a firing test with the exact gun and same ammunition to reproduce the same stippling diameter on the target. Close range shooting is an emotionally charged event. As a writer, you can funnel this emotion into the backstory of your criminal and motivation for his crime.

Grimsrud shoots a cop at close range in this scene from *Fargo*, MGM, 1996.

Contact Shot

What is it?

When the muzzle of a gun touches the body, it is considered a contact shot. As the gun is fired, the muzzle heat brands a ring into the clothing or skin. Gun smoke and gases from the burning powder will often enter the wound or be found on the outside edges of it. If the contact is through fabric, synthetic fabric will melt; cotton or wool fabric will be torn apart and frayed where the bullet entered. The fabric may enter the wound.

Where do I see it?

This victim in *CSI*, episode 121, received a contact shot to the heart.

How can I use it?

A coroner will closely examine the wound and determine how far the gun and shooter were from the victim. Suicides are usually contact shots, as can be murders of passion. There is something intimate and vicious about a contact shot. Contact shooting is an emotionally charged event. As a writer, you can funnel this emotion into the backstory of your criminal and motivation for his crime.

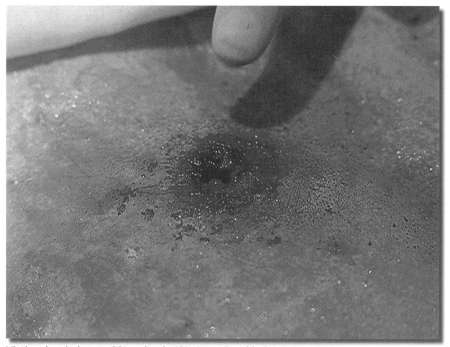

Victim shot in heart. *CSI*, episode 121; Jerry Bruckheimer TV, 2000.

Contusions

What is it?

A contusion is a fancy word for a bruise. In a contusion, the skin doesn't break but the blood vessels underneath sustain damage and cause a hemorrhage. Not all contusions are fatal. We get them frequently from benign activities like bumping into furniture or an open drawer. But when trauma is inflicted on our brain, contusions are often deadly. Contusions on the brain come in three strike types: tears, hemorrhages, and necrosis (dead cells). Just as bruises to our body don't usually penetrate the skin, neither do contusions to the brain. The skull may be cracked, but the dura (the next layer) remains intact. However, if the skull is penetrated, it is considered a laceration or open fracture, not a contusion.

Where do I see it?

An unfortunate young man becomes the victim of a gang who beat him and give him a contusion in *Bones*, season 1, "The Woman in the Garden."

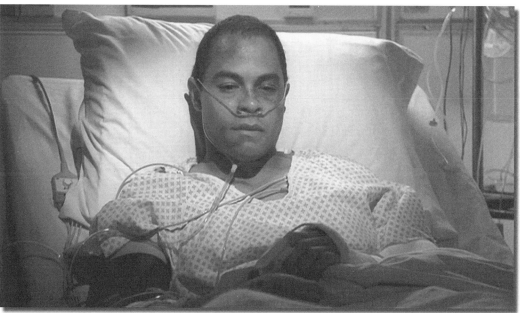

This young man was beaten by a gang and suffered a contusion. *Bones*, "The Woman in the Garden"; 20th Century Fox, 2006.

How can I use it?

Contusions are caused by blows to the head or by a fall. An autopsy will reveal where the contusion is, what kind it is, and possibly what caused it. You can't tell what caused it by looking at the brain outside the skull. You won't see the bruise on the brain until you peel back the scalp. Once you see the area of impact, you can pattern-match the area on the scalp to the instrument used. For example, if the bruise on the scalp came from a pipe, it would look long and narrow; but if the bruise on the scalp came from the head hitting a sidewalk, it would be wide and contoured to match the flat shape of the pavement.

Or, for example, if a victim were whipped with an extension cord, two red, bruised lines, like a train track, would appear on the flesh. The rush of blood directly where the cord hits the flesh causes these two lines. To make a match, simply place the cord on the train tracks and it should be a perfect fit.

Coroner

What is it?

Here is where we splice open the very common misconception that coroners and medical examiners are interchangeable. They are not. A coroner:

- is appointed or elected by the county commissioners
- is not required and usually does not have a medical degree
- could be your local plumber, bee keeper, or car mechanic
- investigates the corpse at the scene of death
- identifies the body
- notifies next of kin
- is the first one allowed to touch the body
- authorizes the death certificate if no medical examiner is present

Where do I see it?

The classic toe tag scene is representative of the coroner's office. This is taken from the opening credits of *Six Feet Under*.

How can I use it?

Start by understanding the difference between a coroner and a medical examiner. One of the main differences is that a coroner is not a medical doctor and is appointed or elected by her constituents.

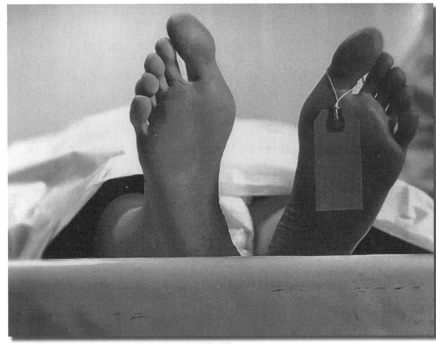

Toe tag. *Six Feet Under* pilot; HBO, 2000–05.

Crypt

What is it?

Crypt is another name for morgue. Crypts in small counties may only have one room for one body. Large crypts in major metropolitan cities can hold hundreds. The Los Angeles County morgue stores an average of 250 bodies on any given day.

Where do I see it?

New CSI, Holly Gribbs (Chandra West), loses her cookies as she accidentally steps into the crypt in the *CSI* pilot.

How can I use it?

Crypt is a good term to use in dialogue or scene headings.

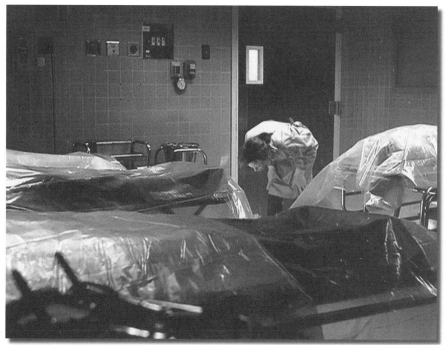

New recruit Holly Gribbs loses her cookies as she accidentally steps into the crypt. *CSI* pilot; Jerry Bruckheimer TV, 2000.

Decapitation

What is it?

Decapitation occurs when the head is severed from the body. It's such an obvious cause of death that I couldn't find a reference for it in the index of Spitz and Fisher's definitive manual on death investigation.

Where do I see it?

The CSI team, Catherine Willows (Marg Helgenberger) and Gil Grissom (William Petersen), and the medial examiner investigate the murder of this unfortunate victim who lost his head in *CSI*, episode 121.

How can I use it?

A French study conducted a blink test of convicts who were beheaded and reported that the head remains conscious for up to fifteen to twenty seconds after death — usually expressing shock, confusion, terror, or grief. Do your own research and decide.

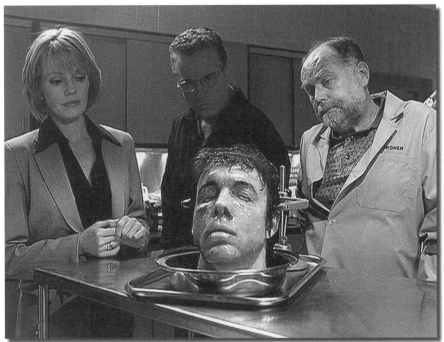

Victim's head on autopsy table. *CSI*, episode 121; Jerry Bruckheimer TV, 2000.

Decomposition

What is it?

Decomposition is the process by which the human body rots after death. It happens in stages that are determined by the health of the deceased, time, atmospheric conditions, humidity, and exposure to the elements. Common variables that affect the decomposition rate are temperature, moisture in the air, sun exposure, and insect or animal activity. The condition of the body is also a factor. Fatter people decompose less quickly than skinny ones. Bodies that are buried, submerged, wearing tight-fitting clothing, or wrapped don't decompose as quickly as those left in the open air.

Where do I see it?

The corpse in a scene from the first season of *Bones*, episode "Two Bodies in the Lab," has reached the skeletonization stage of decomposition.

The corpse in this scene has reached the skeletonization stage of decomposition. *Bones*, "Two Bodies in the Lab"; 20th Century Fox, 2006.

How can I use it?

Decomposition gives investigators clues as to when the person died, where the person died, and how the body was positioned after death. Your investigator should check what the skin is doing, whether there are insects or maggots, and where the blood has pooled on the victim. Blood pooling indicates how the body landed after death. If blood has pooled in the feet and butt (a sitting position), but the body was found lying down, then someone moved it. This raises questions and makes your story more intriguing. Who moved it? Why did they move it? Were they trying to make a homicide look natural or accidental? What if the body has been frozen? Your medical examiner should look for freezer artifact. Tiny bubbles form in the cells as the body dethaws, proving that the body was frozen. By the way, a body rots very quickly after the dethawing process, much like the way frozen fruit turns brown and mushy once it's out of the freezer.

Decomposition Time Line

The following time line is based on a normally occurring exposure:

Death occurs

1st minute — heart and breath stop, eyes dilate, skin sweats out, skin pales and becomes cold and clammy

1 hour — livor mortis sets in, blood begins to pool due to gravity, blowflies lay eggs in moist openings and wounds

2–4 hours — rigor mortis begins, muscles stiffen

8 hours — livor mortis complete, blood stops moving

12 hours — rigor mortis peaks, algor mortis has dropped body temp to ambient temperature at two degrees per hour

13 hours — body temp drops again one degree and continues one degree per hour until it reaches ambient temp

24 hours — rigor mortis declines

36 hours — rigor mortis dissipates

37 hours — the epidermis begins to slip off the dermis layer

48–72 hours — putrefaction: the body literally dissolves itself, releasing liquids and gasses (the predominant gas is ammonia — NH_3); abdomen and extremities bloat; the skin marbles and turns black

72 hours — post-putrefaction: bloating subsides as the body deteriorates; head and body hair falls off the body; fly eggs hatch into maggots; maggots start to eat the flesh and organs

96 hours — decay: increased internal decomposition combined with skin cracks, fluids leaking, hair coming off, and bones exposed

1 week to several months to years — mummification: body dries up; flesh and organs dry up; bone decay

Defense Wounds

What is it?

Defense wounds are those on the body of the victim, caused by the victim as he is trying to escape injury.

Where do I see it?

Dr. Megan Hunt (Dana Delaney) discovers that the victim has defense wounds on his hands in *Body of Proof*, "All in the Family."

How can I use it?

I'm going to ask you to picture some uncomfortable scenarios so you can understand how defense wounds work. Picture someone coming at you with a knife. What's your first instinct? Probably, to raise your hand over your face, right? By trying to protect yourself you would sustain defense wounds to your palm and inner forearm. Now picture being strangled by a scarf. You would reach up and try to release that scarf. In the process your fingernails would dig into your neck causing scratches and bruises. Also remember that defense wounds can happen anywhere on the body where a victim is trying to get away or protect himself.

Delamination

What is it?

Delamination is a splitting or separating of a matter into layers. Forensically speaking, this commonly refers to the way time or extreme heat splits and shrinks the scalp, exposing the skull. Delamination is a form of skin slippage.

Where do I see it?

The victim on this table is not human; it's a gorilla that has been delaminated to fool someone into believing it is human in *CSI*, episode 121.

How can I use it?

Delamination is part of the process of decomposition. You have to look at the skin under a microscope to see what effects the environment has had on it. Delamination is also a common occurrence in fire victims. In normal conditions of 50–90-degree temperatures, delamination will take four to five days. Skin that is delaminated is easy to slip off the hand. Now you can put it on as a glove in order to make a fingerprint identification.

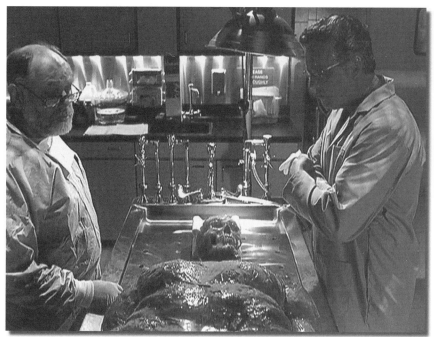

Body of gorilla peeled. *CSI*, episode 121; Jerry Bruckheimer TV, 2000.

Distant Shot

What is it?

A distant shot is a gunshot in which the gun smoke, powder, or residue does not reach its victim. With handguns, this range is usually outside of twelve to eighteen inches. In larger guns, like shotguns, a distant shot will be greater than six feet.

Where do I see it?

Matt Damon trains his weapon and makes the kill on two long-distance outlaws in the 2010 film, *True Grit*.

How can I use it?

Once the bullet has entered a victim from a distant gunshot, the bullet wound will look the same no matter if the gun was fifteen feet or fifty feet away. A gunshot wound resulting from a close range gunshot, but fired through a window or a door, will look like a distant shot because the spread of the pellets will be wider due to a billiard-ball effect. The window will absorb the gunshot powder, so the CSI can swab the window and the crime lab can match the powder to a brand of bullet.

DOA

What is it?

DOA is an acronym that stands for dead on arrival. Usually this pronouncement is made by EMTs or other emergency responders who arrive first at a scene of death.

Where do I see it?

In a scene from *Fargo*, Marge Gunderson (Frances McDormand) and her partner (James Gaulke) arrive on an accident scene where the victims have already been pronounced dead.

How can I use it?

In some counties, Los Angeles for one, laypersons can pronounce or determine

Matt Damon readies a distance shot at two outlaws. *True Grit*, Paramount, 2010.

Marge and her partner investigate the deaths from the prior night; bodies are DOA. *Fargo*, MGM, 1996.

death (note: not *cause* of death, only a medical examiner can do that) if the signs of death are obvious. Decapitation, decomposition, incineration, and evisceration are considered obvious signs. In other jurisdictions, a medical examiner or physician is required to pronounce death.

DMORT

What is it?

Stuck with a large-scale death disaster on your hands? Call in the Disaster Mortuary Operational Response Team. DMORT is a federal assistance program for mass fatalities like airplane crashes, weather-related tragedies, mass suicides, or September 11. DMORT teams provide temporary morgues, identify victims, assist with victim dental records, dispose of remains, give family support, and process paperwork.

Where do I see it?

A DMORT team helps process an airplane crash in the 1999 film, *Random Hearts*.

How can I use it?

DMORT teams present great character studies, as they are comprised of professionals from the forensics field. DMORT work is demanding, messy, high pressure, and often depressing. A team's main objective is to provide answers, remains, and comfort to the living. This is tough work undertaken by tougher people.

DOD

What is it?

Outside the medical examiner system, DOD would stand for Department of Defense. But inside the morgue doors, DOD is an acronym for date of death. This is the official date and time of death recorded on the death certificate by the physician or medical examiner.

Where do I see it?

Lt. Theo Kojak (Telly Savalas) examines an innocent female victim who has just been gunned down in this episode of *Kojak*, "One for the Morgue."

How can I use it?

Know what it means. Use it in dialogue. Don't be fooled. No one really knows the exact time or day of someone's passing. But if you dare to have some fun with it or you are morbidly curious, you can calculate your own DOD on sites like deathdate (*http://deathdate.info/*) or deathclock (*http://deathclock.com/*). A word of warning: Those who know when they are going to die often hit the mark.

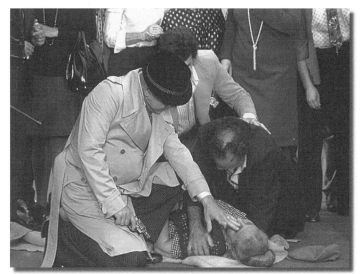

Woman killed in street. *Kojak*; CBS, 1973–78.

Donor Room

What is it?

A donor room is a place where fresh bodies await donorship. This area may be located at the morgue, the coroner's office, or the hospital. A procurement specialist extracts the eyes, organs, or tissues prearranged for donation before the body is released to the family. Sometimes the entire body is procured to universities for research. Badly decomposed bodies or those that have experienced traumatic deaths or communicable diseases are not eligible for donorship.

Where do I see it?

Organs are often harvested in the autopsy room if there is no separate donor room. One victim awaits her autopsy in this scene from *CSI*, episode 120.

How can I use it?

All of us have the option to donate our organs when we check the little box on the back of our driver's license. Some of us go even further and participate in Willed Body programs where universities use human cadavers for teaching purposes. The famous Body Farm started by Dr. Bill Bass at the University of Tennessee regularly accepts cadaver donations to study the effects of weather and insects on the decaying process. And you may even find purpose in the afterlife as a human crash test dummy. The auto industry has used human cadavers to test and improve auto safety since the 1930s.

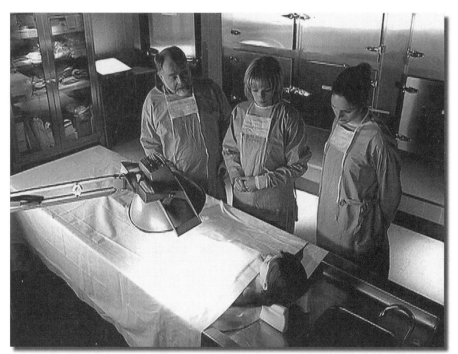

Organs are often harvested during the autopsy if there is no separate donor room. *CSI*, episode 120; Jerry Bruckheimer TV, 2000.

Electrocution

What is it?

Death by electrocution occurs when a human comes into contact with a live electrical source like power lines or lightning. Three things must be in place for electrocution to happen: a ground source (like metal pipes, faucets, or appliances), a live electrical source, and a pathway for the electricity flow — the victim.

Where do I see it?

In the *Body of Proof* episode, "Society Hill," the victim, a magazine editor, is murdered by electrocution in her backyard pool.

How can I use it?

A person who has been electrocuted with a voltage over 1,000 volts will sustain heavy burning patterns. Household appliances such as blow-dryers and toasters with lower voltages of 110 to 120 volts often do not leave visible injuries on their victims.

Victim electrocuted in pool. *Body of Proof*, "Society Hill"; ABC, 2001.

Evisceration

What is it?

One of the four recognized obvious signs of death, evisceration is a disemboweling or gutting of the insides of a human being. It's rather stomach-churning, isn't it? Pun intended.

Where do I see it?

In this gruesome murder in *Bones*, season 1, episode "Two Bodies in the Lab," Dr. Brennan and Detective Booth investigate a murder in which the victim was eviscerated by hungry canines.

How can I use it?

Evisceration seemed to be a more popular, albeit cruel, way to punish offenders and warriors of old. However, evisceration doesn't have to be the cause or result of death. It could happen postmortem. Pregnant women have been killed and then eviscerated to remove their babies. Or evisceration may occur if the body is left outside for a time before it is found and animals disembowel it.

A body has been eviscerated by dogs postmortem. *Bones*, "Two Bodies in the Lab"; 20th Century Fox, 2005.

Exit Wounds

What is it?

The exit wound is where a bullet (or projectile) has passed through the body and out the other side.

Where do I see it?

The victim in the "Hell Hath No Fury" episode of *Castle* was shot in the head. The exit wound is in the rear of the skull.

How can I use it?

More blood can be found on an exit wound than an entry wound. This is because the tissue damage through the entry point of the skin has not caused as much damage as the exit wound. An entry wound is generally smaller and smoother than an exit wound. The exit wound is larger, ragged, and torn because the bullet has pushed the tissue through the body and out the other side as it traveled.

Hole in the head of a victim. *Castle*, "Hell Hath No Fury"; ABC, 2009-present.

Gunshot Wounds

What is it?

It may sound obvious and usually it is: A gunshot wound is a wound caused by a gun. The bullet (or projectile, as they say in copland) penetrates the skin and either stays inside the body or passes through.

Where do I see it?

Brady Kincaid (Edward Norton) is fatally wounded by a gunshot in this scene from the movie *Leaves of Grass*.

How can I use it?

Gunshot wounds can sometimes be disguised as stab wounds or be hidden under layers of fatty tissue. Some may not bleed outwardly very much because of poor circulation or because the bullet missed or only nicked a blood vessel. One sign that a wound is from a gun is gunpowder or discoloration around the skin where it entered. Small gunshot wounds to the head can be missed in people who have lots of hair that completely covers the wound.

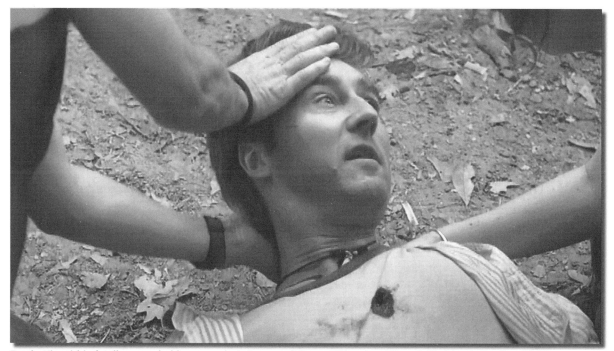

Brady Kincaid is fatally wounded by a gunshot. *Leaves of Grass*, Millennium Films & First Look Studios, 2009.

Hesitation Wounds

What is it?

Hesitation wounds are superficial, incised wounds usually found in suicide cases. The victim repeats the cutting motion in parallel cuts along the wrists or throat as he is trying to build up the courage to make the final death slash.

Where do I see it?

Richie Tenenbaum (Luke Wilson) shows his sister Margot (Gwyneth Paltrow) his attempted suicide wounds in *The Royal Tenenbaums*. His attempt was unsuccessful because he cut vertically instead of horizontally. The many cuts of varying lengths seem to indicate that Richie wasn't really serious about killing himself, but was trying to invoke sympathy and attention from his whacked-out family.

How can I use it?

Note that horizontal (or transverse) cuts along the wrist and forearm are hesitation marks and, therefore, signs of suicide. Sometimes these same markings will be found behind the knees. One exception: drug addicts found dead with vertical, horizontal, and surface scars indicate that they suffered from attention-seeking suicide attempts. In this case, their wounds are referred to as sympathy cuts, not hesitation wounds.

Richie shows Margot the cuts from his attempted suicide. *The Royal Tennenbaums*, Touchstone Pictures, 2001.

Incineration

What is it?

Incineration is one of the four obvious signs of death caused by fire. An incinerated cadaver is one that has been fatally burned, sometimes beyond recognition. Here's a little tip on survival rates of people with third-degree burns: Take the percentage of third-degree burns on their body and add their age; if the number is more than one hundred, they will probably die.

Where do I see it?

The unfortunate lass in the "Smell of Success" episode of *Pushing Daisies* was the victim of an explosion meant to kill another. In this scene, Ned has awakened her to get her story.

How can I use it?

Incineration falls under the category of thermal injury when fire is not the only culprit. Thermal or chemical burn fatalities occur when the victim is exposed to chemicals, hot liquids, hot air inhalation, steam exposure, explosions, toxic smoke, and carbon monoxide inhalation. Another unique type of burn fatality is the flash-over burn. Death occurs when a ball of fire flashes into a room and instantly kills its victims. In these cases, rigor mortis sets in immediately and the dead are found exactly as they were when the flash occurred. One of the most famous examples of flash-over burn is the Las Vegas MGM fire of November 21, 1980.

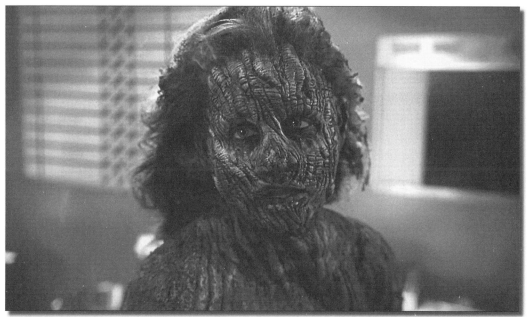

Girl is victim of a scratch 'n sniff bomb meant for her boss. *Pushing Daisies*, "Smell of Success"; ABC, 2007–09.

Incised Wounds

What is it?

An incised wound is the medical name for a cut that extends through the dermis to the subcutaneous layer. An incised wound divides the skin smoothly, not tearing or bruising the tissue. Knives, blades, or glass may cause incised wounds.

Where do I see it?

Several knives are shown as potential weapons in a girl's murder in the "Two Bodies in the Lab" episode of *Bones*.

How can I use it?

Incised wounds occur in many shapes and sizes. When investigating a stabbing victim, note how many wounds; the angle, depth, and shape of the cuts; and the appearance of the broken skin. Your CSI should not forget to swab the exterior of the wound for skin substances — fiber, sperm, assailant's blood, or skin cells — that might tell you something about the attack.

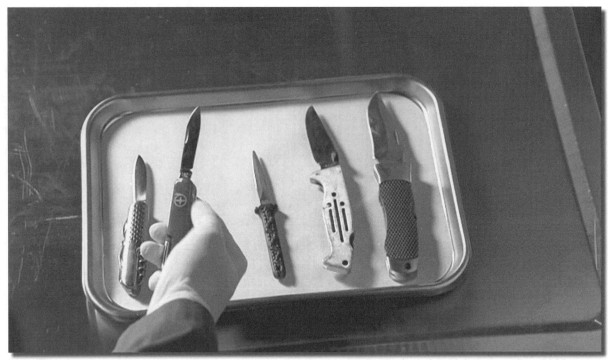

Potential knives used in incised wounds on a dead girl. *Bones*, "Two Bodies in the Lab"; 20th Century Fox, 2005.

Lacerations

What is it?

A laceration is a cut where the skin has been split open by blunt-force trauma. Lacerations are different from an incised wound in that they have ragged or abraded (scraped-away) edges caused by hammers or pistol whipping. Sharp objects cause incised wounds (knives, glass), and they have smoother edges and bridging tissue or strands of fibrous tissue that haven't been separated.

Where do I see it?

Special Agent Seeley Booth (David Boreanaz) sustains a laceration to the forehead when Dr. Temperance Brennan's (Emily Deschanel) refrigerator explodes in an attempted attack on her life in *Bones*, "Two Bodies in the Lab."

How can I use it?

Protruding parts of the face and body are most often the target of lacerations — noses, foreheads, back of the head, elbows, arms, knees, legs. The size and shape of a laceration tells you if a hammer claw or a table lamp hit the person. Finding paint chips, glass, plastic, or gravel inside a laceration may give clues to a hit and run. Lacerations can be internal, such as a karate kick to the chest that tears the heart muscle.

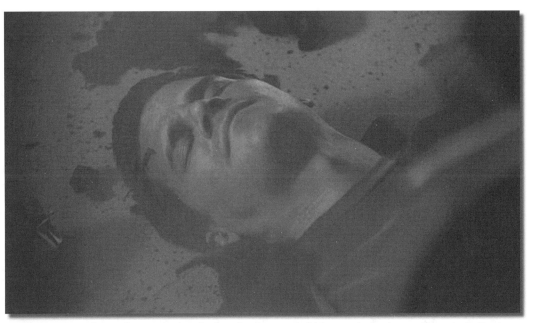

Booth sustains a laceration to the head when Dr. Brennan's fridge explodes in an attempted attack on her life. *Bones*, "Two Bodies in the Lab"; 20th Century Fox, 2005.

Ligature

What is it?

A ligature is a rope or cord (or similar item) used around the neck to strangle or asphyxiate a person. Ligatures are most commonly seen in hangings or strangulations.

Where do I see it?

In Hitchcock's film, *Rope*, two young men attempt to commit the perfect murder when they strangle David Kentley (Dick Hogan) with a rope and stuff him in a trunk before hosting a dinner party.

How can I use it?

We all know the telltale cinematic hanging scenes. A character enters a room. He sees a chair knocked over . . . then, feet swaying four feet off the floor. He looks up, up, up to the ceiling where a body hangs limp from a rafter. Yes, that's certainly one way it happens. But in real life, hangings are much easier to stage. They take place in any position — standing up, sitting down, supine, prone, kneeling. You only need a few inches of noose and the weight of your head to stop blood flow in the neck veins. In less than a minute, you fall unconscious. Death occurs only minutes later as oxygen to the brain ceases.

The boys strangle their victim with a rope as their ligature. *Rope*, MGM, 1948.

Livor Mortis

What is it?

Livor mortis refers to what the blood does after death. Once blood stops circulating, it pools to the lowest point of gravity. If the body is supine (on its back), blood will pool on the back of the legs, arms, buttocks. If the body is prone (on its face), blood pools on the front side — face, chest, front of arms and legs.

Where do I see it?

The body of the victim lies in the trunk next to Rupert Cadell (Jimmy Stewart). Since the victim's body was placed in the box right after he was killed, his blood would have pooled in the position in which he remains in the trunk, thus proving he was killed in that room.

How can I use it?

Livor mortis tells you how long the body has been dead and if the body has been moved after death. Blood starts to pool twenty minutes after death and can be detected several hours later. Because blood clots at the lowest point of gravity on the body, you can move the body and the blood stays in the same place, which is one of many factors used to determine time of death.

Even though you can't see the body of the victim, livor mortis (where and how the blood pooled) would tell investigators that the body was placed in the trunk shortly after death, thus proving he was killed in the room or very nearby. *Rope*, MGM, 1948.

Manner of Death

What is it?

When you die, your death certificate will list the cause of death and one of five modes: natural, accidental, suicide, homicide, and undetermined.

Deaths occurring from **natural** causes such as old age, cancer, or other disease usually do not require an autopsy, especially if the deceased was attended at death.

An **accidental** death includes a vehicle crash, a drowning, exposure, aspiration, complications from old wounds or operative procedures, or wrong diagnosis.

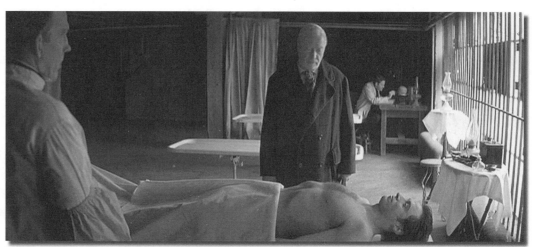

It can be argued that Robert Angier's death in his magic trick is homicide, accidental, and suicidal. *The Prestige*, Touchstone & Warner Bros. Pictures, 2006.

Suicidal deaths are deaths that occur when a person deliberately takes his own life. These can occur in a number of ways. Violent manners of suicide may include hangings, jumping from heights, or gun-inflicted deaths. Less violent manners are drug overdoses, carbon monoxide poisoning, or drowning.

In the forensic realm, **homicide** means the taking of one person's life by another. Homicide does not necessarily mean murder. Homicide may happen under involuntary or unplanned circumstances or be lawfully justified, such as in cases of war or self-defense.

Undetermined death means that the medical examiner is unable to figure out why or how a person has died. It's rare, but occasionally you can't find evidence of natural, suicidal, homicidal, or accidental causes. This is probably the hardest forensic pill to swallow of all — in real life, you cannot solve every death.

Where do I see it?

In *The Prestige*, it could be argued that Robert Angier's (Hugh Jackman) death in the water tanks is classified as homicidal, suicidal, and accidental.

How can I use it?

Most crime or procedural stories center on a protagonist who is trying to solve a homicidal death. Sometimes the death is set up to look accidental or suicidal; therefore, provide a string of red herrings for the investigator. Sometimes the homicide is unintentional, other times brutally premeditated. This doesn't mean that you can't build a good story around a natural death. But death by natural causes is a better bedfellow with dramas.

Medical Examiner

What is it?

There is often much confusion regarding the distinction between medical examiners and coroners. Put simply, medical examiners have at least ten more years of professional schooling than coroners. So, please, never make the mistake of calling a medical examiner just a body butcher. A medical examiner:

- is appointed or hired
- has a medical degree, MD, DO, or DDS
- is often a forensic pathologist
- may investigate the corpse at the scene of death
- performs autopsies
- identifies the body
- notifies next of kin
- determines cause and manner of death
- is the first one allowed to touch the body
- authorizes the death certificate

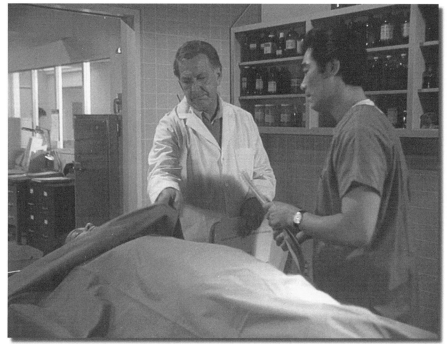

Quincy M.E., "Hit & Run at Danny's"; NBC, 1976–83.

Where do I see it?

The quintessential Quincy M.E. (Jack Klugman) was the first medical examiner who got a show entirely devoted to death investigation.

How can I use it?

On TV the medical examiners and coroners are almost interchangeable. But now you know the main difference: that medical examiners are medical doctors, usually pathologists.

Postmortem

What is it?

Postmortem means after death. Antemortem means before death.

Where do I see it?

Zack Addy (Eric Millegan) performs a postmortem examination on a victim in *Bones*, "The Woman in the Garden."

How can I use it?

We can learn much about the cause of death from the postmortem clock and postmortem artifacts. The postmortem clock, which tracks the changes in the body after death, helps us determine the time of death (see Decomposition). Postmortem artifacts tell us what was relevant to the cause of death before or after it occurred — for example, the weather, the natural environment where the body was found, or animal or insect scavengers.

Zack Addy does a postmortem examination on a victim. *Bones*, "The Woman in the Garden"; 20th Century Fox, 2006.

Processing Room

What is it?

When a body first enters the morgue, it goes through a processing room where it is checked in, much like at a doctor's visit. The cadaver is weighed, measured, photographed, disrobed, given a processing number, and put into the fridge or crypt to await an autopsy. Any evidence left with or on the body is removed, given an evidence tag, and placed in an evidence locker.

Where do I see it?

David Fisher (Michael C. Hall) and the medical examiner move a body from the processing room in the pilot of *Six Feet Under*.

How can I use it?

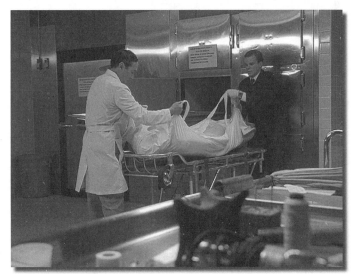

Lifting body bag. *Six Feet Under* pilot; HBO, 2000–05.

Smaller morgues or medical examiners' offices may not have a separate processing room, but bodies are processed in a similar manner. Death is the great equalizer among humanity. Once a body enters, no one gets a rush autopsy or placed on a priority pile. Even the great Michael Jackson had to wait his turn — although he did get to stay in a special, locked celebrity cage to prevent staff looky-loos from sneaking photos and selling them to E-TV.

Pugilistic Pose

What is it?

Referred to as the boxer's stance, the pugilistic pose occurs in fire victims. As the body heats, the muscles in the arms and torso shrink and contract. The body sits up, the hips and knees bend, and the arms rise into fighter position. This happens because the bigger the muscle group, the stronger the pull.

Where do I see it?

Special Agent Jethro Gibbs (Mark Harmon) and team examine a burn victim whose arms are in a pugilistic pose in *NCIS*, "Enigma."

How can I use it?

Pugilistic pose happens during the fire as the body heats up. It can be confused with rigor mortis if not properly recognized for what it is.

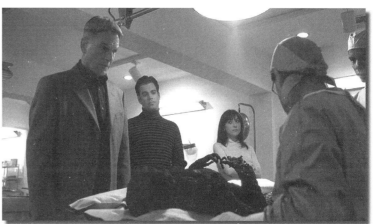

Charred body in morgue. *NCIS*, "Enigma"; CBS, Belisarius Productions 2003–present.

Puncture Wound

What is it?

Also referred to as a stab wound, a puncture wound is sharp force injury created by a pointed object. To be considered a puncture wound, the exterior length of the wound on the skin must be smaller than the depth of the wound under the skin.

Where do I see it?

Billy Kincaid (Edward Norton) suffers from an arrow wound that punctures his torso in *Leaves of Grass*.

How can I use it?

A stab wound usually indicates homicide. And multiple stab wounds are a dead giveaway of murderous intent. Stabbing doesn't usually cause a lot of bruising or bleeding to the exterior of the skin, and the skin will look smooth where the object entered, unless the handle of the weapon strikes the skin and breaks blood vessels, causing a bruise.

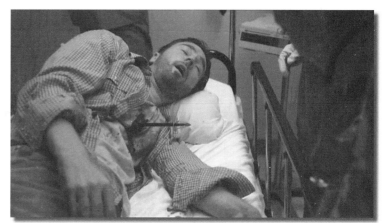

Bill Kincaid is shot by an arrow that punctures him straight through from back to front. *Leaves of Grass*, Millennium Films, 2009.

Putrefaction

What is it?

Putrefaction is another term for the process of decomposition.

Where do I see it?

Bugs collected in evidence containers from the scene of death will tell investigators what stage of decomposition the body was in when it was found and will help narrow down how long ago the person was killed. This scene is taken from the opening scenes of the *CSI* pilot.

How can I use it?

The speed of a body's putrefaction is dependent on air temperature, moisture, humidity levels, and animal or insect intervention. However, Spitz and Werner state that the rule of thumb for decomposition is one week in the air equals two weeks in water equals eight weeks in the ground (1 week air = 2 weeks water = 8 weeks ground). This rate may be sped up by extreme heat or animal activity. It may be slowed down or completely stopped by freezing water temperatures or water with a high salt content and therefore fewer bacteria.

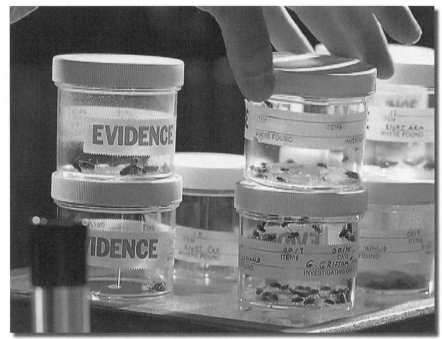

Bugs in jar. *CSI* pilot, CBS, 2000.

Raccoon's Eyes

What is it?

Black circles or shading under the victim's eyes are called raccoon's eyes (not to be confused with a bad hangover). This usually happens when the base of the skull is fractured and bleeding has moved to the tissue around the eyes.

Where do I see it?

Medical examiner Dr. Megan Hunt (Dana Delany) could quickly rule out blunt-force trauma to the skull of the magazine editor and murder victim from *Body of Proof*'s "Society Hill" because she does not have raccoon's eyes. We learn at the end of the episode she was electrocuted in her pool.

How can I use it?

Raccoon's eyes provide evidence to the investigator of trauma to the victim's head (specifically, the base of the skull) that caused a brain hemorrhage . . . trauma that someone may be trying to cover up.

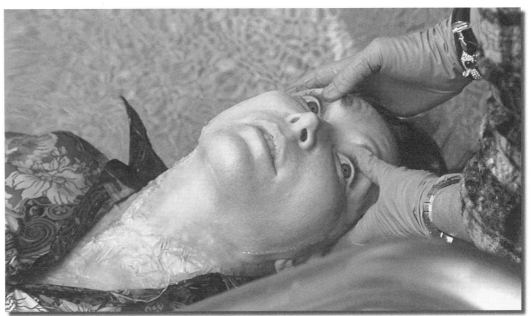

Victim close-up. *Body of Proof*, "Society Hill"; ABC, 2001.

Rigor Mortis

What is it?

Rigor mortis refers to the stiffening of the muscles after death, which causes the body, for a time, to become rigid. Rigor mortis is one of the first stages of decomposition. It can start as early as fifteen minutes after death, peaks at twelve hours, and declines after twenty-four.

Where do I see it?

The body of the victim from *NCIS*'s "The Good Samaritan" was found after rigor mortis took place, meaning he was dead for at least twenty-four hours.

How can I use it?

Rigor mortis is one of the many ways you can estimate time of death. If you encounter a body in full rigor mortis, you can safely determine that the person has been dead for less than twenty-four hours. Cold weather decreases the rate of rigor. Drugs and poisons can either slow or quicken the rate of rigor. People who die in a state of tension or anxiety (drowning or homicide) are sometimes found clutching something nearby — grass, seaweed, hair. This doesn't mean that the victim made one last, desperate struggle to grasp at his last moment of life. Instead, it may reveal a cadaveric spasm, during which the body goes limp before it goes rigid. It passes immediately from death to rigor mortis. When this happens, the muscles in the hands curl instantly, grabbing whatever is between them. Another instance of a quick onset of rigor mortis is when a person has been exercising hard right before death. The muscles contain lactic acid, which needs oxygen to release, but if the person dies before the oxygen can reach the muscles, rigor will set in very quickly.

Wide shot of victim on lawn. *NCIS*, "The Good Samaritan"; CBS, Belisarius Productions, 2003–present.

Self-Inflicted Wounds

What is it?

Self-inflicted is another way of saying, I hurt myself. Self-inflicted wounds may be intentional, as in the case of suicide, or accidental, as in the case of one young man who was killed while cleaning his shotgun. It was ruled an accidental, self-inflicted, fatal wound.

Where do I see it?

View the *CSI: Miami* episode "Paint It Black" to see a victim/suspect who, as a result of a personality disorder, inflicts deep abrasions on her arms.

How can I use it?

When looking at a victim, your investigator needs to decide whether the wounds on his body are self-inflicted or caused by someone else. Are there hesitation wounds or sympathy cuts? And how do you distinguish between homicide, suicide, or accidental shooting? If the shot was at a distance, this points to a homicide or an accident. Is the bullet hole in an area the victim wouldn't be able to reach — like the back of the head? If so, rule out self-inflicted and look to homicide. Was the shot to the heart, mouth, forehead, or temple? If so, these are classic signs of suicide.

Skin Slippage

What is it?

Skin slippage is another term for delamination of the skin. Skin slippage is part of the process of decomposition and starts, on average, thirty-six to seventy-two hours after death, depending on ambient conditions. As the body decomposes, the outer layer of the skin separates. It can literally be peeled away, much like a snake molting its skin.

Where do I see it?

A dog finds the missing foot of a person accidentally chopped up in an industrial-sized blender on *Six Feet Under*, "The Foot." The skin of the foot is marbled and nearing slippage stage.

How can I use it?

Skin slippage can be very useful in getting a clear set of fingerprints from a victim. There's a slight creepiness factor in how it's performed. The skin from the victim's hand is slipped off the body. It now looks like a glove. The fingerprint examiner can then slip her own hand inside the skin glove and roll the fingers to get a good set of prints.

Dog with foot. *Six Feet Under*, HBO, 2000-05.

Smudging

What is it?

Smudging is a type of stippling (see Stippling). When a gun is fired at close range (less than six inches from the victim), the gun smoke from the weapon expels a cloud of gunpowder and soot that leave a smudge around the outside of the gunshot wound. Unlike tattooing, it can be wiped off or swabbed off the skin for testing.

Where do I see it?

The first victim in the *NCIS* episode, "The Good Samaritan," has some smudging around the bullet wound, indicating that he was shot at close range.

How can I use it?

Smudging leaves gunshot residue (trace elements from the primer, aka gunpowder and soot) that can be swabbed and tested at the lab to determine what kind of bullet and gun were used. Smudging also tells you that the gun was in close proximity, but not touching, the victim.

Note: Tattooing is another form of smudging but it remains permanent, like a tattoo, and cannot be wiped off. In tattooing, the unburned gunpowder and soot have been embedded into the skin. This is a good indicator that the gun was shot at close range and that the powder charge is greater (more powerful) than if the stippling could simply be wiped away.

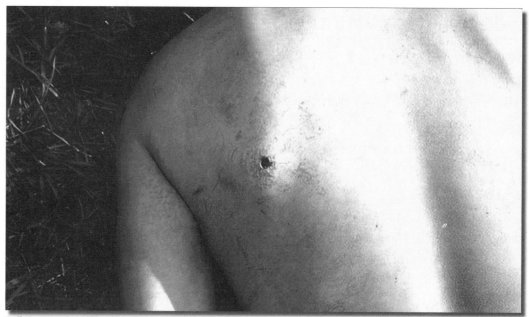

Bullet wound. *NCIS*, "The Good Samaritan"; CBS, 2003–present.

Stellate Pattern

What is it?

Stellate means star. When a bullet penetrates human flesh, it can leave a star-shaped pattern on the skin or bone. This is because the gases from the gunshot get behind the skin and push it back against the gun until it splits and tears the skin in a star pattern.

Where do I see it?

The stellate pattern on the victim shows what would have happened if the victim had actually committed suicide, as investigators originally assumed in the pilot episode of *CSI*.

How can I use it?

Stellate patterns occur when the gun is pressed directly into the flesh in a contact shot. After the explosion the tissue opens, lets in the gases from the gunshot, then cavitates or closes back up. What remains is the torn skin in a star pattern.

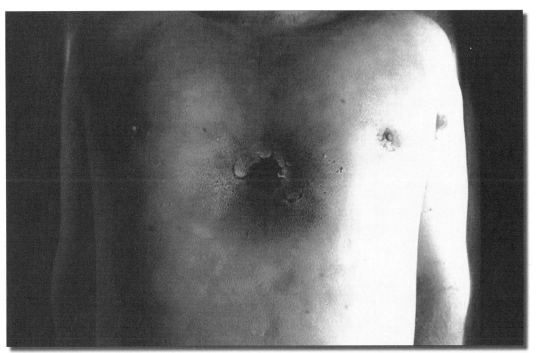

Stellate pattern of gunshot on murder victim. *CSI* pilot; Jerry Bruckheimer TV, 2000.

Stippling

What is it?

When a gun is fired, the gun smoke from the weapon expels a poof of gunpowder and soot in the direction from which the bullet was fired. This unburned gunpowder and soot burns into the skin or clothing and is called stippling. There are two general types of stippling: smudging and tattooing.

Where do I see it?

In season one, episode 110 of *CSI*, the medical examiner and investigator Sara Sidle (Jorga Fox) investigate a gunshot victim. The shot from that scene is an extreme closeup of the bullet wound with stippling around it. CSIs comment on the stellate pattern of the wound, but if you look closely at the picture, there is no stellate pattern shown.

How can I use it?

Stippling tells you something about how close the gun was when it was fired. Guns fired at a distance greater than half a foot will leave scattered stippling in a broad diameter. Guns fired at close range, less than six inches from the victim, will produce lots of stippling in a small diameter. As the bullet goes through the skin a little lead is left on the skin (aka lead wipe). Your CSI should swab this and have it tested. Also, your medical examiner will note the beveling of the bone, which will tell him which direction the bullet traveled when it went through the skin.

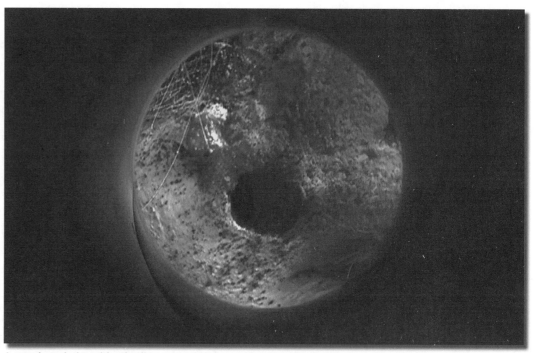

A gunshot victim with stippling around the wound. *CSI*, episode 110; Jerry Bruckheimer, 2000.

Suicide Notes

What is it?

A suicide note is a visible form of communication that a suicide victim leaves for his survivors. It may be written, taped, or recorded. Suicide victims more commonly leave a note than not. About 66% leave a note; 33% do not.

Where do I see it?

In the pilot episode of *CSI*, investigator Gil Grossom (William Petersen) finds the victim's apparent suicide note — in this case, a tape-recorded message.

How can I use it?

There's no one formula for composing suicide notes. They may give clues to why the person killed herself. Or the note might express the victim's feelings towards her friends, family, or the world at large. Some suicide notes may give a last will and testament, explaining to survivors what to do with possessions left behind. However, this is not legally binding.

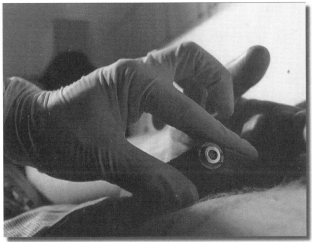

A suicide victim has tape-recorded his suicide note. *CSI* pilot; Jerry Bruckheimer TV, 2000.

X-ray Room

What is it?

The X-ray room is located in the morgue and is used to take a look inside a cadaver without (or before) cutting it open.

Where do I see it?

Medical examiner Donald Mallard (David McCallum) and Special Agent Jethro Gibbs (Mark Harmon) consult about a victim's broken bones in the *NCIS* episode, "The Good Samaritan."

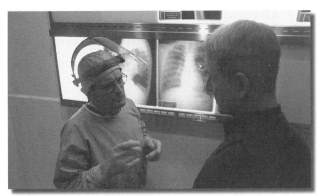

Examination room, Harmon and medical examiner. *NCIS*, "The Good Samaritan"; CBS, 2003–present.

How can I use it?

X-rays of the body can reveal broken bones that may be consistent with external injuries or reports from witnesses. Let's say a witness states that the victim was beat across the chest. An X-ray could show broken ribs or sternum and confirm the witness' testimony. X-rays also detect bullets left inside the body. If it looks like the victim was shot, the medical examiner would want to X-ray the body to find the bullet before he started cutting into it. It's also common to X-ray the bodies of children to see if any bones have been broken or are in various stages of healing. This may indicate physical abuse.

■ *Exercise 1.*

Watch a scene from one of your favorite procedural shows or movies whose story takes viewers inside a morgue (or try *Body of Proof*, *Crossing Jordan*, *Quincy M.E.*). Pause the scene. Take out a pen and paper and note what you observe in the scene. What can you identify in the morgue? Who is there? What tools of the trade are the occupants using? What kind of lighting? Unpause. Watch the scene through and pretend you are in the room during the scene. Write a brief report of what just happened in the scene. Read over the report. Based on what you learned in this chapter, how true to life is this scene? List three things you would do to make the scene more authentic. List three things you could do to make the scene more dramatic or emotionally charged (i.e., adding or removing sounds, visuals, dialogue; enhancing forensic content or setting).

■ *Exercise 2.*

In this exercise you will focus on building knowledge about the body of your victim. We'll start with the assumption that your victim is found dead. Remember the definition for *corpus delicti*? We're going to apply this concept by starting with the body of the victim. First, determine the manner of death – natural, accidental, suicidal, or homicidal. Next, decide what kind of wounds, lacerations, bullet holes, smudging, stippling, raccoon's eyes, or other damage to the body is found. What does this damage say about how the victim was killed? When the body is found, what is the condition of livor mortis, rigor mortis, or algor mortis? What does this tell us about the victim and when she died? In other words, at what stage of decomposition is your victim?

Now, add to the corpus delicti: Add different types of evidence (see Types of Evidence from chapter 1). Start with what you find immediately around your victim at the scene of the crime. Are there bullets? Electrical cords? Rope? A suicide note? Tire impressions? Shoeprints? Tool marks? Then add blood-spatter patterns, DNA evidence, or any drug use (prescribed or illegal). The biggest challenge is to make sure that these all relate to the body of the victim. Use the victim's body to lead the investigator protagonist to the larger body of evidence. You shouldn't reveal all of the corpus delicti right away in your story. One way to unwind a mystery is to start with the body and see what it tells your investigator protagonist about the crime. (See *Body of Proof* or *Quincy M.E.* for some great examples of how to do this.)

III.
Toxicology
Tête-à-Tête

"Drugs are a waste of time. They destroy your memory and your self-respect and everything that goes along with your self esteem."
— *Kurt Cobain*

The Toxicologist's World

Toxicology is the middle child in the forensic family. It's always hanging around, but often ignored or misunderstood. On TV, we catch glimpses of shiny chrome labs filled with whirring machines. We see people working in labs. Test results are spit out of machines and computers in milliseconds. But do we really know how this world works? What really goes on in a "tox" lab? How are drugs recovered from a crime scene or a body? What part does the toxicologist play?

Toxicologists are chemists. They are experts in how drugs, poisons, and alcohol affect the human body. The goal of this chapter is to open the door into their world and explain what happens in a tox lab and what a toxicologist actually does. The chapter also covers basic drugs and poisons. In The Druggie's World we make a brief foray into street terms of illegal drugs. The last section covers drugs from a CSI's perspective. It answers questions about when searches and seizures are permitted and how CSIs recover drug evidence.

Forensic Toxicology

What is it?

Forensic toxicology measures the use or abuse of drugs, alcohol, or poisons in violation of criminal law. It's the job of the forensic toxicologist to examine how toxic substances and poisons are absorbed, distributed, and eliminated in the body. This is done by testing a person's blood, hair, or urine. Forensic toxicologists may work for county health departments, crime labs, or medical examiners' offices.

Where do I see it?

A CSI and toxicologist await blood test results in the toxicology lab in the pilot episode of *CSI*.

How can I use it?

On TV, toxicologists are portrayed as lab gods. A sample comes in and in five minutes the results spill forth. In reality, it takes four to five hours to process a sample. Toxicologists' work is hardly glamorous. They run the samples, interpret the results, and then rinse and repeat. Many crime labs are scraping by, and often times the toxicologist must apply for grants to keep the doors open.

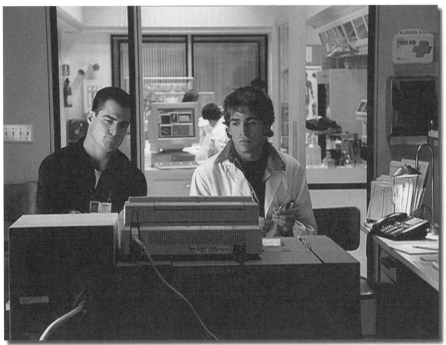

Tox lab — examining results. *CSI* pilot; Jerry Bruckheimer TV, 2000.

Toxicology Lab

What is it?

The lab is the place where the samples are sent and tested for drugs, poisons, and alcohol. A basic, meagerly funded toxicology lab will contain a gas chromatographer-mass spectrometer (GCMS) to test for body fluids. Labs with better funding have new technology including a liquid chromatographer-mass spectrometer (LCMS) and gas chromatographers (GC) for testing blood-alcohol levels. Infrared spectrometers work with polarizing light microscopes to test substances in pill, powder, crystal, leaf, or liquid form.

Mass Spectrometry

Mass spectrometry is one of the methods of screening for substances in the body. It works in conjunction with gas chromatography. After the components are separated by gas chromatography, they head into the mass spectrometer where they undergo a process that produces a readable pattern. That pattern tells the toxicologists which substances and what quantities were in the body.

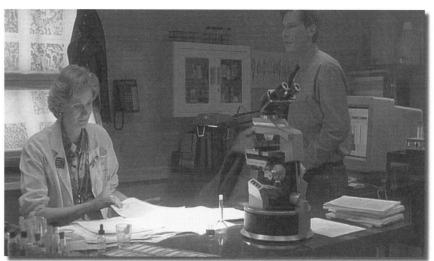

Dr. Richard Kimble visits the lab to review falsified samples. *The Fugitive*, Warner Bros., 1993.

Gas Chromatography

Gas chromatography separates the components of a substance so they can go through the mass spectrometer and be identified.

Where do I see it?

Dr. Richard Kimble visits his friend, Dr. Kathy Wahlund (Jane Lynch) at the lab in *The Fugitive* and learns that his nemesis, Dr. Lentz (David Darlow), was falsifying liver samples, evidence Kimble uses later to take Lentz down.

How can I use it?

We've all seen the CSI moment when the investigator gingerly hands a lab tech a blood sample and instructs her to "run a complete screen on this." Contrary to popular belief and TV myth, you can't "run a complete screen" on a person. There are just too many drugs to test for. So the lab conducts a common drug panel run to check for the presence of amphetamine, methamphetamine, cocaine, and opiates (heroin, codeine, morphine, hydrocodone, and oxycodene.) However, the investigator can help the case and the toxicologist if he knows to look for substances at the scene. If he finds a prescription drug or other paraphernalia, he should take it to the lab and alert the toxicologist.

This section familiarizes you with common drugs and poisons and their effect on the body.

DRUGS AND POISONS

Acute Poisoning

What is it?

Acute poisoning happens quickly and is induced after eating, drinking, inhaling a poisonous substance, or taking a toxic medicine. The person experiencing acute poisoning vomits, convulses, and may end up in a coma or dead.

Where do I see it?

A man in prison was poisoned, and Monk has to find out why and who did it in "Mr. Monk Goes to Jail," *Monk*.

How can I use it?

Acute poisoning may be accidental or intentional. One toxicologist I spoke with tested a case in which an entire family died from liver failure when they mistakenly ate poisonous mushrooms. Many of us are familiar with acute poisoning in cases of fire victims. Most don't die from being burned to death, but from carbon monoxide poisoning. In these cases, the body color changes to a cherry red. Sometimes acute poisoning is intentional suicide, as when Socrates drinks a cup of poison hemlock. Solving an acute poisoning case is a lot easier than solving one in which the person was poisoned slowly (chronic) because the substance in acute cases can be found in high levels in the body. What you have to remember is that many poisons are not part of a routine postmortem drug screen. If someone is poisoned with arsenic or mercury, it will not be found unless the family requests specific testing.

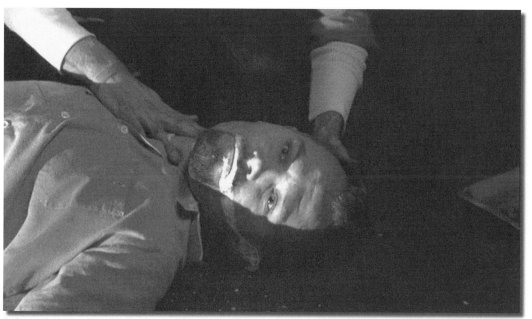

Poisoned victim foams at mouth. *Monk*, "Mr. Monk Goes to Jail"; Universal, 2002–09.

Chronic Poisoning

What is it?

Chronic poisoning takes place over a long period of time. The person may feel ill or suffer from malaise, but doctors find it difficult to uncover a cause.

Where do I see it?

The film *The Chumscrubber* provides an excellent study of toxicology and the slow poisoning of our bodies and minds. In *Chumscrubber* you will find everything from illegal drugs to prescription medications to innocuous-looking vitamins that Dean's mom sells to her friends.

How can I use it?

The classic chronic poisoning case is the wife who wants her husband dead for his life insurance and feeds him very small doses of rat poison over a long period of time until he finally grows sicker and sicker and dies. Chronic poisoning is a deliberate, heartless method of killing. It's methodical, calculated, and downright chilling. How do you prove it? One method is the hair shafts. The drug seeps into the hair shaft and stays there. As the hair grows, toxicologists can tell when the drug was given. Hair normally grows about 1 cm per month. If drugs are detected in the hair up to 10 cm from the scalp, you can deduce that the person was being poisoned for about ten months.

Vitamins on table. *Chumscrubber*, Newmarket Films, 2005.

Poison

What is it?

A poison is a substance taken or given to a person that causes illness or death. It may be introduced in small quantities over a long period of time or may be given as an overdose just once. Below are some examples of common types of poisons. Of course, almost any substance given in an overdose quantity could cause poisoning, even a basic nutritional supplement like iron.

Irritants

Sulfuric acid, hydrochloric acid, ammonia, Lysol

Metallic Poisons

Arsenic, antimony, mercury, lead

Organic/Vegetable Poisons

Belladonna, strychnine, opium derivatives, barbiturate, chloral hydrate

Gases

Hydrogen sulfide, cyanide, phosgene, carbon monoxide, carbon dioxide

Food Poisoning

Botulism (food poisoning), amanita poisoning (mushrooms)

Walter introduces Pinkman to Ricin, a poison in a bean. *Breaking Bad*, season 2, episode 1; Sony & AMC, 2008.

Where do I see it?

Walter introduces Jesse Pinkman (Aaron Paul) to a very deadly form of poison found in certain beans in *Breaking Bad*, season 2, episode 1.

How can I use it?

When writing a crime story, just pick your poison — pun intended. Just remember your points of proof. Your suspect needs to have access to the poison, access to the victim, and knowledge that the poison will cause harm or death.

Psychoactive Drugs

What is it?

A psychoactive drug affects the central nervous system and brain activity. Taking these drugs changes your mood, behavior, or consciousness. Below is a just a sample list of the different types of the most common psychoactive drugs.

Central Nervous System Depressants

codeine, morphine, methadone, heroin, Percodan (oxycodene)

Central Nervous System Stimulants

cocaine, amphetamine, methamphetamine, Ritalin, theophylline

Hallucinogens

mescaline, psilocybin (magic mushrooms), LSD (lysergic acid diethylamide), PCP (phencyclidine)

Cannabis

marijuana

Designer Drugs

MDMA – ecstasy/love drug (methylenedioxymethamphetamine)

MDA (methylenedioxyamphetamine)

GHB – date rape drug (gamma-hydroxybuteric acid)

Steroids

testosterone, Dianabol, durabolin

Inhalants (huffing, taggers)

glue, gasoline, paint, solvents

Veronica drinks a ruffied beverage at a party. *Veronica Mars* pilot; Warner Bros., 2004.

Where do I see it?

In the pilot episode of *Veronica Mars*, we learn that someone ruffied (or, roofied) Veronica's (Kristen Bell) drink and then raped her at a party. This event changes her from self-conscious good girl to hard-boiled teen detective.

How can I use it?

We live in a drug culture. We take drugs for recreation, for medicinal use, or to enhance our bodies or minds. Sometimes drug use is legal, sometimes illegal. Search the headlines on Yahoo or Google any day of the week and you will discover a drug-related story. Look around you at those you know. How are they using or abusing drugs — legal ones or illegal ones? Drugs can easily become the source of poor decision-making, rapes, traffic accidents, homicides — just to name a few. It shouldn't be too difficult to create a trail of evidence that leads to drug involvement.

Unless you're heavy into the illegal drug world already (and I hope you are not), you need to arm yourself with druggie vernacular so that you sound authentic. There are thousands of slang words and they vary from region to region. Here are a few terms I will share from my own A-Z list. I chose them because they refer to common drugs or practices, they make me laugh, or they surprise me. I've included a brief, "What is it" description and a tongue-in-cheek "Where do I see it." As for "How can I use it," I really don't think you need me to tell you that. Besides, I would only be uselessly repeating the cornucopia of druggie information at *http://www.erowid.org*. This is a site maintained by drug users with a complete slang dictionary of thousands of terms. While you're there, check out the testimonials from drug users.

THE DRUGGIE'S WORLD

Author

What is it?

Authors are doctors who write illegal prescriptions for druggies.

Where do I see it?

A doctor from the local hospital supplies teens with prescription drugs that they sell to each other in *The Chumscrubber*.

Beat Artist

What is it?

A beat artist sells inferior or bogus drugs.

Where do I see it?

Twin brothers Billy and Brady Kincaid (both played by Edward Norton) toke it up in *Leaves of Grass*. Brady Kincaid is a beat artist who started selling inferior drugs and has risen to become an accomplished marijuana farmer.

Doctor dealing drugs. *Chumscrubber*, Newmarket Films, 2005.

Twins Bill and Brady Kincaid, a beat artist turned professional weed farmer, enjoy a toke. *Leaves of Grass*, Millennium Films & First Looks Studios, 2009.

Chipping

What is it?

Crushing methadone and mixing it with heroin is called chipping. The term also refers to using drugs occasionally — a chipper.

Where do I see it?

Claire Fisher (Lauren Ambrose) and her boyfriend smoke meth at a party right before she learns that her father has been killed in the pilot episode of *Six Feet Under*.

Clandestine Lab

What is it?

This term refers to an illegal drug lab.

Where do I see it?

Brady Kincaid (Edward Norton) surveys his clandestine marijuana lab in *Leaves of Grass*.

Claire Fisher and her boyfriend smoke meth at a party. *Six Feet Under* pilot; HBO, 2000-05.

Clandestine pot lab, with Ed Norton as Brady Kincaid. *Leaves of Grass*, Millennium Films & First Look Studios, 2009.

93

Cutting Agent

What is it?

A cutting agent is a substance added to a drug to increase the quantity or to dilute it. It's also referred to as cutting. For instance, some common cutting agents for cocaine include caffeine and benzocaine (a topical pain reliever).

Where do I see it?

A prostitute cuts the drug scopolamine into eyedrops and drugs her clients so she can steal their money in the *CSI* pilot.

Dollar

What is it?

A dollar refers to $100 worth of drugs in druggie land.

Where do I see it?

Talk about a great marketing campaign. I can see the flyer now: "Look what a dollar buys you."

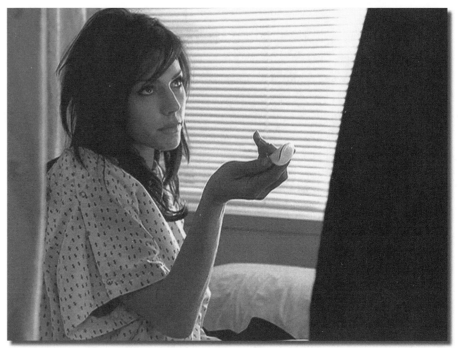

A prostitute cuts the drug scopolamine into eyedrops. *CSI* pilot, Jerry Bruckheimer TV, 2000.

Going 90 MPH

What is it?

If you're going 90 mph, you are at the peak of your high or your trip.

Where do I see it?

Believe me, this is the only way you'll ever reach speeds that fast on the Los Angeles freeways.

Herb and Al

What is it?

Herb and Al refers to the twins, marijuana and alcohol.

Where do I see it?

The name sounds like a new sitcom series you could see on Fox next season.

Ice

What is it?

Ice refers to the drugs crack, meth, cocaine, ecstasy, or PCP.

Where do I see it?

Have you checked that thirty-year-old skateboarder's backpack down by Game Stop? Or maybe at the high school campus of *The Chumscrubber*, where drug use is normal and expected?

High school campus of *The Chumscrubber*, where drug use is normal and expected. *Chumscrubber*, Newmarket Films, 2005.

I-tuning

What is it?

Popular with tweeners and teens, I-tuning is an audio-induced state of euphoria set on by cranking up music and watching iTunes laser shows on the iPhone. It never really caught on . . . or that's what they want us to think.

Where do I see it?

This is a cheap, easy high. Whenever you see an iPod user ignoring pedestrians, signal lights, or telephone poles, you've got to wonder . . . I-tuning?

Jungle Juice

What is it?

Jungle juice is methadone. Originally used to treat heroin addicts or pain, it has now become an abused substance.

Where do I see it?

During my college years, jungle juice was a large tub filled with Kool-Aid, Hawaiian punch, and cheap vodka. Kids these days. . . .

Keistered In

What is it?

This term refers to muling drugs through the anal cavity into prisons.

Where do I see it?

Hopefully you never have to see it.

Kelly's Day, Keller, or Special K

What is it?

A fairly new drug of choice, this refers to Ketamine, an animal anesthetic. It's used mostly for cats, dogs, or horses. In people it is considered the date rape drug of choice. It is ingested through the nose, muscles, or mouth.

Where do I see it?

It is commonly used in Europe at clubs and raves, or any house party where frat guys are looking for a quick score.

Lunchbox

What is it?

Kids who do drugs are called lunchboxes.

Where do I see it?

In the world of the film, *The Chumscrubber* kids use drugs like candy. In this scene Dean (Jamie Bell) studies the prescription drug his dad provided for him to give him a little lift after his best friend committed suicide.

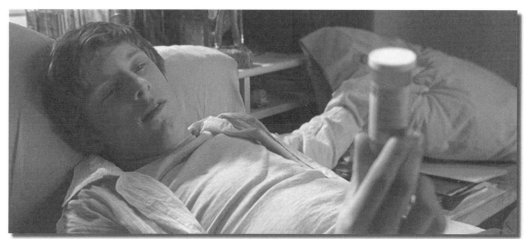

Dean with prescription drugs. *Chumscrubber*, Newmarket Films, 2005.

Munchies

What is it?

Having the munchies means that you are headed for a snacking binge after smoking weed.

Where do I see it?

It's not to be confused with the female snack attack during PMS.

Necking

What is it?

Necking refers to swallowing drugs in order to hide them.

Where do I see it?

Maria (Catalina Sandino Moreno) readies herself to swallow dozens of heroin tablets in a scene from *Maria Full of Grace.*

On a Mission

What is it?

A druggie on a mission is searching for crack.

Where do I see it?

I'm on a mission almost every day, but it's usually to find my keys or to stay ahead of some deadline.

Maria Alvarez in a Columbian pharmacy swallowing half a kilo of heroine bundles. *Maria Full of Grace*, HBO Films, 2008.

Puller

What is it?

We all know what a pusher is, but what about a puller? This crack addict picks or pulls at his body excessively.

Where do I see it?

A puller might look like a tweeker who also picks at her body, leaving scabs, sores, and scars.

Queeted

What is it?

Queeting is every pot smoker's dream. It means you've gotten way too high off half a bowl. Maybe because it was snow capped? (See Snow Cap.)

Where do I see it?

Not to be confused with tweeted.

Roid Rage

What is it?

Taking too many steroids does not make Johnny a very nice boy. Roid rage is caused by excessive use of steroids.

Where do I see it?

If you've ever driven the L.A. freeways, you've experienced roid rage.

Snow Cap

What is it?

A delicacy in the world of illegal drugs, a snow cap is a sprinkling of cocaine on top of the weed you're about to smoke.

Where do I see it?

Now you know what to expect when someone invites you in for a little snow cap. In this preview scene from season 2 of *Weeds*, Heylia (Tonye Patano) weighs her weed.

Weighing weed. *Weeds*, season 2, preview; Lions Gate, 2006.

Tweeker

What is it?
A tweeker is a person who regularly uses methamphetamine.

Where do I see it?
Tweekers have bad acne, stringy hair, and sunken eyes — not to be mistaken with teenagers having a bad hair day and taking their SATs.

Uncle

What is it?
Uncles refer to federal agents.

Where do I see it?
The point is not to see them. They operate undercover.

DEA agent, Hank Scrader (Dean Norris), busts drugs dealers in *Breaking Bad*, "And the Bag's in the River"; AMC, 2008–present.

Vega (aka Space Base)

What is it?
Split open a cigar and fill it with marijuana. Badaboom, you've created a vega.

Where do I see it?
Cuba. No wonder those Cuban cigars are banned in the United States.

Wake 'n Bake

What is it?

When the first thing you do in the morning is get high, you've waked 'n baked.

Where do I see it?

Most of us get by with Starbuck's, but a few of us need a little extra nudge.

X-ing

What is it?

Another name for Ecstasy.

Where do I see it?

In this scene from *Kojak*, "One for the Morgue," an undercover cop pretends to sample a drug dealer's stash.

Kojak partner sniffing coke. *Kojak*, "One for the Morgue"; CBS, 1973–78.

Yale

What is it?

Yale is yet another name for cocaine.

Where do I see it?

This is the only time you'll see a Yalie step foot at Harvard.

Zoinked

What is it?

Zoinked is being intoxicated to the point at which you are useless. No one likes a bad drunk.

Where do I see it?

Any Southside Chicago bar on the weekends will do.

Recovering drugs or drug paraphernalia from a crime scene or scene of a death requires the same caution and chain of custody guidelines as recovering any piece of evidence. Investigators should use gloves, masks, and other protective gear. Samples and substances are placed in paper evidence bags, labeled, sealed, and delivered to the crime lab where they enter the toxicologist's care. From a legal point of view, it may be helpful to understand how and when drugs can be recovered.

DRUGS AND THE CRIME SCENE

INVESTIGATIVE TECHNIQUES TO RECOVER DRUGS

Exigent Circumstances

What is it?

An immediate search and seizure of property for drugs is warranted when law enforcement officers feel that action is needed to spare a life or evidence.

Where do I see it?

Javier Rodriguez (Benicio Del Toro), a Mexican policeman, conducts a drug sweep and discovers cases and cases of cocaine in the opening scenes of *Traffic*.

How can I use it?

We've all seen the drug-house raid scenario. We might have even asked, how can they do that without a search warrant? Exigent circumstance is one exception to the warrant laws. Typically, police or DEA have already investigated and found reasonable proof to believe that there is drug activity in that house. If they aren't allowed to act surreptitiously, key drug evidence could be destroyed.

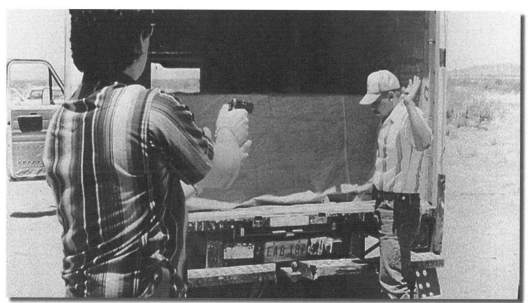

A Mexican policeman makes a protective sweep of a suspicious truck and discovers cases of coke. *Traffic*, USA Films & Universal, 2000.

Plain View

What is it?

An immediate search and seizure of property for drugs is warranted when the drug is in plain view of law enforcement.

Where do I see it?

DEA agents are constantly on Nancy's (Mary-Louise Parker) trail in *Weeds*, season 2.

How can I use it?

Let's say the perp in your story is pulled over for a busted taillight. If the cop looks over on the front seat of his car and sees a Ziploc bag of marijuana, he can legally enter that property and seize that drug.

Protective Sweep

What is it?

An immediate search and seizure of property is warranted if law enforcement officers feel they are in danger of criminal activity. During this protective sweep, if cops find drugs they can confiscate them for evidence.

Where do I see it?

In the pilot episode of *Veronica Mars*, Veronica takes revenge on Logan (Jason Dohring) by planting a bong in his locker. Later, acting on a tip, the principal and local police officer do a protective sweep and bust Logan.

How can I use it?

Other exceptions to Fourth Amendment rights occur when law enforcement officers encounter known drug houses or enter drug trafficking areas. They are allowed to raid. They are allowed to search and seize. And, in schools, random urine drug testing and locker searches are allowed because the school is acting *in loco parentis*.

Police and principal find a bong in Logan's school locker. *Veronica Mars* **pilot; Warner Bros., 2004.**

Probation Search

What is it?

An immediate search and seizure of property for drugs is warranted if the suspect in question is on court-ordered probation.

Where do I see it?

In *The Fugitive*, Dr. Richard Kimble (Harrison Ford) panics when a Chicago SWAT team surrounds his apartment building. He assumes that they are after him, but instead they bust his neighbor, a repeat offender and drug dealer.

How can I use it?

If the perp in your story wears an ankle bracelet and is suspected of having illegal substances, it's fair game for the cops to search and seize his property.

Chicago police SWAT team busts a drug dealer living in the same apartment building as Richard. *The Fugitive*, Warner Bros., 1998.

■ *Exercise 1.*

Let's assume that your criminal is involved in drugs. Select your suspect's drug of choice and do a little research on how the drug works, where it comes from, how it can become compromised, how it's recognized in the body. Create a one-page story synopsis for this character that includes the points of proof for his drug-related crime: how the criminal has access to his drug of choice, how he obtains access to the victim, and his motive or intent for killing this victim.

Now, take a look at the same crime and criminal from the POV of the investigator protagonist. What does the investigator do to stop the crime, discover the drug use/abuse, and redeem the situation? Consider this: Could your investigator be a toxicologist? What would drive her out of the lab to investigate? What steps would she take in the investigation?

■ *Exercise 2.*

For a fictional look into the druggie's world, watch *Breaking Bad* (the pilot), *Traffic*, *Maria Full of Grace*, *The Fugitive*, or *Weeds*, seasons 1 and 2. In what ways do drugs serve as characters? What kind of character — hero, ally, or villain? Does this change during the story? How do drugs shape or change the protagonist? What part do the drugs play in the protagonist's story?

IV.
Fingerprint Talk

"Jekyll's finger patterns remain the same when he transforms himself into Hyde!" — Dr. Henry Faulds (1843-1930)

I f you watch a lot of crime TV, you may be quick to believe that DNA has replaced fingerprint identification or that fingerprinting is a limited, somewhat outdated method. Not true! After taking more than forty hours of fingerprint training and consulting with L.A.'s leading fingerprint specialist, I can assure you that fingerprinting has a strong foothold in forensic science. It works hand-in-hand with DNA identification and on occasion may even trump it. Just like each snowflake is unlike any other snowflake, so fingerprints are unique to each person. No two people have the same pattern. And our prints don't change from year to year. You won't find this in the DNA world where identical twins share the same DNA.

Fingerprinting came into practice in law enforcement in the United States in the early 1900s, in other countries in the 1800s, in Greece and China as early as 3,000 years ago, and before that in ancient Babylonia. Francis Galton published the first textbook on fingerprinting, titled *Finger Prints*, in 1892. Since then, fingerprinting has been accepted as a reliable means of identification. We fingerprint almost everyone. Children are fingerprinted for safety reasons. Adults working for government agencies or in school systems or with foster care or adoptions are printed. Suspects and criminals are printed.

It's important to understand what fingerprinting is; this chapter covers a wide range of fingerprint science in alphabetical order.

ACE-V

What is it?

ACE-V is an acronym that stands for analysis, comparison, evaluation, and verification of fingerprints. ACE-V is a process used by fingerprint specialists in the courtroom when testifying. Analysis refers to how the fingerprint specialist explains the process of looking at a print for ridges and Galton Details (see Ridgeology and Galton Details). Comparison refers to the process by which fingerprints are compared to similar prints. Evaluation is the process by which the specialist confirms that a suspect's fingerprint is a yes or no match to a print in the system. Verification is a process whereby three fingerprint experts do a blind comparison to confirm an identification of a print.

Where do I see it?

In this scene from episode 122 of *CSI,* investigator Sara Sidle (Jorja Fox) uses a magnifying lens to search for prints. Later, if she were called to testify in this case, she would have to be able to explain how she found the prints, the chain of custody, and how the prints were analyzed and compared. This is the process of ACE-V.

How can I use it?

ACE-V is useful when writing courtroom scenes or when you want your fingerprint specialist to explain to other characters what they are seeing in a suspect's fingerprint.

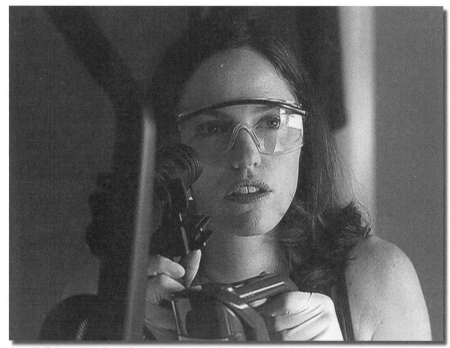

Sara Sidle searches for prints using a magnifying lens. *CSI,* episode 122; Jerry Bruckheimer TV, 2000–present.

AFIS

What is it?

AFIS stands for Automated Fingerprint Identification Systems. The U.S. was not the first to use AFIS. It started with the Royal Canadian Mounted Police in 1977. Seven years later, the U.S. caught on in San Francisco. AFIS uses an algorithm to match fingerprint minutia in terms of ridge characteristics (see Ridgeology). This means looking at and comparing ridge flow, ridge bifurcations, and ridge endings of fingerprints. About a dozen software companies create AFIS software. The FBI has the largest AFIS system — more than 70 million criminal prints and 31 million civilian prints. IAFIS, or Integrated Automated Fingerprint Identification System, is the name of the FBI's AFIS system. NAFIS, or National Automated Fingerprint Identification System, is the name of Australia's AFIS system. INTERPOL is an international police organization that also uses AFIS to track fingerprints of criminals and suspects.

Where do I see it?

In *Call Northside 777*, P. J. McNeal (Jimmy Stewart) paws through old police records by hand, the way things used to be before AFIS.

How can I use it?

Television has propagated the myth that there is one central AFIS bank where all fingerprints are stored and easily accessed by law enforcement. Not so. Each city, county, state, and federal agency has its own AFIS. There is no central bank of fingerprints. Therefore, let's say a criminal from Phoenix commits a crime in Phoenix and the police lift his prints at the scene of the crime. If our criminal then flees to New Jersey and commits another crime and the police there lift his prints at the New Jersey crime scene, there is no easy or central system in place to cross-check prints from both states.

P. J. McNeal paws through old police records by hand, the way things used to be before AFIS. *Call Northside 777*, 20th Century Fox, 1948.

Bertillon System

What is it?

Named after its French inventor, Alphonse Bertillon, this identification system uses a series of body measurements to create a signature stamp on a person's identity. Bertillon used calipers, rulers, and gauges to measure eleven bony parts of the head, arms, fingers, feet, legs, and face. He would also note if a suspect had birthmarks, scars, or tattoos. Bertillon's system was in place in Europe, New Zealand, and North America for almost thirty years, from the late 1870s until 1903. After a strange case of double identity involving Will West and William West in Texas, it was proved that Bertillon was not nearly as reliable as fingerprinting, which was rapidly emerging as science and system around the same time.

A photograph from Alphonse Bertillon's exhibition at the 1893 World's Columbian Exposition in Chicago. Taken from National Library of Medicine online exhibit http://www.nlm.nih.gov/visibleproofs/media/detailed/ii_c_304.jpg.

Where do I see it?

In this photograph taken from the National Library of Medicine at the 1893 World's Fair in Chicago, Alphonse Bertillon demonstrates the equipment and method of obtaining Bertillon measurements.

How can I use it?

If you are writing an historical piece dating from the late 1870s to 1903, you'll want to incorporate the Bertillon system when your detective tries to identify criminals. This will give your crime story historical accuracy. Fun fact: Bertillon was also the father of the mug shot.

Biometrics

What is it?

Biometrics is a way to identify and measure particular anatomical or behavioral characteristics that are unique to you: in this case, your fingerprint details. Your fingerprints are like tread patterns. They have ridges and valleys. Ridges are short or long. They form islands and they split off (see Galton Details). The unique pattern of your ridges identifies you as you, and no one else. This biometric information about you can be used as a passcode to give you added security in certain situations.

Where do I see it?

The *CSI* pilot introduces biometrics in fingerprint comparisons. Both images are loop patterns.

How can I use it?

Let's visit some pros and cons of fingerprint biometrics. Pros: fingerprints are almost impossible to copy; you can't misplace your fingerprint or forget it like a password. Cons: If someone really wants your fingerprint biometric, they could make a picture of it, create a mold of it, or, worst case, chop off your index finger. And if some crook does pull off a fingerprint falsification, you can't order up a new one.

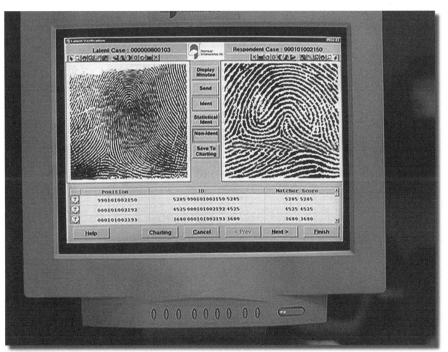

Computer comparison. *CSI* pilot; Jerry Bruckheimer TV, 2000.

111

Core

What is it?

The approximate center of your fingerprint is called the core. It is determined by counting the number of ridges from the delta. This number is used to help classify a person's print. The location of the core is different on each person's print and varies from finger to finger on the same person. It's just one more way to determine the uniqueness of each person's fingerprints.

Where do I see it?

The murderers in *Rope* wore leather gloves to conceal the intricacies of their fingerprints at the crime scene. Two of the most important details of the prints are found in the core and the delta of each print.

How can I use it?

Fingerprints are classified based on ridgeology (see Ridgeology). Finding the core is part of the process of reading a print so that it can be classified and the investigator can find out to whom it belongs — victim, suspect, or casual observer. If you can't find the core, it's very difficult to read the print.

The murderers wear gloves to ensure that the details of their cores and deltas are masked. *Rope*, MGM, 1948.

Delta

What is it?

Each print that is a loop or whorl has a delta. Arch fingerprint patterns do not have deltas. The delta is the place where the ridges part to make way for the loops or whorls of the print. Usually it's located at the left or right bottom of the print. The delta is the first thing to look for when trying to classify a print. Find the delta and count from there the number of ridges between the delta and the core. The number you get is placed into a Henry Classification formula. And because each person's prints are different from everyone else's, each person has a unique formula.

Sara lifts a palm print in *CSI*, episode 306, Jerry Bruckheimer TV, 2000–present.

Where do I see it?

In this scene from *CSI*, episode 306, Sara Sidle lifts a palm print from a murder scene. Incidentally, palm prints have deltas just as fingerprints do.

How can I use it?

Fingerprints are classified based on ridgeology (see Ridgeology). Finding the delta is part of the process of reading a print so that it can be classified and the investigator can find out to whom it belongs — victim, suspect, or casual observer.

Dissociated Ridges

What is it?

Fingerprint ridges that aren't fully formed or connected are called dissociated. There's really no rhyme or reason to the pattern. It's like a box of mixed puzzle pieces. They're not really ridges at all and they look like the lines on a dog's snout. Dissociated ridges could have been caused by a genetic anomaly.

Where do I see it?

A technician in *Pushing Daisies*, "Bitter Sweets," examines fingerprints brought in from the local bakery where the baker was murdered.

How can I use it?

Dissociated ridges are rare and will stand out as highly unique when trying to identify someone. Dissociated ridges are also very, very, very rare, so if you create a suspect with dissociated ridges, his fingerprints should give him away fairly quickly.

A technician examines the fingerprints brought in from the sweet shop bakery. *Pushing Daisies*, "Bitter Sweets"; ABC, 2007–09.

Elimination Prints

What is it?

Let's say a crime occurred in your home. Your fingerprints, along with those of the criminal, will be present. The detective investigating the case should ask you and others who live in your home as well as recent visitors, to be fingerprinted so he can rule you all out as suspects. These are elimination prints. And once they are established, the police can concentrate on matching the perp's prints.

Where do I see it?

Investigator Warrick Brown (Gary Dourdan) in the first season of *CSI*, episode 110, takes elimination earprints from the owner of the house in order to rule out that anyone in the house was the art thief who stole his artwork. Watch the whole scene around minute 14.

How can I use it?

In the past, elimination prints were done at the police station. Victims were asked to come down and give their prints via ink and paper. It was time-consuming and a hassle. Today it's more common for police to use a LiveScan machine or bring a small fingerprint kit so they can get the prints right on the spot.

Investigator Warrick Brown takes elimination earprints from the owner of the house. *CSI*, episode 110; Jerry Bruckheimer TV, 2000.

Fabrication

What is it?

Fabrication is a form of print forgery committed by someone to make another person look guilty.

Where do I see it?

Gil Grissom (William Petersen) follows a fingerprint lead which directs him to a novelty store owner who made 10,000 fake bloody hands that have his own finger-print imbedded in them in *CSI*, episode 110. The fabrication of the store owner's fingerprint wasn't intended to be criminal, but ended up in criminal hands.

How can I use it?

Good guy scenario: If you want to portray an upstanding detective, make sure he photographs the print first and has a witness when he lifts the print at the scene of the crime. Bad guy scenario: If you want your character to be a fabricator, his fake print should look too good to be true. It should be free of background noise, like dirt, fibers, grooves, or lines on the print. This will be a dead giveaway that the print is phony.

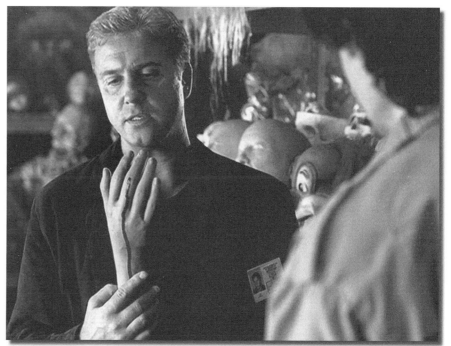

Fake hand. *CSI*, episode 110; Jerry Bruckheimer TV, 2000.

Forged print

What is it?

A fingerprint left by a criminal in order to point the blame to an innocent party is considered a forged print. A true forgery is a very rare occurrence and difficult to pull off, at least in real life.

Where do I see it?

As part of his initiation and training, Agent J's (Will Smith) fingerprints are removed via a heated sphere in *Men in Black* so that his identity cannot be discovered. Watch Agent J lose his identity starting at minute 37.

How can I use it?

In fictional life, if you wish for a criminal to commit fingerprint forgery, here's the rub. The criminal has to make sure the guy he's trying to frame laces the crime scene with his prints. Then, after the criminal commits the crime, wearing thick gloves or wiping away any trace of his own prints, the only prints that remain are those from the innocent guy. Another way it could be done is if the criminal transfers the innocent guy's prints from objects like glass, soda can, or polished wood. And if he's really a sophisticated bad guy, he may even make a mold (or glove) of someone else's fingerprints and wear it as he commits the crime.

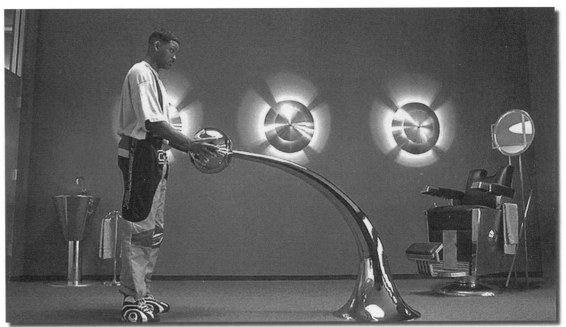

Agent J has his print deleted by a heated sphere so that he becomes truly anonymous. *Men in Black*, Columbia Pictures, 1997.

Friction Ridge or Friction Skin

What is it?

Stated simply, friction ridges or friction skin are found on the fingers, palms, toes, and soles of the feet. They are the raised portions of our prints, which form unique patterns and give our touch some grip. Friction ridges form in the womb by week twelve and can only be altered permanently if the skin is damaged down to the dermis layer.

Where do I see it?

In this computer-generated model of fingerprints from the *CSI* pilot, the formation of the pattern shows the friction ridges of the print. On the left is a loop pattern, on the right an arch.

How can I use it?

Each person is born with a unique, one-of-a-kind set of friction ridges that no one before and no one after will ever have. This is not only incredible and miraculous, but it allows law enforcement to make positive identifications of criminals and victims. Friction skin is a little reminder that we are not anonymous or unaccountable. When grievances are committed by us or to us, nature has a built-in tattletale: the friction ridge.

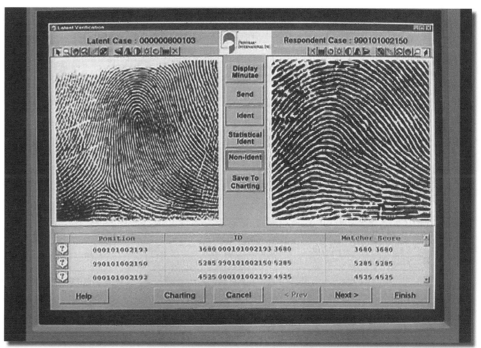

In this computer-generated model of fingerprints, the pattern shows the friction ridges of the print; on the left is a loop, on the right an arch. *CSI* pilot; Jerry Bruckheimer TV, 2000.

Galton Details

What is it?

When trying to match a latent print with a database print, the AFIS uses a system of biometrics that searches for and tries to match up the minutia of each print. This minutia includes the five Galton Details: bifurcations, ridge endings, dots, short ridges, and islands. (See pictures below.)

Where do I see it?

In the opening credits of *CSI*, season 1, an image of a fingerprint marking Galton Details flashes quickly across the screen. The numbers refer to the Galton Details that fingerprint analysts then use to match to prints in question.

How can I use it?

The devil is in the details when it comes to matching prints. For, while it's true that we all have unique and individual prints, there are close similarities between prints. When making a match, the computer spits out the top ten potential matches in geometric form — not the top ten fingerprint matches. Contrary to popular crime TV, the computer does *not* do the match; the fingerprint examiner does. A fingerprint analyst personally inspects each potential geometric match to find the exact fingerprint match in the system. An exact match must have as many as possible number of matching Galton Details. The IAI (International Association of Identification) does not set a required minimum number; it's up to the fingerprint examiner, although some law agencies will require a minimum of ten matching details.

Fingerprint with Galton Details. *CSI* pilot, credits; Jerry Bruckheimer TV, 2000.

Henry Classification System

What is it?

Named after its inventor, Sir Edward Henry, an inspector general of police in Bengal, India, and later Scotland Yard, this was the foremost system for classifying finger-prints dating back to 1897. The Henry System is based on the ridge count of each fingerprint and type of pattern (loop, whorl, or arch). Sometimes it's referred to as the tenprint system because all ten fingerprints are rolled onto one card, classified according to Henry's numbering system, and placed in a card catalog (like the old library cards!).

Where do I see it?

In the olden days and even today in some city police offices, fingerprint cards are still recorded on paper and filed by hand according to the Henry Classification System. It's similar to the Dewey Decimal System at the library. In this scene from *Call Northside 777*, P. J. McNeal (Jimmy Stewart) goes through police files by hand. Under the tenprint system, it could take weeks to find a matching set of prints.

How can I use it?

Even though AFIS and other automated fingerprint systems have taken a front seat during the past thirty years, Henry is still a tried-and-true method that is both taught and used. Smaller agencies or those with less funding use the tenprint card system. Even progressive cities like Santa Monica and Beverly Hills still use tenprint cards and Henry Classification in addition to electronic files.

Jimmy Stewart sorts through old evidence that is stored by hand in paper files. *Call Northside 777*, 20th Century Fox, 1948.

Inked Print

What is it?

Before LiveScan, all fingerprints were inked. And even today, many of them still are. The process of inking a print involves moistening fingers (and sometimes palms, toes, and soles of the feet) in a pad of black ink and then rolling each finger onto a tenprint card. A clear, unsmudged, inked impression will show ridge detail of the fingerprint — loops, arches, whorls, and the Galton Details. Inked prints are also called exemplars or standards.

Where do I see it?

CSIs in *CSI*, episode 121, ink a suspect's foot to solve a case.

How can I use it?

Many in forensic science would argue that fingerprints can be even more valuable evidence than a person's DNA. DNA can easily become tampered with, planted, or broken down by elements. It's difficult to forge a fingerprint, and it can last for years on a surface regardless of weather conditions. Some people, like identical twins, share the same DNA. But no one shares the same fingerprints. And people who are chimeric or mosaic have two completely different sets of DNA, but only one set of unchanging fingerprints.

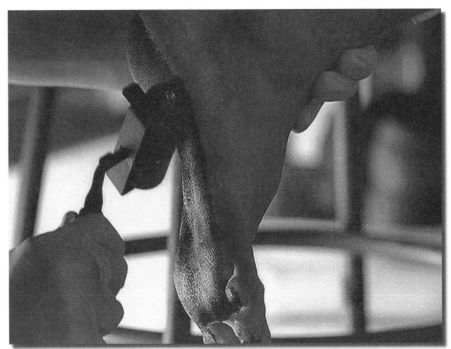

Rolling ink on foot to obtain a print. *CSI*, episode 121; Jerry Bruckheimer TV, 2000.

Latent Print

What is it?

Latent prints are the prints that clean hands and feet leave on the surfaces of things we touch. We know that hands and feet are never clean of perspiration and body oils, and as these form on the ridges of our prints, it causes the impression of print patterns on surfaces we touch. Latent prints are not usually visible to the naked eye and are not intentionally recorded (like inked or LiveScan prints). But they can be enhanced with the use of powders, chemical, and photographs. Latent prints are one of four types of prints investigators look for at a crime scene.

Where do I see it?

Investigators in the "Bitter Sweets" episode of *Pushing Daisies* orchestrated an uncanny (and highly unreliable) method of lifting fingerprints by using a rubber sheet and powdered sugar. But it's a fun use of forensic techniques that fits perfectly into this episode about a candy maker.

How can I use it?

A common misconception is that prints found at a crime scene can be read and matched. Many times, all that is left is a partial print — half of a fingerprint or part of a palm print. (By the way, palm prints make up 40% of latent prints left at a crime scene!) And, contrary to popular belief, gloves do not guarantee that you won't leave a print. Sweat and oil can seep through, causing an impression to form.

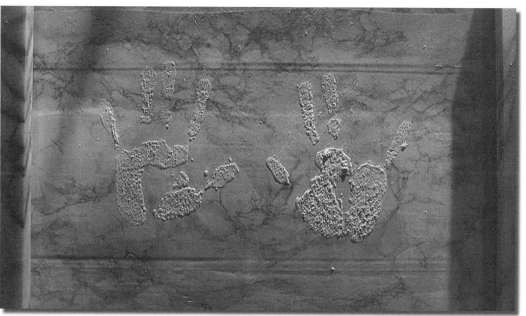

The investigators find and lift prints with powdered sugar. *Pushing Daisies*, "Bitter Sweets"; ABC, 2007–09.

LAW

What is it?

All prints have one of three basic patterns: loops, arches, or whorls (LAW). A loop is where the ridges flow continuously in a steep, upward curve and then back down, making a loop. They may slant left or right. There are two types: ulnar and radial. In an arch, the ridges also flow continuously but in a much less inclined pattern. They rise and fall like a calm wave. There are two types: tented and plain. Whorl patterns make little circles in the center of the print. They are the only pattern that contains two deltas. There are four types of whorls: plain, central pocket, double loop, and accidental.

Where do I see it?

This computer-generated example of fingerprint comparisons from the *CSI* pilot shows a loop pattern on the right and a whorl pattern on the left.

How can I use it?

Arches are the rarest print pattern. Only about 5% of the population has them. Whorls come in second place at 30–35%. The rest of us, about 60–65%, exhibit the loop pattern. I guess you could infer that the majority of us are loopy.

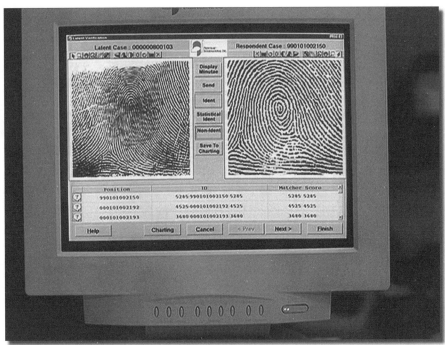

Examples of fingerprint patterns, loop on right, whorl on left. *CSI* pilot; Jerry Bruckheimer TV, 2000.

LiveScan Technology

What is it?

LiveScan technology is a machine that scans fingerprints, creates and records an image of them, and sends them to AFIS. No ink or paper are needed, therefore, no mess.

Where can I see it?

Documentary-based shows like *True Crime* or *Forensic Files* often show suspects being printed via LiveScan technology.

How can I use it?

LiveScans are quick, easy to use, and portable. They don't stain your fingers with ink and they capture an accurate image of your print. (Sometimes inked images can smear, blur, or blob.) Not only that, but the prints are sent directly to AFIS, where they can immediately be searched and matched.

Patent Print

What is it?

A patent print is a print that has been transferred by a substance like blood or grease, substances other than that on humans' skin (i.e., perspiration or skin oils). Patent prints are one of the four types of prints investigators look for at the scene of the crime.

Where do I see it?

Crime scene investigators come across this bloody footprint in *CSI*, episode 121.

How can I use it?

Patent prints are very visible if your CSI knows what to look for. How do you preserve and collect bloody patent prints? First, they are photographed at the scene with a scale. Then the photograph will be taken back to the crime lab and processed in black and white to be scanned into AFIS. Note: After the print has been photographed properly, it can be swabbed for DNA.

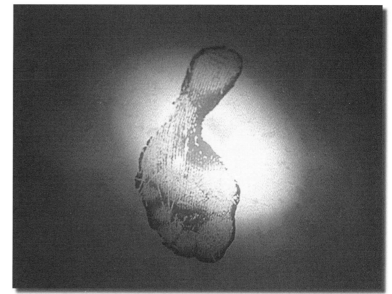

Bloody footprint. *CSI*, episode 121; Jerry Bruckheimer TV, 2000.

Plastic Print

What is it?

Pressing a finger into a soft surface like clay, putty, wax, soap, or mud causes a plastic print. It's an impression print rather than a patent print. Plastic prints are one of four types of prints investigators look for at the scene of the crime.

Where do I see it?

In crime shows sixty years ago, a fingerprint was one of the key pieces of evidence that fictional investigators uncovered. Today, the writers of most film and TV are more savvy, and rarely do criminals leave a plastic print in something so permanent as dust or a melted chocolate bar.

How can I use it?

Plastic prints are easy to see with the naked eye. If you want to plant an obvious seed of evidence, have your criminal touch something at the scene of the crime that leaves a mold of his print — maybe something food-related — peanut butter or frosting? It's not unusual for a perp to work up an appetite after committing a crime and help himself to a snack.

Poroscopy

What is it?

The skin is covered in sweat pores, and when we touch something the sweat residue transfers to that object, leaving a print. The study of the shape, size, and arrangement of pores that determine the uniqueness of a fingerprint is called poroscopy. Poroscopy is rarely used because pore size changes due to the pressure applied as we press down or clamp something with our hands, and due to how much or how little we sweat. Using pore patterns in comparisons occurs only when there isn't enough friction skin detail to make a complete print. And then it's used as a supplement to ridgeology and Galton Details. It's important to note that poroscopy is never as reliable as ridgeology.

Where do I see it?

Feet sweat a lot more than the hands. Since the ridgeology is lacking in these prints, sweat patterns from the pores would be one way that investigators from *CSI*, episode 121, could narrow a match.

How can I use it?

Getting a good print at the scene of a crime is harder than it looks on TV. Criminals are often nervous at the scene of a crime, and nerves produce sweat. If they're sweating a lot, their fingerprints will become distorted. This means that ridge lines are blurred or connected — not a good print. Also, sweat is 98–99% water and only 1–2% solids. The solids are left after the water that forms the print evaporates. Since most people have some oils on their hands (in addition to sweat solids), the prints will form when the oils in the print rise to the top after evaporation. A few folks out there, called non-secretors, don't sweat (wouldn't that be a nice bonus on first dates!). This doesn't mean that they can't leave a print, nor does lack of a print mean the criminal was a non-secretor.

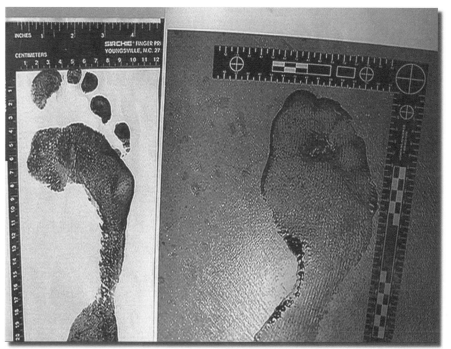

Sweat patterns from the pores of the feet are one way investigators could narrow a match. *CSI*, episode 121; Jerry Bruckheimer TV, 2000.

Ridgeology or Ridge Characteristics

What is it?

Fingerprints are made of ridges and valleys. Ridgeology is the study of the ridge structure of a print to determine its uniqueness. Fingerprint ridges have ridge endings (where they stop and start), ridge bifurcations (where they split), and ridge flow (short, long, parallel, looped, whorled, arched).

Where do I see it?

Catherine Willows (Marg Helgenberger) and Warrick Brown (Gary Dourdan) process prints at a victim's home in the pilot episode of *CSI*. They are most concerned about protecting the ridgeology of the print so they can get an accurate read. Of course, prints are usually not processed on-site at the victim's home; this usually happens at the lab.

How can I use it?

Even though every person's fingerprint is unique, there can be similarities to patterns. The AFIS uses a numerical score to measure the Galton Details (see Galton Details), and the higher the score the more likely the match. AFIS uses an algorithm to match fingerprint minutia in terms of the ridge characteristics each print contains. Warning: myth-buster! The computer doesn't make fingerprint matches; fingerprint examiners do. The computer generates ten geometric forms that are similar to the print in question. The examiner takes those top ten suggestions and finds the one that is most closely matched.

Willows and Brown process prints at a victim's home. *CSI* pilot; Jerry Bruckheimer TV, 2000.

Vacuum Metal Deposition (VMD)

What is it?

VMD is a method of lifting fingerprints from hard-to-lift materials like plastic bags, synthetic cloth, and paper. In this process, a layer of gold is evaporated and settles onto the print. Then a layer of zinc is vaporized and deposits itself into the ridges and valleys of the print rendering the print readable. VMD is effective in materializing older prints or those that have been exposed to environmental conditions, including being waterlogged. It has been used by the Royal Canadian Mounted Police since the late 1970s, but we in the States have been a little behind in employing the process, probably because the machines are expensive and take up a lot of space.

Where do I see it?

A few larger law enforcement agencies around the country use VMD, but seeing VMD on TV or in movies seems to be rare. However, you can read about VMD and see pictures of its results in the book, *Bad Trick: The Hunt for Spokane's Serial Killer*, by Bill Morlin and Jeanette White.

How can I use it?

When other means of lifting prints aren't successful, VMD has a very good chance of revealing a print. Build a case where fingerprint identification is crucial to discovering your suspect. Add hurdles to your investigation by placing the closest VMD chamber in the next state or country. For example, in the mid-1990s the San Diego sheriff jumped through international hoops to solve eight cold cases when he sought the use of the only VMD available in North America, across the U.S. border in Ottawa, Canada.

Visible Prints

What is it?

Visible prints are those you can see with the naked eye. They are created when someone gets a substance like ink, blood, grease, oil, or mud onto their hands or feet, and then touches another surface. Visible prints are one of four types of prints investigators look for at a crime scene.

Where do I see it?

In a rather unorthodox manner of dusting and lifting prints, Chuck (Anna Friel) and Emerson Cod (Chi McBride) use powdered sugar to recover a full set of the suspect's prints in *Pushing Daisies*, "Bitter Sweets."

How can I use it?

Crimes of passion are usually messy. The killer will have blood on his hands or feet that will get transferred to countertops, door handles, and furniture. Investigators: Look here for visible prints. Also, if the killer was bare- or stocking-footed, he will leave identifiable footprints. Even if he wipes up the blood, prints will not remain but the blood hemoglobin will. It's possible that a luminol test (see Chemical Processing) will enhance a print that was once there.

Chuck and Emerson Cod use powdered sugar to recover suspects' prints. *Pushing Daisies*, "Bitter Sweets"; ABC, 2007–09.

Volar Skin

What is it?

Volar skin is the raised, puffy skin on the fingertips, palms, toes, and soles of the feet. In the womb, volar skin starts off as volar pads during the first eleven weeks of fetal development. The volar pads soon become volar skin or friction skin, and unique ridge patterns form on each human being.

Where do I see it?

The part of our hands that creates prints is the volar skin. In a scene from the *CSI* pilot, Sara Sidle (Jorga Fox) dusts a telephone for prints. You can see where the volar skin left print impressions on the side of the receiver.

How can I use it?

Prints are left because of residue that transfers from the volar skin to the surface area it touched. The residue on the volar skin may be naturally occurring like sweat or oil from the hair, or it could be environmental like grease from potato chips or hand lotion.

Sara Sidle dusts for prints from a telephone. *CSI* pilot; Jerry Bruckheimer TV, 2000.

■ *Exercise 1.*

Watch the scene from your favorite crime-related film or TV show where investigators are first processing the scene. As you watch, make a list of all the places where the criminal/villain could have left her fingerprints or palm prints. Are these full or partial prints? What kind of prints might they be? Latent, patent, plastic?

■ *Exercise 2.*

Take one of the stories you are working on. Place yourself in the scene or moment when the crime occurred. Walk yourself around this scene, this setting, and make a list of all the potential places your criminal/villain could have left fingerprints. Now select three to five of these places and circle them on your list. These are places where your investigator protagonist will eventually find prints. Decide if you want them to be discovered all at once or if you want to leave one or two for discovery later. Are they full or partial prints? What kind of prints are they — latent, patent, or plastic?

V.
DNA Lingo

"Our genetic differences are at the heart of one of the most fascinating paradoxes of the human condition: that we are all different, yet we are all the same." — Geneticist Mary-Claire King, 1993

We hear the acronym DNA thrown around these days like a beach ball at a Dodger game. We think we know what it means and how it works based on what we've seen on TV procedurals. But stop for just a second. Can you tell me right now what DNA actually stands for? Can you, as a writer of crime stories, say exactly how it's collected at a crime scene and processed in the lab? What's the name of the equipment lab techs use to process DNA? If you're not sure now, you will be after reading this chapter.

First off, DNA stands for deoxyribonucleic acid. It is found in the cells of all living things (plants and animals included). A complete set of DNA is unique to each individual; only identical twins share the same DNA. DNA contains a set of gene codes arranged along 25,000 chromosomes that contains all the information about a person's genetic makeup and well-being from birth to death. Your hair and eye color and what diseases you're prone to are found in DNA.

DNA was first discovered in 1868, but it wasn't until the 1950s that scientists figured out what DNA looked like. And only in the late 1980s was DNA first used forensically to link suspects and victims to crimes.

This chapter delves a little deeply into chemistry (my only C grade in high school!), so I decided not to arrange it in alphabetical order, but in order of how DNA works. We'll start off with the building blocks of DNA science and then see how it applies to forensic science. At the beginning of this chapter, I will omit the "How can I use it?" section when defining basic DNA terminology. Once we start applying DNA to forensic science, I'll bring that section back into play.

Broken into its simplest parts, this section explains the structure of DNA for all of us who scored Cs or lower in high school chemistry.

THE SCIENCE OF DNA

DNA

What is it?

Within each gene is a complete DNA structure. DNA is the boss of the gene that controls genetic traits. Genes are the microscopic beads of information about our makeup that sit along the chromosomes like water droplets on a spider's web. We have up to 25,000 genes. Genes are carried via chromosomes. As you'll see in the model on this page, the chromosome is made up of bundles of DNA. DNA is made up of thread-like chromosomes strung together within a cell. This structure first loops over itself to form a histone. From here it winds tighter to create a nucleosome bundle and then coils even tighter to form a chromatin chain. This chain forms a chromatid spring. Finally, it winds itself into a chromosome (X or Y). In each cell are 46 mated chromosomes, twenty-three from the father and twenty-three from the mother (except for reproductive cells, which only contain twenty-three chromosomes).

DNA is found in the cells of all living things (not just humans, but plants and animals too). A complete set of DNA is unique to each individual; only identical twins share the same DNA.

Where do I see it?

You cannot see genes, chromosomes, or DNA through a microscope. They are just too small. Rather, they show up as values when you run them through the Short Tandem Repeat process (see later in this chapter).

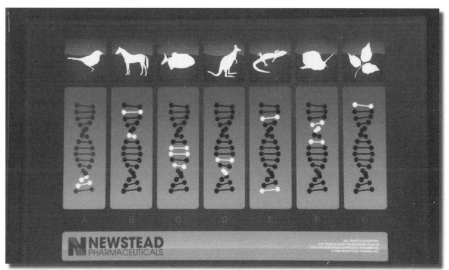

Animal DNA strands. *Splice*, Warner Bros., 2009.

Nucleotide

What is it?

At the core of a DNA unit is a base attached to a sugar-phosphate strand. The four bases contain nitrogen; they are: adenine, cytosine, guanine, and thymine. Adenine always pairs with thymine. And guanine always pairs with cytosine. This core unit of DNA repeats itself over and over and over in one long double-helix configuration.

Where do I see it?

In the 2009 movie *Splice*, two geneticists create a half human, half creature from DNA samples.

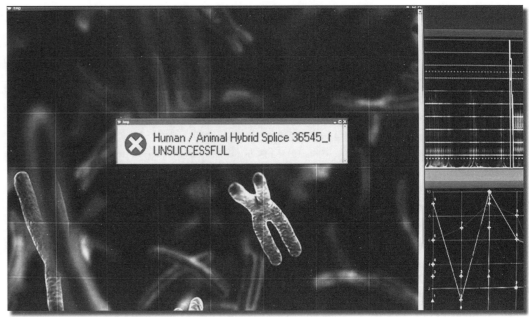

Computer screen with x chromosome. *Splice*, Warner Bros., 2009.

Adenine/Thymine

What is it?

Adenine and thymine are nucleotides that always pair together in the DNA structure. Along with guamine and cytosine, these two nucleotides are the instruction manual of DNA. The way they are arranged tells the cell how to act and what to become (i.e., blue eyes, brown hair, diabetes). The arrangement of these base pairs is unique to each individual and creates the DNA fingerprint (see DNA fingerprint).

Guamine/Cytosine

What is it?

Guamine and cytosine are nucleotides that always pair together in DNA structure. Along with adenine and thymine, these two nucleotides base pairs are the instruction manual of DNA. The way they are arranged tells the cell how to act and what to become (i.e., brown eyes, blonde hair, freckles). The arrangement of these base pairs is unique to each individual and creates the DNA fingerprint (see DNA fingerprint).

Where do I see it?

In this scene from *Body of Proof*, "Society Hill," pathologists look at the DNA of a hair strand and determine that it's more than one hundred years old.

Pathologists look at the DNA of a hair strand and determine that it's more than a century old. *Body of Proof*, "Society Hill"; ABC, 2011.

Genotype

What is it?

When people refer to someone's genotype, they are talking about this person's physical and biological makeup. When we are conceived, two sets of cells from two different people form as one. This new cell holds all the new information about us and who we're going to be physically and biologically. We call this cell structure our set of genes.

Where do I see it?

You can really only see this under a microscope and then only as a pattern. These cells don't look like a blue-eyed, brown-haired, five-foot-eight-inch woman with one foot larger than the other and crooked teeth.

Phenotype

What is it?

A person's phenotype refers to the outward characteristic of the inward gene combination: hair color, eye color, skin tone. It's what happens when cells start to reproduce, grow, and take shape as a human being.

Where do I see it?

When you see a person, you see her phenotype. The cells in genotypes take on the phenotype of a blue-eyed, brown-haired, five-foot-eight-inch female with one foot larger than the other and crooked teeth.

Before investigators collect blood-like substances at the scene of a crime, they test them to see if they are or are not blood. This section explains several types of tests used to find out if a substance is blood or just a little spilled tomato sauce.

IS IT REALLY BLOOD?

Presumptive Testing

What is it?

Presumptive tests are performed at the scene of the crime to test for the presence of blood. I bring this up in this section because often DNA samples will come from blood, and before you leave that crime scene you need to be sure that what you've collected for DNA testing is, indeed, blood. There are several commonly used types of presumptive testing methods: Hemastix, luminol or BlueStar (see the CSI chapter), Kastle-Meyer, and precipitin.

Where do I see it?

An investigator in *CSI*, episode 121, swabs a blood sample for a presumptive test.

How can I use it?

The Hemastix and phenolpthalein tests are first determiners of blood presence. They are quick, easy to use, and non-disruptive, but they don't indicate whether the blood is solely human. The precipitin test, on the other hand, does indicate if the blood is of human origin. Luminol and BlueStar should only be used after the scene is thoroughly investigated because after using these chemicals, the blood evidence will be completely compromised or destroyed. After you've collected the blood and determined it's human, it can undergo DNA testing to be given a DNA profile and then matched to a victim, witness, or suspect.

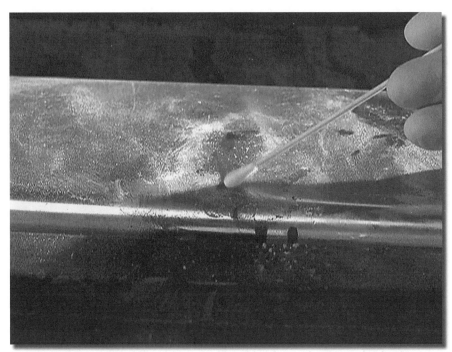

An investigator swabs this car bumper for a blood sample. *CSI*, episode 121; Jerry Bruckheimer TV, 2000.

Hemastix and HemaTrace Test

What is it?

When you're at the scene of a crime and you see red liquid spatter all over the walls, you naturally assume it is blood. How can you be sure? What if it's a food-coloring experiment gone awry? A quick test with Hemastix or HemaTrace will tell you.

Hemastix are thin paper strips about three inches long and a quarter-inch thick. The stick detects the like-like activity found in the hemoglobin of the blood. You wet the strip with distilled water and dip it into the blood-like substance. If the substance is blood, the strip will turn green.

The HemaTrace kit also tests for human hemoglobin and works much like a pregnancy test. You collect a swab of the blood in question, add the buffer, and in less than two minutes results show up on the strip. Two pink lines indicate positive for human blood.

Where do I see it?

A lab technician in *CSI*, episode 120, waits for a HemaTrace sample to turn green.

How can I use it?

The Hemastix test is quick and easy, but it *cannot* distinguish between animal and human blood. You will need the HemaTrace or precipitin test for that. You can buy a kit online and become your own CSI. It comes with fifty test strips.

HemaTrace will identify human blood and therefore is taking precedence in the forensic field over Hemastix tests. Online you can purchase your very own HemaTrace kit for about $17.

If the sample turns blue, it's blood. *CSI*, episode 120; Jerry Bruckheimer TV, 2000.

Phenolphthalein Test

What is it?

The phenolphthalein test is another presumptive test for blood. It's sometimes called the Kastle-Meyer (K-M test for short) test. Like the Hemastix, it detects the like-like quality in blood. Using a filter paper, you rub it on the substance you believe to be blood. Then you add a drop of alcohol, a drop of phenolphthalein, and a drop of hydrogen peroxide. If it turns a bright pink color, it's blood.

Where do I see it?

In the first season of *CSI*, episode 110, Nick Stokes (George Eads) uses a phenolphthalein test on the carpet of a suspect's vehicle to test for blood.

How can I use it?

One little pitfall of the K-M test is that horseradish and potato juice can turn the paper pink. But seriously, how many criminals do you know who sit around juicing potatoes and horseradish at the scene of a crime? As I write this, I'm wondering how many new criminal characters with a penchant for potato-horseradish smoothies are going to pop up because of this reference. And it must also be mentioned that the Kastle-Meyer test has its own Facebook page. Just in case you want to friend it.

Nick Stokes tests carpet for blood. *CSI*, episode 110; Jerry Bruckheimer TV, 2000.

Precipitin Test

What is it?

The precipitin test reveals whether the blood you've collected is human or animal. Human blood carries a specific antigen different from animal blood. To discover if the blood is human, the blood sample to be tested is run next to a nonhuman sample of blood (often rabbit serum). An electrical charge is applied, much like the gel electrophoresis. If the proteins attract toward each other and form a line, it's human blood.

Where do I see it?

Two lab techs on *CSI*, episode 120, test an evidence sample for the presence of human blood.

How can I use it?

Before conducting a precipitin test, you should test the substance to make sure it's actually blood. However, HemaTrace kits are quickly replacing precipitin testing because they kill two birds with one stone, testing for blood and human hemoglobin.

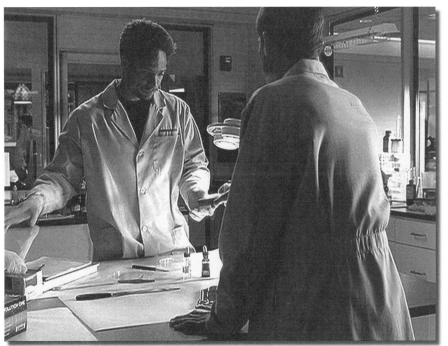

Back at the lab, Warrick tests an evidence sample for human blood. *CSI*, episode 120; Jerry Bruckheimer TV, 2000.

DNA testing is not as straightforward as most crime shows portray. There are three types of DNA tests that can be run: nuclear, mitochondrial (mDNA), and YSTR. Each has a distinct use in forensic investigation. For instance, YSRT testing is most commonly performed in rape cases. mtDNA is least commonly used because you share it with everyone who has a mother, grandmother, or great-grandmother in common with you.

TYPES OF DNA TESTING

Nuclear DNA (nDNA)

What is it?

Crime labs currently use three common types of DNA tests: nuclear, mitochondrial, and YSRTs (or Y testing). The test for nuclear DNA is the broadest form of DNA testing. Nuclear DNA (nDNA) is found in the nucleus of the cell and is comprised of forty-six chromosomes — twenty-three each from mom and dad. Remember, reproductive cells only have twenty-three chromosomes.

Where do I see it?

Scientists who work at N.E.R.D. splice nDNA samples from animals and human beings to create new life forms in *Splice*.

How can I use it?

nDNA is sometimes called touch DNA. This is the kind you hope to find at the crime scene in the form of blood, urine, semen, saliva on a cigarette butt, or glass. nDNA is the most tested form of DNA in crime labs because, compared to mDNA and Y testing, it yields the best statistical results on a suspect. Let's say you wanted to run an nDNA test on yourself; it would cost upwards of $1,500. Those online DNA kits that run a couple hundred dollars only test for mDNA or Y chromosomes. The next few sections will cover why they are less evaluative than nDNA and how they are effective in specialized cases.

Mitochondrial DNA (mtDNA)

What is it?

As mentioned previously, crime labs currently use three common types of DNA tests: nuclear, mitochondrial, and YSRTs. The test for mtDNA is used less often and here's why. Mitochondrial DNA is inherited from the mother only. Because mtDNA is shared through the maternal line, it is not uniquely you. The mtDNA you have is the same as your mother, grandmother, great-grandmother, great-great-grandmother, and so on. So you and your fourth cousin, if you come from the same maternal line, will have the same mtDNA. mtDNA testing can help you narrow down a suspect to a family line, but it's not a definitive test. Also, because a thousand mtDNA cells live on a single cell (compared with just one nDNA in each cell), mtDNA suffers from mutation and error. mtDNA is extracted from hair shafts, teeth, bone, organs, and tissues

Where do I see it?

Geneticists Clive Nicoli (Adrien Brody) and Elsa Kast (Sarah Polley) mix human DNA with animal DNA in the 2009 movie, *Splice*.

How can I use it?

mtDNA testing is commonly used when the body has been completely broken down (charred, dismembered, highly decomposed) and there is no nDNA left to test. In these cases, mtDNA is extracted from teeth and bones. mtDNA testing is also limited in that in order to make an identification, you also must have a DNA sample from the deceased's maternal line. In addition, mtDNA testing is expensive, only a few labs do it, and no organized mtDNA database exists.

Test tube. *Splice*, Warner Bros., 2009.

YSTR
....

What is it?

YSTR refers to a testing method that extracts only the Y chromosome in order to identify a male presence in the sample being tested. Y is for the Y chromosome, and STR stands for "short tandem repeats." This is the process used to test the sample and is covered later in this chapter.

Where do I see it?

Catherine Willows (Marg Helgenberger) examines an unusual sperm sample in *CSI*, episode 122.

How can I use it?

YSTR is used in cases of gang rape to prove multiple Y chromosomes or when there isn't much male DNA present, but you know that a male was involved. In this case, a regular nDNA test of the sample may not show the male DNA because the female's DNA will overshadow it. YSTR testing is rare, few labs do it, and no organized Y-chromosome database is maintained in the United States.

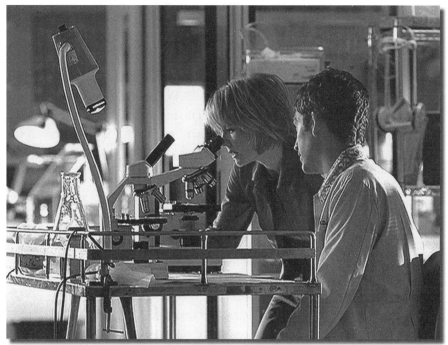

Looking into the microscope to examine a semen slide. *CSI*, episode 122; Jerry Bruckheimer TV, 2000.

DNA testing works much like a copy machine, but much more slowly. Crime shows suggest that scientists can run a full DNA test between commercial breaks. In reality, it takes a minimum of two days to get DNA test results.

HOW DNA TESTING WORKS

Polymerase Chain Reaction (PCR)

What is it?

PCR is the copying process for DNA. Each side of the double-helix structure of DNA is the same. The process of PCR unwinds the helix and copies it millions of times over so that it can be stored, tested, read, and eventually matched. PCR is done through a series of heating and cooling processes in a thermal cycler. The thermal cycler is like a copy machine. First, it separates the DNA strands, binds them to new strands, and then copies them over and over and over. Each of these cycles takes two minutes and cycles twenty-eight to thirty-two times. The final step is adenylation, which adds an adenine to the end. The entire process takes two hours.

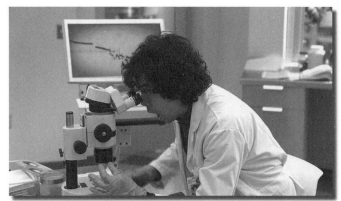

Ethan discovers the DNA code in *Body of Proof*'s "Society Hill"; ABC, 2010–present.

Where do I see it?

Forensic scientist Ethan Gross (Geoffrey Arend) uses STRs through a PCR process to discover the DNA code of a victim in the episode "Society Hill" from *Body of Proof*.

How is this used?

Even if only a small sample of DNA is retrievable from a crime scene, PCR can find a value. PCR can take less than one-billionth of a gram of DNA and copy it. It's important to note that the PCR process doesn't copy the entire DNA chain, but only one section.

Short Tandem Repeat (STR)

What is it?

In a DNA strand, 30% of the strand contains the important coding region where base pairs form a repeating pattern three to seven times. This pattern is called short tandem repeat. The other 70% are non-coding regions that fill space between the coding regions, much like packing peanuts in a shipped box.

Where do I see it?

Forensic scientist Ethan Gross (Geoffrey Arend) uses STRs through a PCR process to discover the DNA code of a victim in the episode "Society Hill" from *Body of Proof*.

How is it used?

How is this helpful in forensic work? The STR is the part of the DNA copied in the PRC process (see Polymerase Chain Reaction). Thankfully, the DNA sample doesn't have to be very big or fresh in order to find an STR.

Gel Electrophoresis

What is it?

Electrophoresis was one of the first methods developed to create and compare a DNA profile. It works by separating the four bases of DNA (adenine, thymine, guanine, and cytosine) using chromatography. In chromatography, the substances in DNA carry a negative electrical charge that move along a gel bed toward a positive electrical charge when the bed is given electrical current. Different DNA strands respond differently and, therefore, travel different lengths (short strands travel more quickly than longer strands of DNA). After they've stopped traveling, the pattern they form in the gel bed represents a person's DNA profile or fingerprint.

Where do I see it?

In this scene from *Splice*, geneticists use a form of gel electrophoresis where the DNA sample is inserted into gel so the electrophoresis process can be run.

How can I use it?

Forensically speaking, electrophoresis is outdated. It is used more in science labs than in crime labs, which now use capillary electrophoresis. Additionally, a portable microchip is being developed to take into the field to run DNA tests.

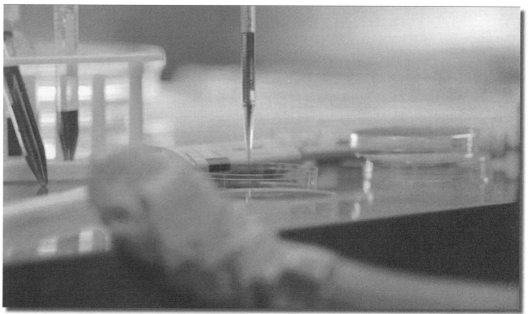

DNA sample is Inserted into gel. *Splice*, Warner Bros., 2009.

Capillary Electrophoresis

What is it?

Capillary electrophoresis (CE) is a machine that finds DNA values based on electrokinetics. Proteins with a positive charge in DNA head towards a negative charge via an electro-osmotic flow through the capillary. The smaller strands travel faster toward the negative charge than the larger one. This creates a DNA pattern that is unique to each person, since each person's strands are different lengths and sizes.

Where do I see it?

Geneticists in the 2009 film, *Splice*, use short tandem repeats, polymerase chain reactions, and electrophoresis in their DNA experiments.

For real-life demonstrations, view a series of short videos demonstrating electrophoresis published by the University of Michigan. *http://www.umd.umich.edu/labtv/modules/agarosegel/agarose .html*

Brody at lab station. *Splice*, Warner Bros., 2009.

How can I use it?

Capillary electrophoresis is more widely used in crime labs to test for DNA than the original gel electrophoresis. It takes a minimum of two days from the time a DNA sample enters the lab until it's processed and reviewed and analyzed, if the lab isn't backlogged. Compare this to TV time, which produces a DNA result between commercial breaks. Learn more about the CE process online from the company QIAxcel's video, "Say Goodbye to Gel Electrophoresis." Or try a kitschy video at *www.Glogster.com*, an online education platform. The video is student-level, but clearly explains and demonstrates the whole process of DNA processing from crime scene through CE.

The world of DNA is continually evolving, expanding, and creating new possibilities. In the future we will be able to take printed books and give them DNA codes. These codes will give us the ability to fit the DNA codes for millions of books on the tip of a pin. This section takes you into some of the applications of DNA science.

OTHER DNA INFO

Artificial DNA (aDNA)

What is it?

Genetics labs engineer DNA all the time in order to run tests to learn how viruses work. But it wasn't until recently that a company in Tel Aviv engineered an artificial DNA and cloned blood. The amplified DNA cells were mixed with DNA-less red blood cells to create fake blood. They sent it off to America for DNA testing and it fooled the American labs. It looks like we've come a long way since the days of cornstarch, food coloring, and syrup. All you need to clone blood is a sample DNA or a DNA profile from the database. There are currently two processes for manufacturing fake DNA. One is called whole genome amplification and the other is a cloning process. So far, current forensic testing has failed to tell the difference between nDNA and aDNA.

Where do I see it?

In an odd twist on artificial DNA, geneticists Clive Nicoli (Adrien Brody) and Elsa Kast (Sarah Polley) mix human DNA with animal DNA in the 2009 movie, *Splice*. The outcome is less than pleasing.

How can I use it?

High-tech criminals, or even those with just some college-level knowledge of genetics, can engineer a crime scene or sell aDNA on the black market to other criminals. Do you want justice to be served in this case? A prosecutor can now contest the reliability of biological versus artificial DNA and save the case if he thinks the perp was faking it. Or a defense attorney can try to get DNA evidence thrown out if she believes someone planted fake DNA evidence against her client.

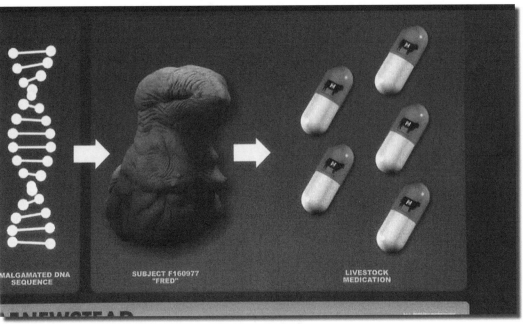

Successful and unsuccessful slide. *Splice*, Warner Bros., 2009.

Chimeric

What is it?

Chimeric people have two separate and distinct DNA strands in their makeup. Typically, chimera happens during very early stages of gestation when two fertilized eggs are created, and then one is absorbed by the other. It can also happen from a blood transfusion or a bone marrow transplant.

Where do I see it?

View the *CSI* episode, "Bloodlines," season four, which centers on a killer who is chimeric.

How can I use it?

Is there a way to identify chimeric people physically? Sometimes chimeric people will have patches of different color on their skin or two different colored eyes. Or, as in the case of hermaphrodites, both sex organs. Some studies estimate that less than .2% of the population is chimeric, whereas other studies say as many as 50–75% are chimeric. However, microchimerism may be an even more common form of chimera. This happens when some of the cells from the fetus remain in the mother after birth, abortion, or miscarriage. According to Catherine Arcabascio's article in the *Akron Law Review*, these cells can stay in the mother for decades. She claims that chimeras are on the rise because of the number in vitro fertilization procedures and births (see "Chimeras: Double the DNA — Double the Fun for Crime Scene Investigators, Prosecutors, and Defense Attorneys?" in *Akron Law Review* 40:3 [2007]).

CODIS

What is it?

CODIS stands for Combined DNA Index System, which is an FBI support system and software program that runs the database for DNA profiles of criminals, offenders, and missing people. A match made on CODIS is called a hit.

NDIS (National DNA Index System) is a part of CODIS that was implemented in October 1998 and is used by all fifty states, the FBI, the U.S. Army, and Puerto Rico.

SDIS (State DNA Index System) is a state laboratory that runs CODIS and is a connecter between the national and local DNA Index Systems. The state's bureau of investigation, department of corrections, or division of justice operates it.

LDIS (Local DNA Index System) is the local laboratory, operated by police and sheriff departments, that runs CODIS and feeds the information to the state and national DNA Index Systems.

Where do I see it?

Go right to the source: *http://www.fbi.gov/about-us/lab/codis*.

How can I use it?

Let's extol the benefits of CODIS: It aids criminal investigations, helps to make the case for convictions, or exonerates innocent folks. It can be used to identify remains and find missing people. But CODIS isn't perfect; it has limitations. For instance, degraded DNA samples have led to misleading matches. In some states, arrestees are required to give a DNA sample, which violates the presumption of innocence before proven guilty. And the prosecution rate of cases in which offender matches have been made is shockingly low — less than 10%.

DNA Fingerprint

What is it?

Each person's DNA contains a slightly different code. The code is found in the way the bases are arranged. Remember the bases — adenine, thymine, cytosine, and guanine? The way in which these pairs (A-T and C-G) are arranged along the double helix creates a unique DNA fingerprint. This fingerprint can be replicated and used to make matches. A DNA fingerprint is also called DNA typing, DNA blueprint, or a genetic profile.

Where do I see it?

The victim or suspect who bled on the T-shirt that Warrick Brown (Gary Dourdan) examines in *CSI*, episode 121, is chock-full of DNA fingerprinting.

How can I use it?

In all humans, 99.9% of our genomes or DNA look exactly the same as everyone else's. It's that 0.1% that distinguishes us. When trying to make DNA matches, technicians look for thirteen different loci (or regions) on the human chromosome. It's not uncommon that a majority of these thirteen loci look the same from one person to the next. According to Jason Felch and Maura Dolan in the *Los Angeles Times* (July 8, 2008), "Although a person's genetic makeup is unique, his genetic profile — just a tiny sliver of the full genome — may not be. Siblings often share genetic markers at several locations (loci), and even unrelated people can share some by coincidence." We've been trained by CSI to rely on the absolute validity of DNA evidence. But in reality DNA evidence can get stuck on the boggy soil of doubt, thereby providing fertile ground for storytelling twists.

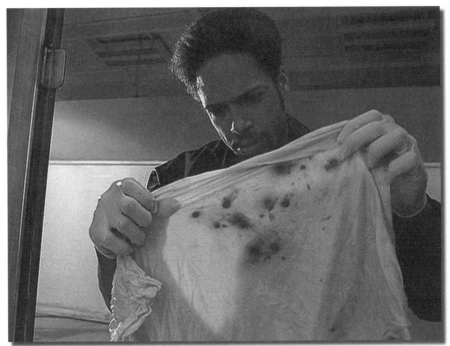

Warrick finds a bloody shirt. *CSI*, episode 121; Jerry Bruckheimer TV, 2000.

Familial DNA

What is it?

In cases of extremely violent, ongoing crimes, law enforcement officials seek requests to conduct familial DNA searches. In these situations, they run DNA harvested from the scene of a crime through the DNA databases to see if it's compatible with parents or siblings who are in the DNA database. If they do find a match, detectives can use this information to deepen their investigation and find potential suspects.

Where do I see it?

The *Body of Proof* forensic team of Dr. Megan Hunt (Dana Delany), Peter Dunlop (Nicholas Bishop), and Dr. Ethan Gross (Geoffrey Arend) catches a killer through a familial DNA search when the murderer left a skin sample on the victim in the episode, "All in the Family," season one.

How can I use it?

Familial DNA testing is not widely used or accepted in the U.S. Such a search requires a formal request to the Department of Justice and this request is rarely granted. The United Kingdom, however, has been conducting familial DNA searches since the mid-2000s.

Flake of suspect's skin, a close match to his son's DNA. *Body of Proof*, "All in the Family"; ABC, 2011.

Human Genome Project

What is it?

The Human Genome Project was started in 1990 to discover the entire gene sequence of a human being. And in thirteen years, they did it! The project's goal was to identify the sequence of all three billion subunits of DNA (made up of adenine, thymine, guanine, and cytocine). A genome is all the information in the DNA. If the human genome were stored on a computer, it would take up three GB of storage space minimum!

Where do I see it?

Elsa Kast (Sarah Polley) injects a human female egg with animal sperm as part of a human genome project gone bad in the 2009 thriller, *Splice*.

How can I use it?

The Human Genome Project isn't concerned with using DNA to solve crimes; rather, it uses DNA information to make us healthier

Kast injects sperm into egg. *Splice*, Warner Bros., 2009.

humans and to prolong our lives. More than thirty genes have been found and associated with diseases like diabetes, cancer, arthritis, deafness, and blindness. Now that scientists have constructed the complete genome structure, they can predict disease and hopefully someday be able to create new tissue and organs. This brings up the subject of cloning, which includes DNA cloning, reproductive cloning, and therapeutic cloning.

The Human Genome Project is only loosely connected to the field of forensic science. It informs forensic testing, but mostly concerns itself with genetics. However, it's possible, forensically speaking, that the human genome could provide a complete gene sequence on a suspect or victim. It would be costly, but it would give insight into that person's makeup. For example, it could indicate a person's race or what diseases they suffer from.

Innocence Project

What is it?

DNA profiling is not just used to prove guilt, but also to prove the innocence of those wrongly accused or convicted. This is the focus of the Innocence Project. In 2012, the Innocence Project turned twenty, and during that time has reported that 250 people (post-conviction) in thirty-four states have been exonerated using DNA evidence.

Where do I see it?

Learn more at *http://www.innocenceproject.org.*

How can I use it?

The Innocence Project is a superb resource when researching how good guys have suffered from bad lawyers, improper forensic evidence, lying informants, or coerced false confessions. The project is loaded with case studies and stories of people who were set free after DNA evidence proved them innocent. It's very moving and inspiring — the stuff great stories are made of.

Surreptitious Sample

What is it?

A surreptitious sample is a DNA sample taken without the suspect knowing it. It's legal and permissible if the sample taken is collected from the public domain. For example, if I throw away my Coffee Bean cup in a public trash can, it is legal for a detective to extract it and swab the lid for my DNA.

Where do I see it?

The use of familial DNA made history in Los Angeles' Grim Sleeper case of 2010. A court allowed familial DNA testing to catch a serial killer, Lonnie Franklin Jr., through a surreptitious sample of napkins he left at a pizza joint. He was tried on ten counts of murder.

How can I use it?

In the 2010 Grim Sleeper case, an undercover detective posed as a busboy in a pizza joint that Franklin frequented. After Franklin tossed his plate, cup, napkin, and pizza scraps, the "busboy" collected the surreptitious samples and brought them to the crime lab. The DNA samples taken from Franklin's leftovers matched DNA samples found on his victims. Busted. You can use similar techniques in your own crime stories. People leave DNA everywhere. A suspect blows his nose and tosses the tissue. Hair sheds onto the floor of a coffee shop. Fingernail clippings or nail files are tossed from a nail spa. The ideas are endless.

■ *Exercise 1.*

Watch a scene from your favorite crime-related film or TV show. As you watch, make a list of all the places where the criminal/villain may have left his DNA. What kind of DNA — skin, saliva, hair, semen?

■ *Exercise 2.*

Take one of the stories you are working on. Place yourself in the scene or moment when the crime occurred. Walk yourself around this scene, this setting, and make a list of all the potential places your criminal/villain could have left DNA. Now, select three to five of these places and circle them on your list. These are places where your investigator protagonist will eventually find DNA. Decide if you want them to be discovered all at once or if you want to leave one or two for discovery later.

VI.
Blood Spatter
Speak

"Blood . . . sometimes it sets my teeth on edge. Other times it helps me control the chaos." — Character Dexter Morgan in Dexter

Blood spatter interpretation has been a part of the *CSI* franchise since its first season, but I would posit that most of us didn't pay much attention until *Dexter* showed up. Suddenly, blood spatter was not just disturbing, but sexy and intriguing. As we know from TV, blood spatter can tell us the type of crime, what instrument may have been used, if the victim was moved after injury, if the attacker bled, and where the attacker was positioned when he struck the victim.

This chapter starts by identifying the difference between spatter and splatter. Then we look at spatter terminology and finally, we examine the six main types of bloodstain patterns: drops, splashes, pools, spurts, trails, and wipes. By the way, you can try this at home by replicating David Katz's blood spatter experiment found at *http://www.chymist.com/BLOODSTAIN%20PATTERNS.pdf*.

157

Serology

What is it?

Serology is the study of blood serum for antigen-antibody reactions. These tell us blood type and the health of the blood. In forensics, serology focuses mostly on red blood cells and the blood serum, which looks like a pale yellowish liquid. Serology may also take into account other bodily serums such as sweat, saliva, fecal matter, mucus, and semen.

Where do I see it?

Dexter Morgan (Michael C. Hall) is a serologist of sorts. In this scene, he files a blood slide from his most recent kill in the *Dexter* pilot.

How can I use it?

In forensic science, serology is most used when trying to identify human blood and to link blood type to a person. When you come across a crime scene covered in red, sticky liquid, you shouldn't automatically assume that what you are seeing is blood or that it's from a human source. Presumptive tests on the blood using BlueStar or luminol (see BlueStar and Luminol) will reveal whether the liquid is blood. Precipitin testing will show whether the blood is human or animal. If it's human, test the DNA next so that you can match the blood source to a victim or suspect.

Dexter examines a slide of a drop of blood. *Dexter* pilot; Showtime, 2006.

If you're going to speak blood spatter, first learn the different between spatter and splatter. Contrary to popular misuse, they are not the same.

SPATTER VERSUS SPLATTER

Blood Spatter

What is it?

Spatter refers to the shape, size, and consistency of the blood as it leaves the body and flies through the air. It may come out in sprays, drops, spurts, streams, or strings depending on the impact and type of weapon used. Once it hits a surface, it becomes splatter, something you can step in or wipe your hand across.

Where do I see it?

Rose Lorkowski (Amy Adams) observes the result of blood spatter on the shower wall of her first crime scene clean-up job in *Sunshine Cleaning*.

How can I use it?

Please start by knowing the difference between spatter and splatter and using the terms correctly. The rest of this chapter lays out the different types of spatter and what they say about the suspect or the victim.

Rose sees the bloody crime scene for the first time. *Sunshine Cleaning*, Overture Films, 2008.

Blood Splatter

What is it?

Splatter is different than spatter. It's a subtle difference, but splatter is what blood becomes once it lands or pools on the floor. You can step in splatter. You can wipe your hand across splatter. Spatter (no "l") refers to the shape, size, and consistency of the blood as it comes out of the body and flies through the air; it may be a spray, stream, drop, or spurt.

Where do I see it?

Rose Lorkowski (Amy Adams) cleans her first crime scene, a shower of blood spatter, in the 2008 film, *Sunshine Cleaning*.

How can I use it?

Please, just know the difference between splatter and spatter and use them correctly.

Splatter on shower. *Sunshine Cleaning*, Overture Films, 2008.

How fast was the blood traveling? From what point of the room did it originate? What kind of surface did it fall on? The terms in this section help you answer those questions and reveal how Dexter does his job.

BASIC BLOOD SPATTER TERMINOLOGY

Angle of Impact

What is it?

The angle of impact is the angle at which blood strikes its target. The higher and more acute the angle is (90 degrees), the flatter and rounder the drop; the less acute the angle (10 degrees), the longer and narrower the drop.

Where do I see it?

Dr. Ethan Gross (Geoffrey Arend), Dr. Megan Hunt (Dana Delany), and Detective Peter Dunlop (Nicholas Bishop) examine the angle of impact of a knife in ABC's *Body of Proof*, "All in the Family."

How can I use it?

Angle of impact can tell you about the position of the victim when blood was released.

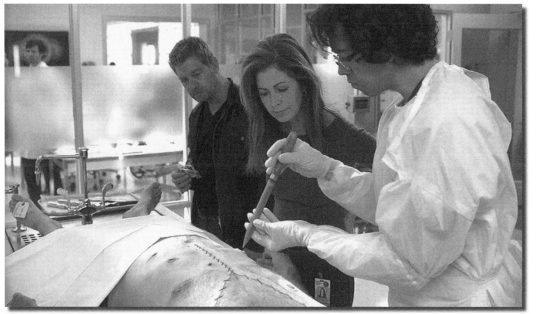

Matching knife to wound. *Body of Proof*, "All in the Family"; ABC, 2011.

Blood Drippings

What is it?

Blood drippings are blood droplets found outside a pool of blood. They serve to point back to the main pool of blood.

Where do I see it?

View the opening credits of *Dexter* for a great visual example of blood drippings.

How can I use it?

Blood drippings can tell you if the victim was moving or if the blood had time to drip out and pool.

Opening credits, blood running down in drips. *Dexter* pilot; Showtime, 2006.

Blowback

What is it?

Blowback is the effect or force of causing back-spatter: the explosive air, pressure, or gas that forces the blood backward.

Where do I see it?

After Bolger (Tim Blake Nelson) shoots a thug in Pug Rothbaum's (Richard Dreyfuss) office, the blowback spatters his blood against the wall and pictures in *Leaves of Grass*.

How can I use it?

Blowback causes backspatter. Examine the criminal and crime scene for backspatter. See Backspatter for more.

Tim Blake Nelson shoots two thugs in Pug Rothbaum's office. *Leaves of Grass*, Millennium Films & First Look Studios, 2010.

Low Velocity

What is it?

Low velocity refers to how fast the blood flows out of the victim in relation to the size of the blood droplet. Low velocity is generally considered to travel less than five feet per second. Blood droplets from a low-velocity altercation will be three millimeters or greater in diameter. Freefalling drops, cast-off from a weapon, and light blood splashing are considered low velocity spatter.

Where do I see it?

Medical examiner Megan Hunt examines the body of a stay-at-home dad in the episode, "All in the Family," from the first season of *Body of Proof*. Not only has the blood pooled, but you can see low-velocity drops around the pooled blood, proving that the victim was moving at no or low velocity.

How can I use it?

In your story, have the blood-pattern analyst determine the type of crime that has taken place by measuring how far the blood has traveled and how large the droplets are.

Low velocity drops. *Body of Proof*, "All in the Family"; ABC, 2011.

Medium Velocity

What is it?

Medium velocity refers to how fast the blood flows out of the victim in relation to the size of the blood droplets. Medium velocity is generally considered to travel five to twenty-five feet per second. Blood droplets from a medium velocity altercation will be one to three millimeters in diameter. Blunt force trauma, stabbing, or arterial spurting are considered medium velocity spatter. Stamping through a pool of blood is also considered medium velocity.

Where do I see it?

Gil Grissom (William Petersen) experiments with blunt force trauma to a dummy and creates a medium velocity blood spatter pattern in the pilot episode of *CSI*.

How can I use it?

In your story, have the blood pattern analyst determine the type of crime that has taken place by measuring how far the blood has traveled and how large the droplets are.

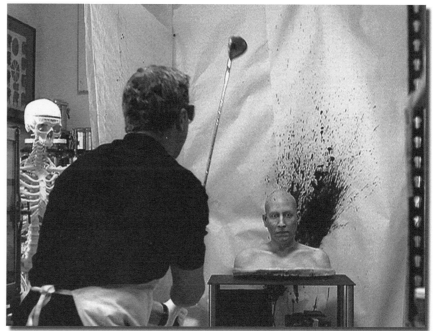

Grissom experiments with blunt-force trauma on a dummy. *CSI* pilot; Jerry Bruckheimer TV, 2000.

High Velocity

What is it?

High velocity refers to how fast the blood flows out of the victim in relation to the size of the droplets of blood. High velocity is generally considered to travel greater than twenty-five feet or one hundred feet per second. Blood droplets from a high-velocity altercation will be less than one millimeter in diameter. Spray from a gunshot wound, backspatter, blowback, or mist from a machinery accident are considered high-velocity spatter.

Where do I see it?

See a rather graphic example of high-velocity spatter in *Fargo* when Gaear Grimsrud (Peter Stormare) puts the pieces of his accomplice Carl Showalter (Steve Buscemi) in the wood chipper. See photo under Misting on page 179.

How can I use it?

In your story, have the blood-pattern analyst determine the type of crime that has taken place by measuring how far the blood has traveled and how large the droplets are.

Nonporous

What is it?

Surface texture determines the shape of the bloodstain. Nonporous surfaces like glass, marble, smooth metal, or shiny tile are smooth, unlike porous surfaces which are rough. Nonporous surfaces allow blood to flow easily and to round out in pools with even edges.

Where do I see it?

In *Leaves of Grass*, starring Edward Norton and Tim Blake Nelson, the blood from a thug's shooting is spattered on the porous and nonporous surfaces of Pug Rothbaum's (Richard Dreyfuss) office wall. The nonporous surface of the glass in the frames causes the blood to wash down the glass, leaving a thin, watery trail, whereas the blood on the wooden wall, a porous surface, has more sticking power and leaves a thick, distinct trail.

Blood on porous and nonporous surfaces: On wood it leaves a trail, on glass it flows over. *Leaves of Grass*, Millennium Films & First Look Studios, 2009.

How can I use it?

Avoid making the mistake of confusing blood droplet shape with velocity. The shape of a blood droplet, once it settles onto its surface, has to do with the texture of that surface and not how fast it hits that surface. However, the size has everything to do with how fast the blood hits its surface. See Low, Medium, and High Velocity for more information.

Porous

What is it?

Surface texture determines the nature of the shape and size of the bloodstain. Porous surfaces like wood, carpet, and cloth are rougher in texture than nonporous surfaces. When blood falls on porous surfaces, the stains splatter in irregular, jagged edges.

Where do I see it?

In *Leaves of Grass*, starring Edward Norton and Tim Blake Nelson, the blood from a thug's shooting is spattered on the porous and nonporous surfaces of Pug Rothbaum's (Richard Dreyfuss) office wall. The nonporous surface of the glass in the frames causes the blood to wash down the glass, leaving a thin, watery trail, whereas the blood on the wooden wall, a porous surface, has more sticking power and leaves a thick, distinct trail.

How can I use it?

Avoid making the mistake of confusing blood droplet shape with velocity. The shape of a blood droplet, once it settles onto its surface, has to do with the texture of that surface and not how fast it hits that surface. However, the size has everything to do with how fast the blood hits its surface. See Low, Medium, and High Velocity for more information.

Point of Convergence

What is it?

The point of convergence (POC) is the two-dimensional place represented by the X and Y axis. It is the distance from the victim to her blood.

Where do I see it?

In the pilot episode of *Dexter*, Dexter (Michael C. Hall) uses string method to examine the point of convergence (or location on the floor) where the victim was standing during an injury.

How can I use it?

POC tells you where the victim and suspect were positioned when the injury or fatality took place.

In this crime scene, Dexter raises his hands directly above the POC, which he has marked with the metal pole. *Dexter* pilot; Showtime, 2006.

Point of Origin

What is it?

The point of origin (POO) is the three-dimensional space (or Z axis) where the victim was standing during injury. POO established the height of the victim at the time of bleeding.

Where do I see it?

In the *Dexter* pilot, Dexter (Michael C. Hall) uses string method to determine the vertical level of the injury to the victim.

How can I use it?

Use POO and POC like Dexter does to figure out where the victim was located and the height at which the blood was coming out of the victim.

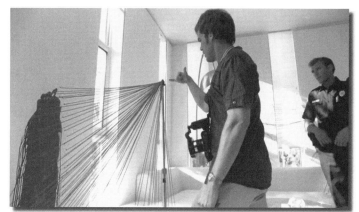

Dexter demonstrates POO with string method. *Dexter* pilot; Showtime, 2006.

You can tell a lot about a crime by looking at the actual blood droplets. If you learn the anatomy of a drop, you can draw conclusions about which way the victim was moving when the crime happened, the angle of impact, and how fresh the blood is. In this section, we follow the blood drop from the moment it exits the body until after it's remained on its surface for a time.

ANATOMY OF A BLOOD DROP

Surface Tension

What is it?

Surface tension refers to the shape of the blood drop as it leaves the body. When blood leaves the body, it pulls itself into a perfectly spherical shape and stays in this shape until some force intervenes (floors, walls, ground, the human body)

Where do I see it?

Dr. Megan Hunt (Dana Delany) notes the condition of blood from a victim in *Body of Proof*, "Buried Secrets," season one.

How can I use it?

The investigator is not concerned with the surface tension of falling blood, but with what happens to that drop when it loses surface tension and is interrupted by the floor, wall, and other objects in its way. This interruption happens in angles and patterns that tell the investigator where the victim was when she bled out and how quickly she bled out (see Velocity).

Megan Hunt tests blood. *Body of Proof*, "Buried Secrets"; ABC, 2011.

Teardrop

What is it?

As a blood drop leaves the body, surface tension works on it to form a perfectly round spherical shape. But on its way to the ground, it starts as a teardrop. From here it elongates vertically, then horizontally, and finally, spherically. A typical drop of blood is .05 milliliters.

Where do I see it?

As blood loses its surface tension, it forms a teardrop shape. In this scene from *Homicide: Life on the Street*, season 7, "La Famiglia," it looks like the walls are literally tearing up from the victim's blood after a brutal homicide.

How can I use it?

Blood drops compact and stay together until impact. It's only after impact that we can start to learn from them about the crime that caused them.

Blood forms teardrop shapes as it loses tension in the "La Famiglia" episode of *Homicide: Life on the Street*; NBC, 1993-99.

Elongated

What is it?

Elongated refers to the shape of a blood drop under the force of gravity as it falls from the victim to the ground. When it hits the ground, it retreats into the sphere-shaped drop that we're used to seeing. The exception here is when the blood impacts a surface that is angled less than 90 degrees. The smaller the angle, the more elongated the drop appears when it lands. Think about honey. If you drip some on a flat table, if forms a nice, round circular pool. Now picture dripping honey on a plate you are holding at a 45-degree angle. The honey hits and doesn't pool. It stretches out into an elongated form.

Where do I see it?

The blood dripping down this witness's face in the *NCIS* episode, "One Shot, One Kill," is an example of blood drops that have been elongated because of their angle of impact.

How can I use it?

This term is useful mostly as background knowledge. But you could use it as a cool slo-mo visual effect where you show blood coming out of an area of impact.

Elongated blood spatter on the face a young man who just witnessed a murder. *NCIS*, "One Shot, One Kill"; CBS, 2003.

Parent Drop

What is it?

Like its name suggests, the parent drop is the main drop from which other satellite drops or tail whips point back to. The best way to understand this is through an illustration.

Where do I see it?

In this picture from *CSI*, season 3, "Abra Cadaver," note the series of parent drops that start at the top of the window. The light marks coming off them are the tails.

How can I use it?

If a parent drop is elongated and looks like a question mark with a tail whip (see Tail Whip), then you can tell which way the blood was traveling by following the pointy end. If the parent drop is rounder and has satellite drops (see Satellite Drops) surrounding it, the blood was dripped closer to a 90-degree angle and from a height greater than six feet.

Parent drops and tails in "Abra Cadaver," *CSI* **season 3; Jerry Bruckheimer TV, 2000–present.**

Satellite Stain

What is it?

Satellite stains (or drops) surround the parent drop or main pool of blood. They are like the stars and moons that orbit planets.

Where do I see it?

When a sniper kills an armed forces recruiting officer at his desk, the main blood spatter and its satellite spatter form a blood pattern on his clipboard in *NCIS*, "One Shot, One Kill."

How can I use it?

Satellite spatter tells you something about how high the blood was when it fell and landed. A higher source means that it picks up speed (or velocity) and creates more satellite staining. A lower height results in a lower velocity (less speed) and less satellite staining.

Bloodstain on clipboard. *NCIS*, "One Shot, One Kill"; CBS, 2003–present.

Tail

What is it?

Picture a single, round blood drop. Now picture it flying through the air and landing on a wall. As it makes contact, it skids across the wall. Once it hits, it loses its round shape and takes on an elongated shape that looks a bit like sperm, except that in blood spatter, the tail leads the way; it doesn't follow in the rear. It sounds backwards, but the tail points toward the parent drop in the direction from which the blood flew. To gain a better understanding, see the picture below.

Where do I see it?

Faint tail marks can be seen in this picture from *CSI*, season 3, "Abra Cadaver." Locate the larger parent drops first. The tails trail the drops and look like little sperm.

How can I use it?

You can pinpoint where in the room a victim was hit and which direction the hit came from by the way the tails lead you to the parent drop and point you in the direction of blood travel. Blood will form tails as it travels in medium-velocity impacts such as blunt-force beatings or when a body collides with a rough surface such as concrete or asphalt.

Note the satellite stains on the clipboard in this scene from *NCIS*, "One Shot, One Kill"; CBS, 2003–present.

Whip

What is it?

A whip comes off the tail. It's a second, unattached tail. Like the tail, it points in the direction the blood was traveling when it splattered.

Where do I see it?

When a man in a restaurant is hit by a rogue car in this scene from *CSI*, episode 317, his blood spatter sprays across the windshield creating long tails and whips. Pay close attention to the drops on the perimeter that best depict whips.

How can I use it?

A whip points back to the tail, which points back to the parent drop. It tells you what direction the blood was headed when it flew from the victim and helps identify where the victim was positioned when the attack occurred.

Perimeter Stain

What is it?

A blood droplet dries from the outside perimeter to the center. If the perimeter dries and then a swipe or wipe occurs, a perimeter stain is left. Even if the blood has been cleaned up, a presumptive test, like BlueStar or luminol, will show that outer skeleton of dried blood.

Where do I see it?

This bloodstain from a scene in the first season of *Castle* shows a bloodstain that has had time to dry. Notice how the outer edges are lighter and drier than the darker interior of the stain that is still wet.

Long whips from blood spatter. *CSI*, episode 317; Jerry Bruckheimer TV, 2000–present.

The perimeter of this bloodstain has begun to dry in this episode from the first season of *Castle*.

A repetitive arrangement of blood spatter patterns forms a bloodstain pattern that points to how the accident or killing occurred. In the 1930s, Scottish pathologist John Glaister identified ways that blood forms patterns after leaving the body: drops, splashes, pools, spurts, wipes, and trails.

When investigating a scene, evaluate the big bloodstain picture, looking for different types of blood formation or patterns. This will tell you about the amount of blood lost, the direction of force or travel impact, what type of instrument was used, how many blows or shots were administered, if the victim moved or was moved, the type of injuries, and where the injuries occurred and in which order.

HOW TO INTERPRET BLOODSTAIN PATTERNS

Backspatter Pattern

What is it?

Backspatter is blood that comes back at you. Let's say you fire a gun in the chest of a person at close range. As the bullet opens up the body, blood spatters onto the gun barrel, your chest, arms, and hands.

How can I use it?

Backspatter on a suspected weapon may prove that the weapon was used in the crime. The same is true with a suspect. If the suspect is found with a victim's backspatter, he was in close range when the shooting happened.

Blood Trail Pattern

What is it?

Bleeding people and bloody weapons leave a trail when they are in motion. This is considered low-velocity spatter. Droplets hit the surface at an angle and have an elongated, scalloped look. They may also create satellite drops.

Where do I see it?

A woman unexpectedly comes across a murder victim who has left a watery blood trail after her brutal murder in *Homicide: Life on the Streets*, "La Famiglia."

How can I use it?

Blood trails show the direction in which the victim or assailant traveled. They can tell you where a perp broke into a home. They can help you find a lost victim. They can lead you to a hiding criminal.

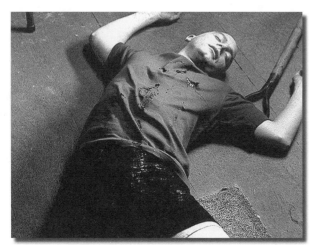

Guy dead on floor with backspatter on shirt. *CSI*, episode 122; Jerry Bruckheimer TV, 2000.

Blood trail from murder victims in "La Famiglia." season 7, *Homicide: Life on the Streets*; NBC, 1993–99.

Cast-off Pattern

What is it?

The pattern that blood makes when it flies off an object in motion is the cast-off pattern. For instance, a killer hits his victim with a hammer. The hammer smashes into the flesh, picks up blood, and as the killer swings the hammer back to administer the next hit, the blood on the hammer releases onto the ceiling. This blood is the cast-off.

Where do I see it?

Dexter (Michael C. Hall) stands in front of a crime scene where blood has been cast off from a knife in a stabbing incident in the pilot episode of *Dexter*.

How can I use it?

Cast-off gives you the location of the victim during an attack. Cast-off indicates how many times the victim was hit.

Drip Stain

What is it?

After blood is released from the body, gravity sends it to the ground or floor, causing a drip stain to appear. Bloodstains that appear on walls or ceilings are not drip stains. They are simply bloodstains.

Where do I see it?

In the film *Sunshine Cleaning*, Rose (Amy Adams) tears up the carpet to find this blood drip stain below.

How can I use it?

Drip stains form various drip patterns. These patterns can reveal angle of impact, area of impact, and velocity of impact.

Dexter at crime scene where blood has been cast off an object and onto the wall. *Dexter* pilot; Showtime, 2006.

Drip stain on wooden floor in *Sunshine Cleaning*, Overture Pictures, 2008.

Expiration Pattern

What is it?

Expiration pattern falls under the category of splash. It happens when blood is forced out of the body or some body cavity. These include the nose, mouth, ears, rectum, or other wounds created on the body.

Where do I see it?

Walter White (Bryan Cranston) comes to after collapsing and exhales a blast of saliva mixed with blood, creating an expiration pattern in the "And the Bag's in the River" episode of *Breaking Bad*.

How can I use it?

Expiration bleeding from wounds shows you where the point of impact occurred, either from a bullet or other weapon. Expiration bleeding from mouth, nose, or anal cavity may indicate internal bleeding. Small air bubbles may be present in the blood if it has come from the lungs. An autopsy will show the extent of the damage and which wounds were fatal.

Fly Spatter Pattern

What is it?

Fly spatter is when flies dip into the blood source and scatter it around the scene via their feet or pooh. At first glance, it looks like high-velocity blood spatter. But a closer investigation will reveal that there is no particular directionality to it. It's fly spatter.

Where do I see it?

Fly spatter probably appears somewhere in the thousands of crime scene shows on air, but I have never stumbled across it. Instead, the quickest way to view an example of fly spatter is to look at this link: *http://hemospat.com/terminology/index.php?cat=misc&sub=fly-spots*.

How can I use it?

You can use it to throw off an investigator. Or you can use it to make your investigator look really, really smart.

Forward Spatter Pattern

What is it?

Forward spatter is bloodstain that has traveled from the exit wound in the same direction as the impact.

Where do I see it?

The blood dripping down the shower wall of a victim's bathroom in the *CSI* pilot opening case is an example of forward spatter from a fatal gunshot wound.

How can I use it?

Use it to determine from which direction the victim was hit.

Blood from a suicide victim on bathroom wall. *CSI* pilot; Jerry Bruckheimer TV, 2000.

Misting Pattern

What is it?

Misting is the form that blood takes during a high-velocity spatter and is in the category of blood splashing. The diameter of the blood droplets is so fine (less than 1mm) that it forms a mist, like that from a spray bottle. Misting occurs from gunshots or high-speed machinery accidents.

Where do I see it?

In this scene from *Fargo*, one of the assailants shoves his accomplice's leg into a woodchipper. A misting pattern sprays from the chipper's front funnel.

How can I use it?

Not all gunshot wounds create misting. But if misting is present, it's likely from a gunshot wound. A fine spray of blood will be present around the direct area of impact from a gunshot or machinery accident. Now your investigator knows where the event took place. This is the focal point. From here your investigator can follow other bloodstain patterns to determine whether the body was moved or what steps the killer took next. Sometimes blood pools in the lungs or sinuses, which, when exhaled, forms a misting pattern that can look like a gunshot wound. However, serology testing will show saliva and mucus present in the blood.

Leg being fed into a wood chipper. *Fargo*, Gramercy Pictures, 1996.

Pooling Pattern

What is it?

Pooling is one of six blood patterns that pathologist John Glaister identified in the 1930s. It happens when blood accumulates in the same place and forms a pool. Pooling forms with a low to no-velocity blood spatter.

Where do I see it?

The victim's blood pools on a semiporous surface in the 121st episode of *CSI*.

How can I use it?

Blood pooling indicates that a victim stayed in the same place long enough for blood to collect. It tells you how long the body lay there from the time the blood ran out until it was discovered.

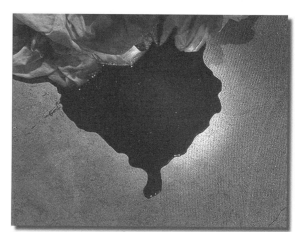

Pooled blood from a crime scene in *CSI*, episode 121; Jerry Bruckheimer TV, 2000–present.

Splash Pattern

What is it?

A splash pattern is the quantity of blood flung through the air that lands onto a particular surface at an angle.

Where do I see it?

Blood from a cop victim that Carl Showalter (Steve Buscemi) has shot splashes onto his face in *Fargo*.

How can I use it?

Splash patterns tell you something about the amount of blood and direction of force or travel of the victim. But it's only a small part of the picture. Splash patterns, along with other forms of bloodstain patterns, tell you more about how many blows or shots were administered and where the impact happened.

Splash pattern on Carl, *Fargo*, Gramercy Pictures, 1996.

Swipe Pattern

What is it?

A little different than a wipe, a swipe pattern suggests the lateral movement of two surfaces (both moving), one bloody, the other not. For example, the bloody hand of an attacker swipes across a victim's arm as she tries to escape his grasp.

Where do I see it?

In this rather comical example from *The Royal Tenenbaums*, the tennis ball boy (Tomm Bauer) waits in the hospital with matriarch Etheline Tenenbaum (Anjelica Huston). His shirt is covered in blood that was swiped from Richie's bleeding arms onto his shirt.

Tennis boy with blood from Richie's failed suicide attempt. *The Royal Tenenbaums*, Touchstone Pictures, 2001.

How can I use it?

Let's say your investigator catches her suspect soon after a crime has been committed. The suspect is bleeding from his shoulder and has blood all over his arms and torso. He tells your investigating officer that he heard screaming and went to rescue the victim and saw that the victim was already dead. He turned to leave, but instead was attacked by the killer. Should your investigator believe him? No way. Don't assume all of the blood on his body is his own. Blood from the victim may be on the suspect, proving he was in direct contact.

Transfer Pattern

What is it?

The pattern that blood makes when it's been transferred from one surface to another is the transfer pattern. This might be accomplished as a hand swipes blood across a countertop, hair sweeps along a wall, or a shoe tromps through blood across the floor.

How can I use it?

Transfer patterns may contain fingerprints, hair samples, shoe tracks, or other evidence that steers you to the person of interest.

Dexter Morgan examines blood transfer across the carpet of a victim's home, where it's unclear whether the victim or suspect transferred the blood. *Dexter*, "Crocodile"; Showtime, 2006.

Void Pattern

What is it?

Void means an empty space. A void pattern is a space in the bloodstain pattern without blood. It indicates that something was blocking the spatter when the incident occurred. Of course, that something also received the spatter, but moved soon after the incident. Often, the thing that moved is a person. And often that person is the assailant.

Where do I see it?

In *CSI*, episode 307, a thug gets blasted away outside a casino and his blood lands on a wall next to him. When investigators remove his body and photograph the scene (yes, they always photograph the scene with and without the body), the area where his body lay will create a void pattern.

How can I use it?

If you see a void of blood spatter at the scene, it is an immediate clue that someone was present when the incident took place. Find that person, match it to the void, and, *voila*, you have completed the puzzle piece and found your killer.

A void pattern will be created when the body is removed, *CSI*, episode 307; Jerry Bruckheimer TV, 2000–present.

Wave Pattern

What is it?

A wave pattern can be caused by two things. The first is an arterial spurt that results from a wound in which an artery is severed. As the victim bleeds, the blood sprays out and casts a wave pattern in accordance with the heart rate. The arterial spatter casts a wave pattern as the blood pumps out of the body through the severed artery.

The second is when a victim has sustained a medium-velocity injury. As the weapon breaks the skin, some of the blood sprays up and out over the main drop. This is wave cast-off. It creates a whip off the tail of the parent drop because of the force of impact. This wave cast-off and the tail point back to the parent drop and tell you which direction the blood was traveling in when it hit.

Where do I see it?

Investigators simulate the moment when a boxer is killed in the ring during episode 307 of *CSI*. During this simulation, the blood expelled from the boxer's mouth during a medium-velocity punch creates a wave cast-off pattern. In this pattern both the tail and the whip will be visible. To see an example of arterial spurting, watch the pilot episode of *Dexter* or view this clip from YouTube: *http://www.youtube.com/watch?v=toilz1kjwjw.*

Victim hit with hammer, leaving a wave pattern. *CSI*, episode 121; Jerry Bruckheimer TV, 2000.

How can I use it?

Arterial spurts tell you that the victim was alive for a time and, if moving, in which direction. When you see a wave pattern across the wall of a bloody crime scene, you can be sure that the victim or suspect sustained an artery injury and was on the move while bleeding.

Wave cast-offs caused from medium-velocity spatter occur in beatings, stabbings, or body drops from long-distance heights.

Wipe Pattern

What is it?

When an object moves through a wet bloodstain and changes the shape of the stain, it's called a wipe pattern. Example: The end of a scarf drags through a pool of blood as the assailant leaves the scene of a murder.

Where do I see it?

CSI, episode 121, demonstrates a wave pattern from a medium-velocity attack with a hammer.

How can I use it?

Remnants of whatever wiped through the blood may be present and could tell you something about the people involved. For instance, let's assume that some fibers from the scarf are found in the wipe. We test the fibers and discover that they are wool — not just any wool, but alpaca wool from an alpaca farm in Arizona. You can trace where that wool was sold, who bought the wool, and who spun it into yarn. Find out where was the yarn was sold, who bought it, who knitted it into a scarf, and who has the scarf now. Bingo. You have your assailant.

■ *Exercise 1.*

Try a little blood spatter experiment for yourself. Instructions for the experiment and how to make fake blood can be found at: *http://www.chymist.com/ BLOODSTAIN%20PATTERNS.pdf*

■ *Exercise 2.*

Watch the pilot episode of *Dexter*. See how many blood spatter terms you can identify and list from this chapter.

■ *Exercise 3.*

When you create your next fictional crime, use blood spatter to give the investigator at least two pieces of key information about the victim and criminal. Use one or more of the bloodstain patterns listed to help investigators solve the crime.

VII.
Gabbing about Guns

"One loves to possess arms, though they hope never to have occasion for them." — *Thomas Jefferson*

The firearm is by far the weapon of choice for most TV and film criminals. On camera they are a visually appealing symbol of power and destruction. Firearms evoke an aura as menacing as the criminal pulling the trigger. When someone flashes a knife, we sense danger, but when someone flashes a gun, the stakes immediately skyrocket to life threatening.

This chapter begins by assuming you have little or no knowledge of firearms. It starts from the ground up discussing the six basic types of firearms, types of gun actions and bullets, and definitions of the main parts of a gun so you can understand how a gun operates. If you've never learned about guns or need a refresher, begin at the beginning.

If you have knowledge of guns and how they work, then skip over the first couple of sections and head to the section addressing how forensic science is applied to firearms. Here you will find information on bullet trajectories, bullet and firearm comparisons, gunshot residue, and more. If you're looking for how bullet wounds affect the body, see the Coroner Chat chapter.

There are hundreds of brands and models of guns, but just seven class types: muskets, shotguns, rifles, pistols, revolvers, fully automatics, and dummy guns. Use this section as a reference to study up on firearm basics; then take it to the next level by investing in *The Shooter's Bible*, arguably the best firearm and ammunition guide out there. It's a candy shop for firearm aficionados ... or those wanting to be.

FIREARMS: COMMON TYPES

Dummy Firearms

What is it?

Dummy firearms are prop guns. They are inoperative firearms, nonworking replicas of any type of firearm used for theatrical purposes. They cannot shoot real ammo.

Where do I see it?

An alien pawnshop owner displays an array of extra-terrestrial firearms in *Men in Black*.

How can I use it?

Use them for theatrical performances, TV, or film. Create real-life effects of shootings using special effects, makeup, and costuming.

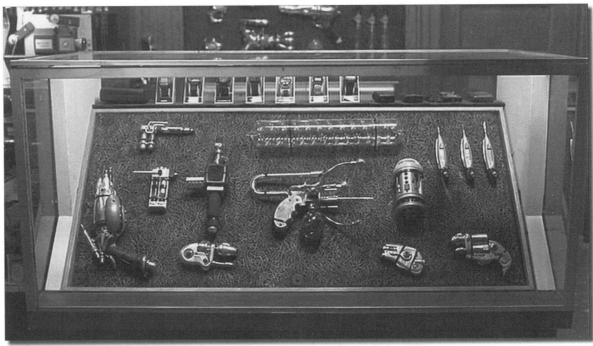

Pawn shop display of extraterrestrial weapons. *Men In Black*, Columbia Pictures, 1997.

Fully Automatic

What is it?

Fully automatic guns keep firing from the moment you press the trigger until you release it. Think machine guns, Gatling guns, and MP5s. They can spray an area and hit more of the target than with other guns. Automatics are used mostly by the police, the military, and, of course, the mob.

Where do I see it?

Shooters surround a criminal who bears his automatic in the pilot episode of *Burn Notice*.

How can I use it?

Automatic guns leave wounds that look like multiple rifle wounds.

Thug with a fully automatic gun. *Burn Notice* pilot; USA Network, 2007.

Muskets

What is it?

Muskets are the first type of guns invented, and they're still popular with gamesmen and war reenactors. They are loaded one shot at a time. Instead of using bullets, the musket is loaded with black powder and a round lead ball the size of the barrel. A flintlock creates a spark, which ignites the powder. Today, a regular primer can replace the flintlock. In muskets, you adjust the fire charge by how much powder is loaded into the barrel. The more powder, the more velocity the ball has in reaching its target. Of course, too much powder and you'll blow up your gun. A musket has a thicker barrel than a shotgun and can withstand higher pressure and, therefore, has greater velocity and distance than shotguns.

Where do I see it?

Ned (Lee Pace) finds a musket pushed between his legs when he makes a visit to Chuck's aunts in *Pushing Daisies*, "Corpscicle."

How can I use it?

Bullet wounds made by a musket have a single round hole at the entrance and exit site.

Ned finds a musket between his legs when he visits Charlotte's aunts. *Pushing Daisies*, "Corpscicle"; ABC, 2007–09.

Pistols

What is it?

Pistols are semiautomatic handguns. You pull the trigger, it releases a bullet, another bullet slides into the chamber, and you pull the trigger again to shoot another bullet. Pistols are fed their ammo automatically by a magazine. Magazines are rectangular or banana-shaped and typically hold seven to fifteen bullets. When a bullet is fired, the receiver slides back, throwing out the empty cartridge and loading the next bullet automatically. Pistols are considered handguns and are small enough to carry easily, some in pockets or handbags.

Where do I see it?

Martin Blank (John Cusack) and Grocer (Dan Aykroyd) engage in a pistol shootout in the final action scene of *Grosse Pointe Blank*.

How can I use it?

A pistol leaves a single entry and exit hole.

Blank and Grocer pull their pistols on each other during a gun fight. *Grosse Pointe Blank*, Buena Vista Pictures, 1997.

Revolvers

What is it?

The revolver is another type of handgun that came into existence around the mid-1800s. Revolvers can be single shots, requiring reloading after each shot. Or they carry multiple shots, as in the early 1800s cylinders. Revolvers contain multiple shots in the cylinder. The cylinder holds the bullets and revolves the chamber to line up with the muzzle so that it can shoot the next round. Typically revolvers will hold five to six bullets. Some call it the most reliable of all handguns because very little can jam in a revolver. Revolvers are used in the game of Russian roulette, with all chambers empty except one.

Where do I see it?

The prosecuting attorney holds up Andy Dufresne's (Tim Robbins) revolver during his trial in the opening of *The Shawshank Redemption*.

How can I use it?

Being shot with a revolver looks like a single entry and exit hole unless it's placed against the head. When this happens, the force of the explosion causes the scalp to split on entry and exit.

Defense attorney holds up a revolver to prove his case in Andy Dufresne's murder trial. *Shawshank Redemption*, Castle Rock Entertainment, 1994.

Rifles

What is it?

A rifle is like a shotgun except that it has a thicker barrel and deep, spiral-shaped grooves that spiral inside the barrel. Rifles shoot single bullets, not shells that contain hundreds of pellets inside. Grooves cause the bullet to spin, giving it higher velocity. The spinning gives the bullet a gyroscopic stabilizing action that keeps the bullet straight on course. Otherwise it might wobble, tumble, or yaw. Unlike shotguns, rifle bullets do not contain a wad. A single bullet is expelled out of the gun and moved singularly to its target.

Where do I see it?

A shooter loads his rifle in *Monk*, "Mr. Monk and the Captain's Wife."

How can I use it?

A rifle shot would leave a single entry hole or it may completely destroy or remove parts of the body depending on velocity and distance. Velocities over 2,500 feet per second act like an explosion that creates a cavity when the bullet hits the target.

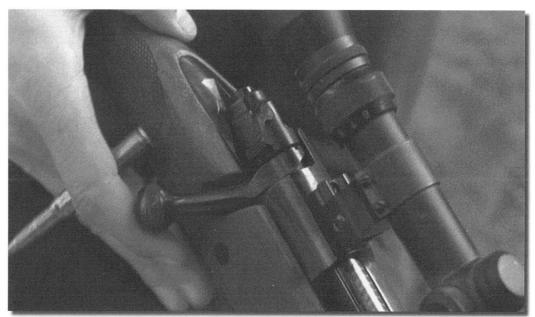

Shooter loading his rifle. *Monk*, Universal, 2002–09.

Shotguns

What is it?

A shotgun is an all-purpose gun. You don't need as much skill to operate a shotgun. Your goal is to point, not aim. The shotgun shoots a long shell packed with pellets of varying sizes. A regular round contains nine pellets. Magnum rounds carry twelve pellets. Sometimes this shell is a slug, which is a single ounce of lead (lead ball), instead of many pellets. After the bullet is released, a hot spray of pellets exits the barrel and sprays out towards the target.

Where do I see it?

A shotgun is mounted in the back seat of Bolger's (Tim Blake Nelson) car as he escorts Billy Kincaid (Edward Norton) to his home in the film, *Leaves of Grass*.

How can I use it?

A person shot with a shotgun would have multiple holes or small bruises because the pellets disperse and spread out as they hit their target. The farther away the gun is, the larger the pellet pattern. They spray out in the same way a showerhead sprays water, more concentrated near the head and dispersed in a wider diameter farther away from the head.

Bill Kinkaid and Bolger ride with Blake's shotgun in the rear window. *Leaves of Grass*, Millennium Films & First Look Studios, 2010.

Let's go over the basic construction of a firearm part by part. Again, if you're not new to firearms, you can use this section as a review or skip over it to the next section on firearms and forensics. I've eliminated the "How do I use it?" section when defining parts, pieces, and bullets because their application is integrated solely in the execution of a firearm. The practical-use section returns in Firearms and Forensics. You'll also note that there isn't a "Where do I see it?" reference for all terms. I've tried to include an image for the terms most helpful to writers employing visual storytelling. For instance, bores, gauges, and breechblocks are part of weaponry and good to learn about. However, we don't usually "see" them in visual storytelling.

FIREARMS: PARTS AND PIECES

Ammo

What is it?

Ammo is short for ammunition. Ammo is what's shot out of a gun to hit a target, commonly referred to as a bullet. There are hundreds of types of ammo. *The Shooter's Bible* is the authoritative resource for what kind of ammo is out there. A new edition is published each year to keep up with shooting products.

Special Agent Seeley Booth and Dr. Temperance Brennan dodge a firestorm of ammo on *Bones*, "The Man on the Fairway"; 20th Century Fox.

Bore

What is it?

The bore is the inside of the barrel before it has been rifled. When you rifle a firearm, it creates a spiral pattern inside the barrel. Think mountains and valleys. The valley is the bore (the original surface) and mountains are the lands (where it has been drilled into a spiral pattern).

Breechblock

What is it?

At the rear of the firearm barrel is a metal piece called the breechblock. It's the place where the cartridge (or bullet) hits as it's being expelled from the gun. The breechblock closes the breech. The pattern made on the back of the cartridge from hitting the breechblock leaves an impression that matches that particular gun.

Bullet

What is it?

We typically refer to the entire piece of ammunition as the bullet. But the bullet is the lead piece that sits atop the casing. The bullet may be flat, round, hollowed, pointy, or jacketed. (See common types of bullets below.)

Butt

What is it?

The butt of the gun refers to rifles and shotguns. This is the bottom of the grip.

The ammunition on the far left shows a bullet and casing intact. The remaining three pieces of ammunition are bullets (on top) separated from their casing (on bottom). Photo by J. Dornbush.

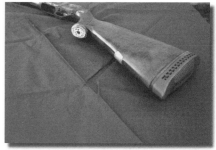

Depicted in this picture is the butt of a shotgun. Photo by J. Dornbush.

Caliber

What is it?

Caliber refers to the bullet size and the diameter inside the barrel of the gun. The diameter is measured on the bore (or original surface). You measure the bore, not the lands, to get caliber. Some are measured in hundredths of an inch, others in millimeters. There are dozens of different caliber guns and bullets. Some of the most common are 9mm, 40mm, .22, 25mm, .38. To get a better idea of the many different caliber bullets, refer to *The Shooter's Bible*.

Casing or Shell

What is it?

The casing is the part of the ammo that holds the primer, wadding, powder, and bullet or pellets. Casings are typically made of brass, nickel, or aluminum. In shotgun shells the material is plastic. Casings come in different lengths and usually have head stamps that indicate size and brand.

Centerfire

What is it?

Centerfire refers to the location of the primer. It means that the primer is located in the center of the base of the casing. The firing pin is positioned to hit the primer in the center to ignite the powder.

Choke

What is it?

Chokes are found on shotguns. The choke is the last few inches of the barrel, which influences the shot dispersion of the pellets. The more constricted the choke, the greater speed and distance the pellets will go.

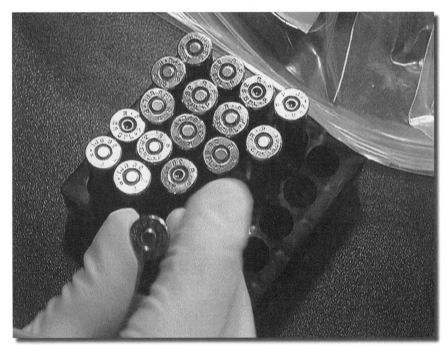

Sara Sidle examines ammunition with centerfire primer. *CSI*, season 1, episode 110; Jerry Bruckheimer TV, 2000.

Ejector Apparatus

What is it?

This is the piece that pushes the cartridge (or bullet) out of the firearm. When the bullet is ejected, the ejector places a mark or scratch in the casing that can be matched back to that firearm.

The ejector apparatus and grip of a semi-automatic gun. Photo by J. Dornbush.

Firing Pin

What is it?

The firing pin works to hit the primer (made of barium and antimony), which ignites the powder and sends the casing or shell out of the barrel.

The firing pin of a semiautomatic gun. Photo by J. Dornbush.

Gauge

What is it?

Gauge refers to the bore diameter and is determined by the number of lead balls in a given diameter. The smaller the barrel diameter is, the higher the gauge. The lower the gauge is, the bigger the diameter of the shotgun. Back in the day, gauge was measured by how many lead balls could fit in the diameter of the barrel and make up a pound. A 12 gauge shotgun barrel could fit 1/12 of a pound of lead balls in its diameter. A 16 gauge shotgun barrel fit 1/16 of a pound of lead in its diameter.

Grip

What is it?

Smaller guns like pistols and other handguns have a grip or a handle. This is where you hold and steady the gun when firing. The grip of a rifle or shotgun is called the stock.

Grooves

What is it?

When a gun barrel is drilled to a hollow tube, the drill creates grooves along the inner surface of the barrel. These grooves are unique to each gun barrel.

Gun Barrel

What is it?

The gun barrel is simply a rod of steel that has been drilled out with lands and grooves. This is the passageway for the bullet to travel and keep stabilized as it heads towards its target.

As Martin Blank fires on an intruder, the explosion from the ignited gunpowder expels from his gun. *Grosse Pointe Blank*, Hollywood Pictures, 1997.

Gunpowder

What is it?

Bullets and cartridges are expelled from the barrel through explosion. The explosion happens inside the casing or cartridge when the firing pin hits the primer, which ignites the gunpowder. The most common gunpowder is black nitro.

Hammer

What is it?

The hammer is at the rear of the barrel and is attached to the pin that strikes the cartridge (or bullet) and ignites the primer.

Turkish waves his revolver in the crime film, *Snatch*. Columbia Pictures, 2000.

Lands

What is it?

When you rifle a firearm, it creates a pattern of lands and bores. Lands are indented into the bore, like spiral rivers along the valley of the bore. Think mountains and rivers. The valley is the bore (the original surface) and the rivers are the lands (where the inside has been drilled into a spiral pattern).

Magazine

What is it?

The magazine is the part of the firearm that houses the bullets before they are fired. Magazines may be built into the gun, as in rifles, or may be detachable, as in semiautomatic firearms.

A punked-out shooter loads the magazine of a pistol in the opening scene of the *Moonlighting* pilot. *Moonlighting* pilot; ABC, 1985–89.

Muzzle

What is it?

The last place the bullet exits is at the very tip of the barrel, called the muzzle. The muzzle places a spin on the bullet so it won't wobble towards its trajectory.

Pellets

What is it?

Pellets are found in ammo for shotguns. They spray out after the cartridge is expelled. Pellets are made of lead or steel and range in size from 9 (the smallest at .08 inches in diameter) to 00 (the largest at .33 inches diameter).

Primer

What is it?

The primer is found at the base of the ammo; when the firing pin triggers it, it ignites the powder causing an explosion. The gases propel the shell or bullet through the barrel of the gun and to the target.

Reloader

What is it?

A reloader is a machine that reloads casings or shells with wadding, powder, bullets, and pellets so you can reuse the bullets. Talk about reduce, reuse, and recycle.

Rifling

What is it?

After the drilling is completed, the gun manufacturer runs a broach cutter in a spiral motion through the barrel to create grooves. This process is called rifling and it's done for two reasons. First, it increases the speed and range of a bullet. And second, it prevents the bullet from yawing (not yawning, which I hope you aren't doing by this point in the chapter). Yawing is when a projectile tumbles end over end. There is no rifling on a shotgun.

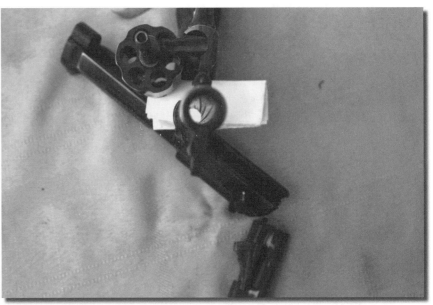

The lines inside the center of the barrel are rifling. Photo by J. Dornbush.

Rimfire

What is it?

Rimfire refers to the location of the primer. It means that the primer is located around the outer rim of the base of the casing. The firing pin is positioned to hit the primer on the outer rim to ignite the powder.

Sights

What is it?

Sights are found on the top of the firearm and assist in aiming at the target. Looking through them gives a proper trajectory toward your target. There are several basic sights: rear, front, open iron, peep, and scope. A scopes is a type of sight that telescopes your view on the target.

Slide

What is it?

The slide is the part of the gun that the bullet lodges into so that it is ready to be fired. When the gun is fired, the slide ejects the spent casing to the rear and loads a new bullet (in semiautomatics). When all the bullets are fired, it locks to the rear.

Martin Blank peers through the sight on his rifle as he prepares for an assassination. *Grosse Pointe Blank*, Hollywood Pictures, 1997.

Striations

What is it?

Striations are simply lines that occur on the inside of the gun barrel from rifling. It's important to note that no two rifling processes look alike. During the process, minute metal protrusions cause striation marks as the broach cutter makes lands. Think of firearms as having faint scars or blemishes along their barrel. Just like no human has the same scars and markings, no two guns have the same striation markings. Thus, this gives each gun individual characteristics (see Individual Characteristics), and when the bullet exits, it carries these lines with it. This is a key method of matching bullets to specific guns.

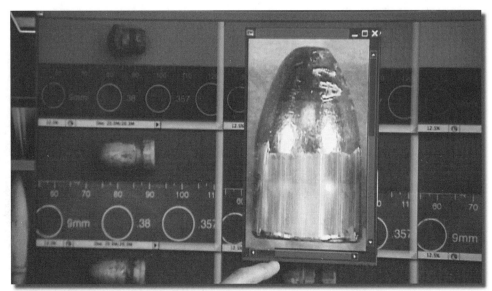

Brennan's anthropology team examines a bullet recovered from a crime scene that contains distinct striations from the gun barrel it passed through. *Bones*, season 1, "Two Bodies in the Lab"; 20th Century Fox, 2006.

Trigger

What is it?

The trigger is the lever under the barrel of the gun, which you press to fire the gun.

Wadding

What is it?

Wadding is found in the cartridge area of shotgun shells. It's made of elastic, felt, plastic, or Styrofoam. Think of it as stuffing that sits between the pellets or powder and bullet.

A shooter is about to pull the trigger. *Monk*, "Monk and the Captain's Wife"; Universal, 2002-09.

This picture shows the wadding found inside shotshell ammo. Photo by J. Dornbush.

As with firearms, there are hundreds of brands and models of ammunition. Use this section as a reference for the basic bullet types; then take it to the next level by investing in *The Shooter's Bible*, where you will find hundreds of types of ammo.

COMMON BULLET TYPES AND HOW THEY AFFECT THEIR TARGET

Ball Bullet

What is it?

The ball bullet has a rounded, spherical top. When shot, it punches a hole through the target but doesn't tear it up. Ball bullets are more humane and therefore sanctioned for military use by international law. They are also called soft point bullets.

Where do I see it?

A clear image of ball bullets is found in the pilot episode of *Moonlighting*, a 1985 TV series starring Cybill Shepherd and Bruce Willis who co-run a private detective agency.

Dummy Bullet

What is it?

A dummy bullet is an empty cartridge used in fictional settings such as theatrical performances, film, and TV. Dummy cartridges do not have primer or powder inside them. The bullet is dead.

Where do I see it?

Frank the Tank (Will Ferrell) accidentally shoots himself in the jugular with a tranquilizer bullet in *Old School*. In the filming of this scene, a dummy tranquilizer dart (same as a dummy bullet) would have been used.

Example of ball bullets and gun. *Moonlighting* pilot; ABC Circle Films, 1985–89.

Frank the Tank accidentally shoots himself with a tranquilizer dart in the jugular. *Old School*, Dreamworks, 2003.

205

Hollow Point Bullet

What is it?

The hollow point bullet is pointed with a hollowed-out middle. When this bullet hits its target, the material it hits flowers out because it catches on the hollow. With the hollow point, the target absorbs more impact, and therefore, more damage is done. The hollow point bullet's top flattens upon impact.

Where do I see it?

Ken Feinman (Josh Pais) waves his gun and carries on about how he has hollow point bullets in his gun in one of the final scenes from *Leaves of Grass*.

Jacketed

What is it?

Jacketed bullets are cream of the crop. A copper layer surrounds the lead bullet to help retain the bullet's shape as it is shot at high velocities. Because lead is a very malleable material, it starts to give and break apart when shot at such high velocity. Sometimes these bullets are referred to as full metal jacket. Typically, jacketed bullets are non-expanding; when they hit the target, they leave a small hole.

Where do I see it?

This photograph shows a copper jacketed bullet torn off the lead part of the bullet after it has been fired.

Ken Feinman waves his gun and yells that he has hollow points. *Leaves of Grass*, Millennium Films & First Look Studios, 2009.

The frayed copper portion shown here is the jacket that was surrounding the lead bullet. Photo by J. Dornbush.

Shotshell Bullets

What is it?

Shotshell bullets are large, flat-topped, and used for hunting game. The primer area is lead, but the casing consists of plastic filled with buckshot or pellets. They are also called shotgun shells, target and field loads, or slugs.

Where do I see it?

A man bent on suicide loads a shell into a shotgun at a gun shop in the opening scene of *Sunshine Cleaning*.

Wad Card Cutter

What is it?

Wad card bullets have flat tops. Shotgun shells and slugs are examples of wad card bullets. When the primer is ignited, it shoots a wad out of the casing. Wad card bullets are cheaper than most bullets and used for target practice, competitions, and on-duty law officers.

Where do I see it?

The picture on this page shows a wad card cutter bullet — aka a shotgun shell.

Shell in hand. *Sunshine Cleaning*, Overture Films, 2008.

Actions: Five Types and How They're Used

Action refers to how the ammo is fed into the chamber.

Single-shot action means that only one bullet at a time is fed into the chamber. You open the bolt, insert the bullet, close the bolt, and fire. The shells remains and needs to be ejected manually before the next bullet can be put into place.

Bolt action uses a magazine that feeds the next bullet into the chamber. Shells or casings are ejected automatically.

Lever action takes out the old bullet and reloads the new. Shells or casings are ejected automatically. The bolt is located underneath the gun.

Gordie defends himself and his friend from their bully Ace. *Stand By Me*, Columbia Pictures, 1986.

Semiautomatic action is found in pistols. You use a magazine to load a round of ammo and pull the trigger. After each release, a new bullet is loaded. The gun fires and reloads as fast as you can pull the trigger. Shells or casing are ejected automatically.

Automatic action is found in machine guns. The gun has a capacity for a great quantity of ammo. Once you pull the trigger, it keeps firing until you stop it. Casings are ejected automatically.

Where do I see it?

In the classic coming-of-age movie, *Stand By Me*, Gordie (Wil Wheaton) uses a single-shot action to defend himself and his friend Chris (River Phoenix) from their bully, Ace (Kiefer Sutherland).

How do they collect gunshot residue? What does a bullet trajectory tell you? Is there such a thing as ballistic fingerprinting? Put it all together in this section where we apply forensic science to firearms and ammunition.

FIREARMS AND FORENSICS

Ballistics Databases

What is it?

DRUGFIRE is an automated firearms database organized by the FBI starting in the early 1990s. It competed with the IBIS system developed by the ATF (Bureau of Alcohol, Tobacco, and Firearms) during the same time period. It focused on capturing and databasing cartridge and case images used in crimes.

IBIS was an automated firearms database organized by the ATF starting in the early 1990s. It competed with the DRUGFIRE system developed by the FBI during the same time period. It focused on capturing and databasing expended (fired) bullets, as well as cartridge and case images used in crimes.

NIBIN

What is it?

In 1999, the ATF and FBI cooperated to create a single system, National Integrated Ballistics Information Network. This system is a database of test-fire entries and ballistics evidence from both IBIS and DRUGFIRE. NIBIN is the AFIS of bullets. But instead of ridges and Galton Details, NIBIN uses the headstamps, the information imprinted on the base of a cartridge that typically indicates the size of the ammo and its manufacturer.

Where do I see it?

In this scene from *Bones*, "Two Bodies in the Lab," Dr. Brennan (Emily Deschanel) uses a ballistics software system to compare bullet striations.

How can I use it?

Today, more than 200 law enforcement agencies all over the world use NIBIN technology. NIBIN contains more than 800,000 casing, cartridge, and bullet images. NIBIN is different from ballistic fingering in that it primarily focuses on matching striation marks on bullet casings to the guns in question.

Computer analysis. *Bones*, "Two Bodies in a Lab"; 20th Century Fox, 2006–present.

Ballistic Fingerprinting

What is it?

Ballistic fingerprinting is a system that is in its infancy. Much like a fingerprint database carries the fingerprints of criminals and those latent prints recovered at a crime scene, so a ballistic fingerprint database would involve compiling a list of casings and cartridges fired at crime scenes, as well as casings and cartridges fired in test rounds from guns used by criminals. The goal is to produce a system that law enforcement could tap into to make matches.

Where do I see it?

You can't see it yet because ballistic fingerprinting is in its infancy. It is a "Coming Soon" attraction.

How can I use it?

Someday it'll be here, but for now prime your imagination to create a fictional universe where ballistic fingerprinting is commonplace, one where matches on casings can happen as instantly as fingerprint matches.

Bullet and Barrel Comparisons

What is it?

Bullet and barrel comparisons have to do with matching the bullet to the particular rifle or gun that it came from (see Rifling earlier in this chapter). A fired bullet bears the pattern of the bores (the raised portions inside the barrel). Firearms examiners perform comparisons.

Where do I see it?

A bullet under the microscope in the opening credits of the *CSI* pilot demonstrates how closely striation markings are examined to find matches to weapons used in crimes.

How can I use it?

Since each barrel is rifled differently, each bullet will carry the markings of that barrel and can be matched back to that rifle. Of course, in order to make the comparison, you have to have both the bullet and the gun that fired it in your possession (see Rifling earlier in chapter). That's why investigators find it so important to recover bullets, casings, and the weapon used for the crime. To make accurate comparisons, investigators fire test bullets from the weapon in question and match them to the found bullets. The exception to this is shotguns. They have smooth barrels and fire cartridges filled with pellets.

What can a firearms examiner tell you about a gun if all she has to go on is the bullet? Using her experience and some comprehensive firearms databases, she can narrow down the search to the type of weapon and caliber of bullet. The FBI has compiled a large database of general rifling characteristics from known firearms.

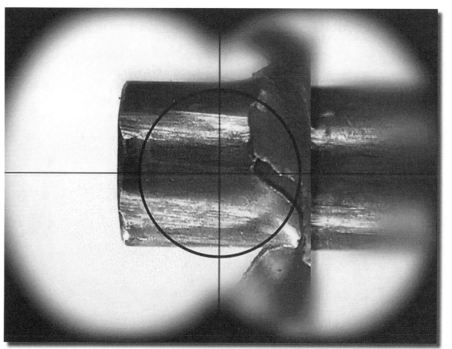

Bullet under microscope in opening credits. *CSI* pilot, opening credits; Jerry Bruckheimer TV, 2000.

Bullet Trajectory

What is it?

Ballistics is often interchanged with the term *firearms*. But the two are very different. Ballistics is the study of the path the bullet takes (its trajectory) to its target.

Where do I see it?

Monk has an uncanny way of determining bullet trajectory in this scene from act one of "Mr. Monk and the Red-Headed Stranger" in season one of *Monk*. Monk sees that the victim's bullet hole and jacket line up. Monk flails his arms to prove that the victim was not raising his arms when he was shot; if he were, the holes from his jacket would not line up to the bullet wound on his body.

How can I use it?

When fired firearms are involved in a crime, CSIs recreate the bullet trajectory to determine where the shooter was standing when he fired. For instance, to find the angle from which a bullet entered a wall, investigators will insert small wooden dowels or aluminum rods into the bullet hole. Using a protractor, they can find the angle, and using trajectory charts, track it back to a point of origin. The oldest method dating back to 1939 is stringing. With this method, string is used to show trajectory lines from the bullet hole to the point of origin. Many investigators argue that stringing is a highly accurate, inexpensive method, one that is easy to demonstrate in court. Today, laser technology is taking over traditional methods because it's highly accurate, saves time, and is easier to set up and take down.

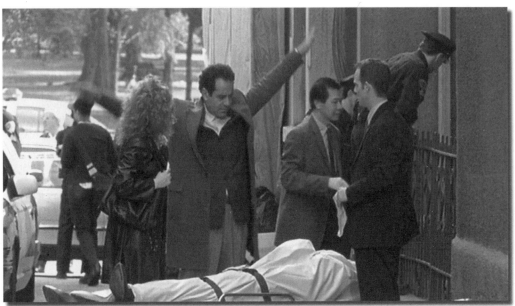

Monk's uncanny way of determining bullet trajectory. *Monk*, "Red-Headed Stranger"; Universal, 2002–09.

Firearm Collection

What is it?

We can't leave this chapter without discussing the proper ways in which to recover bullets, casings, shells, and guns from a crime scene. There is a strict protocol for recovering firearms at the scene of a crime. Safety and evidence retention are top priorities. If you find a firearm at the scene of a crime, do not move the weapon until it has been photographed and documented. Make notes as to its position relative to the other evidence at the scene. When you are given permission to recover it, first make sure that the weapon is safe, meaning that it's not about to fire. With gloves on, pick it up by the grip or trigger guard. Record the gun's serial number, make, model, and how many rounds of ammo are left in the gun. Store items in paper envelopes or bags — not plastic, where condensation can destroy evidence.

Where do I see it?

Lt. Randall Disher (Jason Gray-Stanford) collects a firearm from a suspect's trash in the *Monk* episode, "Mr. Monk and the Captain's Wife." However, even though he wears gloves, Disher manhandles the gun in a way that tampers with fingerprints on the gun.

How can I use it?

Here's how *not* to do it. How many times in cop shows do you see

Disher collects gun. *Monk*, "Mr. Monk and the Captain's Wife"; Universal, 2002–09.

investigators collecting guns by inserting a pencil or stick into the barrel and lifting it from the scene? Knowing what we now know about firearms, why is this a bad idea? Think striation marks. Whatever you stick inside a gun barrel disturbs it and may create new striation marks inside the barrel. You don't want to change the striation markings because when you test fire bullets, they aren't going to match your weapon in question.

GSR: Gunshot Residue

What is it?

When a gun is fired, the primer ignites the powder, which creates gases that propel the bullet. Not all of the powder is burned during this explosion. The leftover or unburned powder puffs out of the cartridge or casing to create gunshot residue (GSR).

Where do I see it?

In this shootout scene from *Call Northside 777*, you can clearly see the gun smoke and residue emitted from the shooters' firearms as they attack a police officer.

How can I use it?

Residue may be found on and collected from a victim's or perp's skin or clothing. GSR can tell us how close the gun was positioned from where it was fired to its target. Look at the distribution pattern of the GSR to determine this. For instance, a halo effect of GSR around a bullet hole indicates that a handgun or rifle was twelve to eighteen inches away. An evenly dispersed, speckled pattern may indicate that the gun was up to twenty-five inches away when fired. A bullet wipe is a type of residue left around a bullet hole that is fired from a rifle or handgun more than three feet from the target. You won't find GSR on the target, but what does appear is a dark ring around the hole made up of lead from the bullet's surface, dirt, primer, lubricant, and carbon.

Gangsters kill a cop in a cloud of gun smoke and residue. *Call Northside 777*, 20th century Fox, 1948.

Range

What is it?

In forensic terms, range refers to how close the victim was to the firearm when it was fired. Ranges are classified in three ways: contact, close, and distant. Contact is touching the victim. Close range is twelve to eighteen inches or less. Distant range is greater than eighteen inches for pistols and greater than six feet for rifles and shotguns.

Where do I see it?

A surprised Will Smith, Agent J, watches Tommy Lee Jones, Agent K, draw his otherworldly weapon at close range on an extraterrestrial in a pawn shop, *Men in Black*.

How can I use it?

Range of fire has differing effects on the human body. It may cause concentric or radiating fractures, decapitation, smudging, stippling, stellate patterning, or tattooing. You'll find information on all of these and how to identify range based on a victim's injuries in the Coroner Chat chapter of this book.

Extraterrestrial weapon collection in a pawnshop that the MIB investigate. *Men in Black*, Columbia Pictures, 1997.

■ *Exercise 1.*

If you don't know much about guns, familiarize yourself with guns and ammo with hands-on activities. Visit a gun shop. Spend some time looking around and talking to the employees and owner about the types of guns they sell. Take a field trip to a local firing range. Many offer lessons for newbies and are eager to educate visitors about gun use. Many shooting ranges offer Ladies Night. Gather a group of girlfriends and go shooting. If there are no gun shops close to you, pick up a copy of the *Speer Reloading Manual*, a hefty reference guide to ballistics. It lists the latest in firearms and ammo. Spend some time online at *NRA.com* or *American Rifleman.org*.

■ *Exercise 2.*

Select two or three of your favorite procedural shows and review the episodes for one season. Make a list of how murders occurred and which weapons were used. How do investigators collect the weapons? How important is ballistics to the investigation? Are bullet comparisons conducted? How often do the investigators swab for and test gunshot residue? Do you see opportunities in these shows to do more forensically with ballistics and firearms? If you were writing the show, where would you add this or how would you do it differently?

VIII.
Courtroom Confabulation

"The real significance of crime is in its being a breach of faith with the community of mankind." — *Joseph Conrad*

Forensic science deals with science as it is applied to the law. Eventually, the evidence recovered from a crime and the persons investigating it may end up in a court of law. If your story moves into judicial territory, it's helpful to know something about this arena. Who are the key players? What are they responsible for? What are some common legal terms? During a trial, what happens first, second, third? And is the CSI effect real? This chapter acquaints you with courtroom people and procedures. For our purposes, in this chapter we'll focus on criminal, rather than civil or federal, trials.

Who should be present in your courtroom scenes and why?

KEY PLAYERS IN A TRIAL

The Judge

What is it?

Think of a judge like a referee at a baseball game. She controls the shape of the game, making sure the rules are followed and that all parties play fairly to ensure that justice is served. In the courtroom, she has several distinct responsibilities during a trial. She maintains order in the courtroom. She determines what evidence can be used in the case. The judge advises the jury on the law and how to apply it to the case. The judge looks at all the facts, guides the jury, and determines the sentence for the convicted defendant. There are two types of criminal case judges. Trial judges only deliberate over cases. They are not usually involved in any of the pretrial proceedings and are concerned with conducting the actual trial. Calendar court judges may look over twenty to twenty-five cases a day, presiding over all of the transactions that happen before the courtroom trial, from arraignment to pretrial.

Where do I see it?

The judge in the 1962 film *To Kill a Mockingbird* bangs on his gavel as his witness and courtroom get out of hand.

How can I use it?

When writing courtroom scenes, know how to stay within the boundaries of a judge's job. Judges don't decide cases; juries do. When writing a judge character, think about some of the common challenges that a judge faces and build those into the story as moments of conflict. For instance, a judge may deal with attorneys who are not prepared, who talk too much, argue with the witnesses, or disrupt the court. The jury may hang and the judge has to retry the case.

Judge hears case. *To Kill a Mockingbird*, Universal Pictures, 1962.

The Prosecuting Attorney

What is it?

Think of the defense attorney and the prosecuting attorney as the kings in a chess match vying for possession of their case. In criminal cases the prosecuting attorney represents the victim of the crime. It's his job to bring to light the truth about the crime and show how his client (the victim) was harmed. The prosecuting attorney bears the burden of proof, which means it's his job to overturn the evidence and testimony presented in favor of the defendant's case. His ultimate goal is to seek justice for the crime committed. If he can do that, he has won the game.

Where do I see it?

The prosecuting attorney, Jim Trotter III (Lane Smith), questions Mona Lisa Vito (Marisa Tomei) in the 1992 film, *My Cousin Vinny*.

How can I use it?

More often than not in legal dramas or courtroom thrillers, the prosecutor is your hero. A hero needs a goal and central conflict, right? Let me make it easy for you. The prosecutor protagonist's sole goal is justice. This may mean putting away the bad guy. The central conflict becomes how he accomplishes this goal. During the course of the story he thwarts all sorts of obstacles to prove his case. He finds the best witnesses and evidence. His own life and livelihood are threatened. In the end, he proves the guilt of his client beyond a reasonable doubt and wins the case. A good prosecutor knows his case, listens to witnesses' answers, and knows when less is more.

Trotter questions Mona Lisa. *My Cousin Vinny*, 20th Century Fox, 1992.

The Defense Attorney

What is it?

Think of the defense attorney and the prosecuting attorney as the kings in a chess match vying for possession of the case. In criminal cases the defendant's attorney represents the person who allegedly committed the crime. It's his job to bring to light the truth about the crime and show how his client (the victim) is not guilty of some or all of the things of which he is being accused. His ultimate goal is to set reasonable doubt that his client committed the crime and reduce any negative results or accusations placed on his client. If he can do that and his client receives a lesser sentence or is freed, he has won the game. His client finds justice. He becomes a hero.

Where do I see it?

Defense attorney Atticus Finch (Gregory Peck) listens to witness testimony with his client in *To Kill a Mockingbird*, 1962.

How can I use it?

A little less common, but just as interesting in courtroom stories, is the protagonist as defense attorney. If the defense attorney is your protagonist, his sole goal in the story is to prove the innocence of a client wrongly accused. His central conflict is how he accomplishes this goal. During the course of the story he thwarts all sorts of obstacles to prove his client's innocence. He finds the best witnesses and evidence. His own life and livelihood are threatened. In the end, he proves the innocence of his client beyond a reasonable doubt and wins the case. His client goes free. He becomes a hero. A good defense attorney is an astute student of human nature, can be pleasant in unpleasant situations, asks intelligible questions, and knows when less is more.

Atticus Finch listens to testimony. *To Kill a Mockingbird*, Universal Pictures, 1962.

The Defendant

What is it?

The defendant is the person accused of the crime. The U.S. justice system operates on the principle that people are innocent until proven guilty. It's the prosecutor's job to prove that guilt. The defendant is guaranteed representation by a defense attorney, either self-appointed or appointed by the state.

Where do I see it?

Defendants Stan Rothenstein (Mitchell Whitfield) and Bill Gambini (Ralph Macchio) wait eagerly during their pretrial hearing in the 1992 film, *My Cousin Vinny*.

How can I use it?

The defendants in your story may be guilty, like Dawson and Downey in *A Few Good Men*, or may have been wrongly accused, like Dr. Richard Kimble in *The Fugitive*. Whether or not you create a guilty defendant, the trick in great storytelling is to sow those seeds of doubt in his character. Whether guilty or innocent, give him access to the victim and the murder weapon, and a motivation for doing it that will keep your audience guessing. Tip: A common mistake defendants make in the courtroom is that they want to testify. Once they do, this usually sows doubt about the defendant's innocence in the minds of the jury. Smart defendants keep quiet and cooperate with their attorneys.

Two defendants in pretrial hearing. *My Cousin Vinny*, 20th Century Fox, 1992.

The Plaintiff

What is it?

Avoid the mistake of using the term *plaintiff* in criminal trials. Plaintiffs belong in civil trials. This is the person who files the complaint — the one who claims that she has been wronged and is requesting a trial to resolve matters. In criminal trials this is called prosecution, and it consists of an attorney or legal team who files a claim on behalf of the victim of a crime.

Where do I see it?

A teenaged plaintiff Eddie Sims (Michael J. Fox) and his girlfriend Carla B. (Rita Taggart) plead their case to Judge Harry T. Stone (Harry Anderson) in the TV series *Night Court*, "Santa Goes Downtown."

How can I use it?

Think of the plaintiff as the person who seeks justice because a wrong has been done to him. A landlord cheated him of his security deposit. A car dealer sold him a lemon. A business owner finds his property defaced by graffiti. When creating a case in which the plaintiff is a main character, remember that he carries the burden of proof. Build a solid case by using the three points of proof. For example, the plaintiff should be able to show that the defendant had access to him, access to the method of delivering the crime, and motivation for the wrongdoing.

Sims and girlfriend. *Night Court*, "Santa Goes Downtown"; NBC, 1984–92, Warner Brothers TV.

The Victim/Victim's Family

What is it?

The victim and her family may or may not play a role in the trial. They may be called upon to testify. They may not. They may be present. They may not. The victim's presence may be only in memory and photographs or it may be a live, physical appearance. One thing is certain: the presence of the victim (if alive) and her family creates a highly charged emotional element in the courtroom. After all, they are the reason why the trial is taking place, they have the greatest interest in the outcome of justice, and they may feel its effects most heavily.

Where do I see it?

The alleged rape victim, Mayella Violet Ewell (Collin Wilcox), and her father, Bob Ewell (James Anderson), await the verdict at Tom Robinson's (Brock Peters) trial in *To Kill a Mockingbird*, 1962.

How can I use it?

Use the emotional angle that a victim and her family feel to raise the stakes of your scenes and introduce tension, anticipation, despair, anger, exuberance, or relief.

Mayella and her father, Bob Ewell. *To Kill a Mockingbird*, Universal Pictures, 1962.

The Witnesses

What is it?

During the trial, each side presents witnesses that shed light on the case, the crime, the victim, and the defendant. Witness testimony is considered evidence.

Where do I see it?

A disgruntled Mona Lisa Vito (Marisa Tomei) serves as an expert witness to help her fiancé, Vinny Gambini (Joe Pesci), win his case in *My Cousin Vinny*.

How can I use it?

Because you are trying to create tension and conflict, your witnesses should deliver either good or poor testimony. Good testimony is clear, easy to understand, clever, even witty. A good witness listens to the questions being asked and speaks slowly. Poor witness testimony is difficult to hear or understand. Poor witnesses try to embellish the facts or impress the courtroom with their hubris. Poor witnesses dance around the question or answer what they think the jury wants to hear.

The Bailiff

What is it?

The bailiff (often a deputy sheriff) is the bouncer of the courtroom. He keeps order, protects witnesses, and guards defendants. His other main job is maintaining custody of the jury. Just as there is a chain of custody for evidence, there are protocols that the jury must follow during a trial so that jurors don't come into direct contact with the defendant, plaintiff, attorneys, or witnesses.

Where do I see it?

The bailiff (Bill Coates) in *My Cousin Vinny* calls the court to rise as the judge enters.

How can I use it?

When things go as they should, the bailiff keeps the jury together, takes roll, and protects them from outsiders during the trial. He maintains safety in the courtroom and serves as liaison between the judge and the jury. If there is disorder in the courtroom, he has the authority to break up scuffles and draw his gun. If you want to shake things up for the safety of your jurors and fictional courtroom, expose a weak link in your bailiff character.

Marisa Tomei serves as an expert witness. *My Cousin Vinny*, 20th Century Fox, 1992.

Bailiff announces judge. *My Cousin Vinny*, 20th Century Fox, 1992.

Court Clerk

What is it?

Think of the clerk as the assistant to the courtroom, its judge, attorneys, and witnesses. She keeps track of exhibits, submitted evidence, court orders, and other important documents. She also swears in the witnesses and keeps a record of what happens in the courtroom every day.

Where do I see it?

The court clerk (Jill Jane Clements) announces the Gambini/Rothenstein case in the pretrial hearing of *My Cousin Vinny*.

How can I use it?

A lot of importance is given to judges, attorneys, witnesses, and jurors, but don't neglect the power of the courtroom clerk. She is privy to every piece of evidence and sensitive material in the case. As a character in your story, the clerk could feasibly tamper with evidence submitted. She could slip in new evidence or leave out a key piece of information in her daily report.

Court Reporter

What is it?

The court reporter sits near the judge, in earshot of the witnesses and attorneys, to record every word spoken during the trial.

Where do I see it?

The court reporter in *My Cousin Vinny* faithfully transcribes the proceedings of the Gambini/Rothenstein murder trial.

How can I use it?

Being the eyes and ears of the courtroom has its advantages. The reporter catches everything that happens. She is a silent but potent observer, probably second only to the judge. Find ways to involve her in your crime story, maybe not inside the courtroom, but outside. A journalist bribes her for an illegal copy of the transcript. A court reporter discovers a loophole that the prosecutor didn't catch and reveals it to him because she wants to see the defendant put away. Don't resort to making your court reporter just a fixture in your set piece. Like they say, it's always the quiet ones.

Court clerk announces case. *My Cousin Vinny*, 20th Century Fox, 1992.

Court reporter documenting proceedings. *My Cousin Vinny*, 20th Century Fox, 1992.

The Jury

What is it?

A jury of twelve members deliberates over criminal, and sometimes civil, cases to hear evidence and decide if the defendant is guilty or not. The defense attorney and the prosecuting attorney choose them. Juries ruling in civil cases must be requested for the court, and the plaintiff or defendant often pays out-of-pocket fees for a jury trial.

Where do I see it?

Wendell Rohr (Dustin Hoffman) addresses the jury in the 2003 film, *Runaway Jury*.

How can I use it?

In a civil trial, only three-fourths of the jury need to reach a verdict. In a criminal trial, all twelve members must reach the same verdict. What happens if the jury can't reach a verdict? They can claim a mistrial and another jury may be selected to try the case. The same judge retries the case.

Wendell Rohr addresses the jury. *Runaway Jury*, 20th Century Fox, New Regency Pictures, 2003.

Want a great example of the trial process and a few good laughs along the way? Watch *My Cousin Vinny*. This movie is literally structured around the criminal trial process from arrest to arraignment to verdict. The only thing missing is the sentencing because, as we all know, Vinny wins his case and his clients are not convicted. Also, *My Cousin Vinny* does not address jury selection. For a solid example of jury selection, watch *Runaway Jury*. It's a bit of a stretch from real-life jury selection, but you'll get the idea.

WHAT HAPPENS IN A CRIMINAL TRIAL?

Jury Selection

What is it?

Also called *voir dire*, the jury-selection process takes place in the courtroom and can last up to several days. Defense and prosecution choose from a pool of about forty jurors who are ordinary citizens like you and me. Both attorneys must agree on each juror. Additionally, two alternate jurors are chosen who listen to the case but are not allowed to deliberate on it. What are attorneys looking for in jurors? Generally, they want people who can listen to both sides, be unbiased, and evaluate testimony. They tend to shy away from people who see things in black and white, are quick to pre-judge, and hold extreme views.

Where do I see it?

Nicholas Easter (John Cusack) awaits jury selection in the 2003 film, *Runaway Jury*.

How can I use it?

Juries are the lifeblood of a trial. Since they make the final verdict, the future of the defendant is in their hands. Use this to add tension to your trial. Is there a moment when something said in the trial turns a jury member toward or away from a guilty verdict? How do jury members' personalities affect the outcome? Do stronger personalities prevail? Is someone on the jury engaging in subversive bullying or bribery? Who on the jury is convinced more by emotion? Who is convinced more by facts?

Nicholas Easter awaits jury selection. *Runaway Jury*, 20th Century Fox, New Regency Pictures, 2003.

Opening Statements

What is it?

As the trial begins, the prosecution opens the trial with a speech in which she lays out the charges against the defendant. Her main goal is to lay pipe to lead the jury to see that the defendant committed the crime against her client. The defense attorney may speak next or may defer his opening speech until he opens his case. The main goal of his statement is to convince the jury that the defendant is innocent of some or all of the charges.

Where do I see it?

Defense attorney Vinny Gambini (Joe Pesci) gives his opening statements in the Gambini/Rothenstein murder trial in *My Cousin Vinny*.

How can I use it?

Opening statements offer a story-cheat opportunity. As a writer, you can lay a lot of story pipe quickly as each attorney introduces his side of the case and evidence. Make each character's opening statement strong (unless you're trying to show that one of the attorneys is unprepared or ill-equipped). Don't tip your hat as to which party is going to win. Start your characters strong. In presenting the main points of evidence via the opening statement, we know where the story is headed and what's at stake.

Vinny gives his opening statement. *My Cousin Vinny*, 20th Century Fox, 1992.

Presentation of Evidence

What is it?

The main course of the trial comes after the opening statements. Again, the prosecution starts this part of the trial, presenting his evidence and witness testimony. The defense is then allowed to cross-examine the prosecution's witnesses. The prosecution now has another chance to reexamine his witnesses and then rests his case. Next, the defense can ask the judge to dismiss the case if she believes that the prosecution has failed to show that her client is guilty beyond a reasonable doubt. But this rarely happens, and the trial continues. Next, the defense attorney brings her evidence and key witnesses. The prosecution is allowed to cross-examine the witnesses. The defense may reexamine them and then rest her case.

Where do I see it?

The prosecuting attorney in *Legally Blonde* presents a male swimsuit as evidence that Brooke (Ali Larter) and her pool boy were having an affair.

How can I use it?

The presentation of evidence is like a highly charged tango. Sometimes the female dancer carries the dance; sometimes the male dancer has the upper hand. And so it goes in trial, back and forth between the defense and the prosecution. First, know how the dance works in the courtroom if you plan to include a trial in your writing. Then add tension between the two attorneys, remembering that they are both equally good and equally flawed. Give them each victories and successes during the trial. Give them each minor failures before one of them loses the *big* battle.

Pool boy's uniform as evidence. *Legally Blonde*, MGM, 2001.

Closing Argument

What is it?

The closing argument is a bookend to the trial. This is when the prosecution reminds the jury of the facts of the case and the consequences of the crime on the victim and others. After he has done this, the defense continues to tear apart the evidence against the defendant and tries to convince the jury that the prosecution's case is bogus. In our court system, the prosecution gets the last word. He can choose to make a rebuttal of the defense's statement and close the trial.

Where do I see it?

Wendell Rohr (Dustin Hoffman) gives his closing arguments in *Runaway Jury*, 2003.

How can I use it?

If your characters have been dancing well, they should end strongly and with completion. We get a deeper satisfaction from watching a closely fought football game than one in which the teams are unequally matched. This is the last great battle of the story, the last time we'll see the defense and prosecution at each other's throats. Make it count. Make it memorable. Make it well matched.

Wendell Rohr gives his closing arguments. *Runaway Jury*, 20th Century Fox, New Regency Pictures, 2003.

Jury Deliberates

What is it?

After the case has been presented, the jury resides together in private to decide if the defendant is guilty or not guilty of some or all of the charges. The jurists don't do this alone. The judge instructs them how to apply the law to the case at hand. Juries are allowed to deliberate as long as it takes to make a decision. If a jury cannot reach a unanimous verdict, the jury is considered hung. To the defendant, a hung jury means no conviction. The judge declares a mistrial and the case may either be dismissed or retried with a new jury. The foreman of the jury leads the deliberating process. If the jury is hung and the decision is made to retry, the same judge must retry the case sixty days later.

Where do I see it?

The jury takes a vote on the murder case they are trying in *12 Angry Men*, 1957.

How can I use it?

Deliberating a case could be an entire movie or mini-series itself, as *12 Angry Men* so brilliantly demonstrates. Here is an arena ripe with character development. Stir in twelve different personalities and twelve different points of view and you have endless conflict and tension. The biggest challenge will be how to resolve it and come up with a verdict. And you do need a verdict. Unlike the real world, in story-land you can't leave your audience hanging . . . pun intended.

Jury deliberates a murder case. *12 Angry Men*, MGM, 1957.

Verdict

What is it?

Once a jury reaches a verdict, the court is reassembled and the head juror reads the verdict out loud to the court.

Where do I see it?

The jury reaches a verdict in the rape case of Tom Robinson in *To Kill a Mockingbird*, 1962.

How can I use it?

If you are involved in a court trial, the verdict is a turning point for all involved. And it should be in your story world, too. For your characters, there is life before this moment and life after. To whom is this moment most important? That will depend on what POV you are using. Are you telling this story from the POV of the victim's mother? The defendant? The prosecutor? What does life after this moment mean for your main character? Does your story start with this moment? Is the verdict the midpoint? Or is it the all-hope-is-lost moment at the end of act two? Maybe you reserve the verdict for the climactic moment just pages before your story ends and loose ends are tied up.

The foreman of the jury in *12 Angry Men* presents the jury's verdict. *12 Angry Men*, MGM, 1957.

Sentencing

What is it?

In a criminal case, the defendant receives his sentence through a sentencing hearing or from a judge. This does not happen immediately after the jury trial, but several weeks or months later. In civil cases, sentencing happens immediately after the trial. Several things the court may consider in sentencing a defendant are: How remorseful is he? How severe was the crime? What is the defendant's criminal past and what are his personal circumstances?

Where do I see it?

Andy Dufresne receives two life sentences for murders he did not commit in the opening scene of *The Shawshank Redemption*.

How can I use it?

The sentencing scene is one of those pivotal moments in your story when a defendant can become unhinged or a victim's family can experience relief or outrage (if the sentence is not long). You may find yourself writing this moment at the close of your story to sum up what happens with the characters and case. You may find that this moment kicks off your story as in *The Shawshank Redemption*, which follows Andy Dufresne through the hardships of prison life.

Andy Dufresne receives two life sentences for murders he did not commit. *The Shawshank Redemption*, Castle Rock Entertainment, 1994.

For anyone who has seen a legal procedural or tuned into *Judge Judy*, the terms in this section will be familiar. So you have an armchair knowledge of TV law. Can you accurately define preponderance of evidence or pro se representation? (You aren't allowed to answer if you're a lawyer!) This section will give you the law lingo needed to write brilliant courtroom scenes and more deeply appreciate the twists and turns of legal thrillers.

COMMON LEGAL TERMS

Admissible Evidence

What is it?

Admissible evidence is the evidence that can be presented in the courtroom during the trial. The judge has the final say on what can be admitted. Generally, it needs to be relevant, reliable, and related to the case. One step further, admissible evidence has to add a fact to the case or have the probability to add a fact that otherwise wouldn't be there if the evidence was left out. Admissible evidence has to have documentation. What was the chain of custody? Under what circumstances was a witness's testimony gathered? How do we know that a forensic sample wasn't contaminated? Who took photographs or video and how were they recorded? Types of evidence that may be admitted include eyewitness, expert witness, circumstantial, direct, trace, physical, and biological evidence. For definitions of these, refer to the Chew the Fat with CSIs chapter. When *does* a judge refuse evidence? See Inadmissible Evidence.

Where do I see it?

Vinny Gambini (Joe Pesci) arrives home with a box full of admissible evidence that Trotter (Lane Smith) has given him to be used in his cousin's case in *My Cousin Vinny*.

How can I use it?

Attorneys and judges spend hours of pretrial time determining what evidence can be admitted. You may not want to take so much story time delving into the minutia of admissible evidence. But you could select one key piece of evidence and create a dispute surrounding its admission. The outcome of this fight (moderated and decided by the judge) provides a win for either your protagonist or antagonist. It also gives us insight as to how your judge character handles conflict and fairness, which will be important as the story unfolds.

Trotter's files. *My Cousin Vinny*, 20th Century Fox, 1992.

Allocution

What is it?

Before the judge offers the defendant his sentence, the accused is allowed to address the judge. In this speech, the defendant may offer reasons for committing the crime, any unknown facts pertaining to the case, and an apology or statement of remorse for the crime.

Where do I see it?

Mark Whitacre (Matt Damon) addresses the judge with his allocution and apology at the end of his trial in *The Informant*.

How can I use it?

An allocution may provide closure of the crime you've created. As a reader or viewer, it can provide some closure or completion to the story, just as it would in real life for a victim and his family. Writing an allocution scene in your story gives your criminal character a chance to speak her mind. We may get new information from her that didn't come out in the trial. She may shed some light on her motivations and how she feels now about her acts. This may be a very personal, intense, and intimate moment in your story.

Mark Whitacre gives his allocution. *The Informant*, Warner Bros., 2009.

Arraignment

What is it?

At the arraignment the person accused of a crime hears a list of the charges, pleads guilty or not guilty, and is given the opportunity to request an attorney. If he can't afford one, the state selects one for him. The judge then sets bail and schedules the next step of proceedings, preliminary hearings.

Where do I see it?

In the arraignment scene in *My Cousin Vinny*, Vinny Gambini (Joe Pesci) has a hard time pronouncing his clients not guilty and ultimately lands himself in contempt of court.

How can I use it?

Writing a brief arraignment scene is a good device for laying story pipe and character development. Right away we learn who the person is, something about him, and where the case is headed. In this scene you, as writer, can hit us on the head with his name, his birth date, his home, and what he's being accused of — car theft, child abuse, rape, murder.

Bench Trial

What is it?

A bench trial is conducted before a judge with no jury. Usually these are civil trials, not criminal, unless the defense and the prosecution agree to waive rights to a jury trial. A bench trial may be held in a criminal case if the defendant has issues with insanity, the witness pool is weak, or the case involves complicated issues that may go over jury members' heads. Typically, bench trials are quicker and less burdensome to the court system.

Where do I see it?

Dan Fielding (John Larroquette) and Public Defender Liz Williams (Paula Kelly) confer with Judge T. Harry Stone (Harry Anderson) in this classic sitcom from 1984, *Night Court*, about a civil courtroom in Manhattan that tries cases 24/7.

How can I use it?

Including a bench trial in your story is probably best introduced as a choice that a defendant is forced to make. One reason she may want a bench trial is because she knows that the judge on her case is lenient and she is hoping for a lesser sentence. Or perhaps the prosecution is pushing for a bench trial, but the defendant believes she can garner more compassion from a jury.

Dan Fielding and Public Defender Liz Williams confer with Judge T. Harry Stone. *Night Court*, "Santa Goes Downtown"; Warner Bros., 1984–92.

Beyond a Reasonable Doubt

What is it?

If there is any uncertainty based on the evidence presented that the defendant did not commit the crime, there exists a reasonable doubt and the defendant cannot be convicted. It is the prosecutor's job to find and remove that doubt so the defendant will be convicted.

Where do I see it?

The judge explains to the jury how they must find a verdict beyond a reasonable doubt in the opening scene from *12 Angry Men*, 1957.

How can I use it?

As a writer you choose what evidence and testimony the prosecutor and defense has access to. What power! You create the crime, the characters, the case. With so much information, how do you (in the form of your characters, evidence, witnesses, and testimony) narrow it down to decide the case?

All your prosecutor needs to do is to find that *one* piece of evidence that erases any doubt in the minds of the jury that the defendant is guilty.

All your defense attorney needs to do is to counter with *one* piece of evidence or testimony that worms doubt into the minds of the jury. This is exactly what happened in the O. J. Simpson trial. Because evidence found at the scene was not transmitted from the crime scene to the crime lab until the next day, this planted a seed of reasonable doubt that the evidence *could have* been tampered with overnight. That little seed let O. J. off the hook, even though the rest of the evidence pointed a guilty finger at him.

Judge explains reasonable doubt. *12 Angry Men*, MGM, 1957.

Civil Trial

What is it?

A civil trial involves a non-criminal case in which an injury or a loss of money, property, or civil rights has occurred. The person filing the complaint is usually an individual and is called the plaintiff. If found guilty, the defendant never goes to jail, but has to reimburse the plaintiff for damages.

Where do I see it?

Judge Harry T. Stone (Harry Anderson) deliberates with his staff on *Night Court*, a sitcom that ran from 1984 to 1992 and was set in a civil courtroom in Manhattan.

How can I use it?

Civil trials are important and in some cases necessary, but the stakes are much lower than in criminal ones. If you include a civil trial in your story, you aren't dealing with the high stakes of rape or murder. But this doesn't mean that the stakes aren't important to your protagonist. When an injustice has occurred, your hero goes on a journey to right his wronged world. He may seek a fair ruling in a civil court. It may be successful and he wins the case. Or he may lose and have to find redemption by other means. Remember, in civil trials the defendant can be found guilty if there is a 50% or higher probability that the offense more than likely happened.

Judge Stone deliberates with his staff. *Night Court*, "Death Threat"; Warner Bros. TV, 1984–91.

Contempt of Court

What is it?

When a person in the courtroom goes against the rules of court established by the judge, he is in contempt of court. This usually involves some unruly or belligerent behavior that interrupts the trial in session or makes some accusation against the judge. It may also be withholding evidence or other important documents needed to try the case.

Where do I see it?

Vinny Gambini finds himself in contempt of court and then in jail for his lack of proper attire in *My Cousin Vinny*.

How can I use it?

What happens if someone is in contempt of court? The court may file charges against her and she may be punished likewise. If your character acts out in court and is charged with contempt of court, it will change the outcome of the trial, cast that character in a negative light, and give the audience more information about that character. This provides an emotional moment for our audience. They may cheer for a character who stands up for something or experience disappointment when a character jeopardizes the justice process.

Vinny gets jailed because of his attire. *My Cousin Vinny*, 20th Century Fox, 1992.

Criminal Trial

What is it?

A criminal trial involves deliberating a case in which a felony or misdemeanor has been committed. The case is filed on behalf of the government, referred to as the prosecution. If found guilty, the defendant pays a fine, is sentenced to jail, or given the death penalty.

Where do I see it?

In *12 Angry Men* the jury tries a felony case of murder.

How can I use it?

Criminal trials involve high stakes. People's lives have been lost or severely damaged and, as a result, the defendant's life is held in the balance. Nothing is more intense than watching the fate of someone's life unfold. Whether you are writing a courtroom thriller or just incorporating excerpts of a criminal trial into your story, the courtroom arena is by nature a battlefield. The conflict is innate. It's hero against villain and there will be casualties. A few tips when writing criminal trial scenes: Keep the evidence and testimony relevant. Lock in the main conflict between prosecutor and defense. Decide who your casualties are and make them fall hard. Maintain fairness, but let justice win in the end. But don't think that means the jury or judge has to administer the justice — they only rule based on reasonable doubt. Sometimes justice arrives post-trial, and recourse follows. Decide if you want a moment of reconciliation and redemption for either hero or villain. This is the moment your hero answers the questions: What was the purpose of all this? Through this journey, did we change anything for the better?

Courtroom. *12 Angry Men*, MGM, 1957.

CSI Effect

What is it?

The *CSI* franchise, which started in the 1990s, has been credited and criticized for creating the CSI effect. The CSI effect is a theory positing that jurors have increased expectations about science presented in the courtroom because of shows like *CSI* and *Forensic Files*. Prosecutors, attorneys, and judges have expressed concern that jurors who watch *CSI* demand elaborate scientific evidence in the courtroom. They think that *CSI*-watching jurors have been fooled into thinking that forensic science evidence should be high-tech and impressive. According to some studies, about 40% of the science in *CSI* doesn't actually exist.

Where do I see it?

The CSI effect happens when normal everyday citizens consume a steady diet of crime and forensics shows and then think they are forensic experts because of what they have seen on TV.

How can I use it?

Several academic studies conducted in the last six years *seem* to prove that the CSI effect is valid. *CSI* viewers enter courtrooms thinking that forensic science is more accurate and more technically advanced than it actually is. According to these studies, those who watch *CSI* believe they have a good understanding of forensics and feel better prepared to examine forensic evidence than non-*CSI* watchers.

At the end of the day, much to the relief of judges and lawyers, other studies show that *CSI* viewers are *not* more likely to deliver guilty or acquittal verdicts than non-*CSI* viewers. So reports about the CSI effect are mixed. "CSI" jurors are more confident about their knowledge of forensics, but this doesn't seem to have a bearing on how they decide cases.

Crime scene tape across a crime scene. *CSI* pilot; Jerry Bruckheimer TV, 2000.

Discoverable Evidence

What is it?

Discoverable evidence is the evidence that each side unearths before the trial in order to prove the defendant's guilt or innocence. It is admitted to the judge prior to the trial, and both sides have the opportunity to review it. No secrets. The biggest factor in determining if discoverable evidence can be admissible is that it has to be relevant to the case and should serve to lead a jury towards a fair verdict. If a judge feels it is misleading, stirs up prejudice, wastes time in court, or confuses the jury, it probably won't make the cut. Some examples of discoverable evidence are depositions, peer reviews, physical evidence, pictures, videos, interrogation reports, medical examiners' reports, doctors' statements, and eyewitness statements.

Where do I see it?

Vinny (Joe Pesci) and Trotter (Lane Smith) explain to the judge why they want a certain piece of evidence added to the trial in *My Cousin Vinny*.

How can I use it?

Prosecutors and defense attorneys have to turn over all discoverable evidence before the case begins. However, they don't have to reveal rebuttal evidence. Rebuttal evidence contradicts or works to disprove the evidence presented. Use rebuttal evidence as a turning-point moment in your legal thriller. Have a prosecutor bring to light information about the defendant that he didn't previously know. The defense attorney tries to smother it with his own rebuttal evidence. Surprise! This keeps everyone in the story guessing — your characters and your audience.

Lawyers conversing with judge. *My Cousin Vinny*, 20th Century Fox, 1992.

Felony

What is it?

A felony is the most serious level of crime with which a person can be charged. It is punishable by imprisonment in a state or federal prison and possibly death. Examples of felonies are robbery, grand theft, rape, arson, illegal drug sales, and murder.

Where do I see it?

Willie Nelson stands for a lineup after he's been detained in a felony homicide charge during the episode of *Monk*, "Mr. Monk and the Red-Headed Stranger."

How can I use it?

Determining the level of crime that your antagonist commits is the first step toward deciding what your story is about. The more serious the crime is, the higher the stakes, the better the drama. You'll be hard pressed to find a crime story in which the villain has committed a misdemeanor. Weak. Stick to the felonies.

Willie Nelson in a lineup. *Monk*, "Mr. Monk and the Red-Headed Stranger"; Universal, 2002-09.

Hearsay

What is it?

Information told to one person by another is hearsay. For instance, a shooting crime occurs and a neighbor witnesses a man running from the house across the street. A police officer interviews the neighbor later for his account of what turns out to be a murder. What the neighbor tells the cop is considered hearsay. The cop didn't actually see it, but the neighbor telling the story did. When the cop writes down the neighbor's account, this written record becomes secondhand hearsay. Hearsay evidence is not accepted in court.

Where do I see it?

All the reports about Chutney's dad's murder were just hearsay until Elle (Reese Witherspoon) gets Chutney (Linda Cardellini) to confess to accidentally killing her father in the trial scene in *Legally Blonde*.

How can I use it?

While hearsay evidence is not admissible in court, your investigator or attorney may use it to explore new leads, new witnesses, and new evidence. The report serves as a guide or tool for the case. It's a starting point. This is also why it's so important that first responders and police officers are thorough and accurate in their reporting. It's easy to overlook details and fail to report them.

It's not hearsay if they confess! *Legally Blonde*, MGM, 2001.

Inadmissible Evidence

What is it?

According to the Federal Rules of Evidence, evidence is prohibited from being presented in a trial when it's in danger of causing unfair prejudice, confusing the issues at hand, misleading the jury, creating undue delay of the case, wasting the time of the court, or needlessly presenting duplicate or cumulative evidence. Inadmissible evidence is evidence that was gathered illegally or without a chain of custody. Hearsay is not admissible. The testimony of an expert who is presenting facts or opinions not accepted in his field of practice is not admissible. What kind of evidence *does* a judge allow? See Admissible Evidence.

Where do I see it?

In this scene from *Kojak*, a police officer is wired to record evidence in a drug case. Let's hope he got permission first or his hard-earned evidence may get thrown out of court as inadmissible.

How can I use it?

One of the most common misunderstandings about inadmissible evidence on TV is the police report. Police reports are not admissible because they are hearsay. Think about it. A police officer arrives on the scene and asks several witnesses for their version of what they saw and heard. The police officer's report is secondhand knowledge. Avoid making the mistake of having an attorney present the police report in trial.

Getting wired to track evidence. *Kojak*; CBS 1973-78.

In Limine Motions

What is it?

In limine (pronounced limonay) means "at the threshold," and in court it refers to limiting evidence or testimony. In limine motions are presented before the trial begins. The prosecutor or defense attorney can present this motion to the judge, and that will affect what is presented as acceptable evidence during the trial. Each is concerned with allowing only evidence and testimony that is relevant to the case. The judge then decides to accept or reject this motion.

Where do I see it?

In this scene from *My Cousin Vinny*, Judge Chamberlain Haller (Fred Gwynne) explains to Vinny Gambini (Joe Pesci) the evidence under consideration for Bill and Stan's trial.

How can I use it?

If you are creating a legal mystery, writing an in limine scene is a great place to lay story pipe. You can set up the stakes and rules of the trial so that the characters know what's expected of them and your audience will understand when someone is playing fair or stepping out of bounds. You can also establish the rules of your story world and introduce the audience to insights about the characters that they wouldn't necessarily learn from a trial. For instance, the fact that the defendant was a gang member may not be important to the case being tried, and a judge may set an in limine motion on this information. But now that you know his past, the chances are that it'll come back to bite someone. You've not only sown plot, but also foreshadowed something dark about your defendant.

Vinny meets with judge. *My Cousin Vinny*, 20th Century Fox, 1992.

Misdemeanor

What is it?

A misdemeanor is a crime of lesser offense than a felony and is not punishable by death. Criminals committing misdemeanors pay fines and serve time in county or local jails. A misdemeanor is still a serious offense, categorized into classes from least to most serious. Misdemeanors include driving under the influence, graffiti of non-federal property, use of a false ID, trespassing, indecent exposure, and possession of illegal drugs.

Where do I see it?

In *Old School*, Frank the Tank (Will Ferrell) gets drunk and goes streaking after a frat party. Both public intoxication and indecent exposure would be considered a misdemeanor offense. Fortunately for Frank, the only authorities who catch him are his wife, Marissa (Perrey Reeves), and her friends.

How can I use it?

Misdemeanors don't make for high-drama crime stories. Save these for your softer dramas or comedies where the stakes of the story don't depend on the seriousness of the crime and putting the bad guy away. Misdemeanor offenses can give a comedy or light drama a story device that allows the protagonist to build on a weakness and handle a new adversity.

Frank the Tank goes streaking, a misdemeanor offense. *Old School*, DreamWorks, 2003.

Personal Knowledge

What is it?

Personal knowledge means that the witness must know something about the occurrence he is going to testify about and that he is competent to testify to that matter. He has to have eyewitness knowledge. This has to be shown to the court before the witness is put on the stand.

Where do I see it?

In a scene from *Legally Blonde*, Elle (Reese Witherspoon) visits murder suspect Brooke (Ali Larter) and learns a tidbit of personal knowledge about her witness. Brooke has a valid alibi for the time of her husband's murder.

How can I use it?

When an attorney interviews potential witnesses, she will test them to see if they are relying on firsthand knowledge or just hearsay. Your prosecutor or defense attorney character can quickly put holes in a witness's testimony by showing how he didn't actually see or hear something critical to the crime.

Preliminary Hearing

What is it?

After the arraignment the judge looks at the evidence from the prosecution and determines if it's adequate to put the defendant on trial for the crime.

Where do I see it?

In *Anatomy of a Murder*, Paul Biegler (James Stewart) attends a preliminary hearing on a murder case that he is representing.

How can I use it?

As a writer you can use this step of the process to cast doubt on the case, either by the defense or the judge. This will make your prosecutor have to work harder to prove the burden of evidence against the defendant.

Friend tells Elle her alibi but Elle can't reveal. *Legally Blonde*, MGM, 2001.

Biegler talks to the judge about his client in preliminary hearing. *Anatomy of a Murder*, Columbia Pictures, 1959.

Preponderance of Evidence

What is it?

Preponderance of evidence is relevant to civil trials. Although this chapter doesn't address civil trials, I mention it in order to compare it to reasonable doubt. In civil trials the plaintiff must prove a case by preponderance of evidence, not beyond reasonable doubt. In civil trials it's the plaintiff's job to prove the offense at hand. He has to give enough probable or accurate proof to show that the offense *more likely than not* happened. Sometimes judges put it in terms of percentages. It has to be 51% or more likely that the defendant cheated the plaintiff of his apartment security deposit. If so, the ruling goes to the plaintiff.

Where do I see it?

In "The Eye of the Beholder" episode from *Night Court*, Dan Fielding (John Larroquette) defends a prostitute and her pimp in Judge Harry's civil court. Fielding wants to prove with a 51% or more possibility that his clients are innocent of their charges.

How can I use it?

If you find your character in a civil suit, remember that you only need to show a 51% probability that the offense happened. This offers a lot of leeway in showing how far your character has to go to prove her innocence or the defendant's guilt.

Night Court, "The Eye of the Beholder"; Warner Bros. TV, 1984-91.

Pretrial Hearing

What is it?

After the preliminary hearing the defense attorney and prosecutor appear before the judge and try to pick apart evidence and witness testimony in a pretrial hearing. This is a dress rehearsal to see if the case should be tried. Attorneys may even practice saying certain things they would say in court. While conducting the pretrial, the judge still holds the authority to determine whether there is sufficient persuasive evidence to try the case or whether to dismiss it.

Where do I see it?

During a pretrial hearing, a witness states to the prosecuting attorney, Trotter, what she saw the day of the murder in *My Cousin Vinny*.

How can I use it?

Audience members don't generally attend dress rehearsals of plays, and since a pretrial is like a dress rehearsal, you don't need to drag us through it. Usually there isn't enough screen time for a pretrial, it's not as dramatic as the real trial, and the duplication of information would bore an audience. However, here are a few instances when you could use a pretrial hearing to build suspense about the upcoming case. Show a flaw in the prosecutor's case that a judge asks him to correct. This becomes an obstacle that your prosecutor must overcome. A pretrial scene could also become a compare-and-contrast device. Show a competent defense attorney in pretrial who later crumbles under the pressure of the real trial and has to rebound. We know he can because we saw him do it in pretrial. Or make the pretrial story point centered around chain of custody, when a piece of evidence used in pretrial turns up missing during the real trial.

Pretrial starts here, reviewing first witnesses. *My Cousin Vinny*, 20th Century Fox, 1992.

Pro Se Representation

What is it?

The defendant has the right to waive an appointed attorney and represent himself. *Pro se* is Latin meaning "for oneself." The law for this is found in U.S. Code, 28 USC Chapter 111, section 1654, and states that anyone may conduct his or her own case personally.

Where do I see it?

A porn star plaintiff pleads her case to Judge Harry T. Stone (Harry Anderson) in the TV series *Night Court*, "The Eye of the Beholder."

How can I use it?

If you want to create a character who wishes to represent herself, here are a few real-life motivations for doing this: lack of finances to hire an attorney, wanting to be in control of one's circumstances, and feeling that one is better served by oneself because she knows her situation the best.

Real-life fact about *pro se*: The economic downturn of the last decade has led to an increase in *pro se* representation, according to an American Bar Association 2010 study of 1,200 judges. Unfortunately, *pro se* seems to backfire on most people. The average Joe fails to provide necessary evidence, doesn't know how to act properly in court procedures, and fails to object to evidence. As a result, such cases clog the court system and fill the court dockets.

A plaintiff porn star pleads her case. *Night Court*, "The Eye of the Beholder"; Warner Bros., TV, 1984–92.

Keep this in mind if you write a character who goes *pro se*. You could create a character who has her legal ducks in a row. Or one whose lack of legal know-how eats him alive during the trial. Maybe going *pro se* is a way to demonstrate your character's growth? By the end of act two, he fails because of his courtroom ignorance, but by act three he's learned from his mistakes, sought counsel, and become a legal leviathan.

Reports

What is it?

Reports are the accounts of an event or crime as told by the eyewitness to an official working on the case. Reports are considered secondhand hearsay. Common reports taken from crime scenes are police reports and interviews, the CSI's study of the crime scene, and the death certificate and medical examiner's report.

Where do I see it?

Vinny Gambini (Joe Pesci) visits a witness to gather his own report of what she saw the day of the murder in *My Cousin Vinny*.

How can I use it?

Since most crimes won't go to trial for months after they occur, reports offer handy reminders of how an offense happened. It would be very difficult for law enforcement and other forensic professionals to remember the minutia of a crime in exact detail. This is also why it's important for those involved in reporting a crime to take good notes and write complete reports. Reports can be subpoenaed for court evidence, but it's always better if the witness or expert takes the stand and explains what happened.

Vinny gets report from woman. *My Cousin Vinny*, 20th Century Fox, 1992.

Swearing of Witnesses

What is it?

When a witness takes the stand, he is asked by the bailiff or court clerk to state his name and swear an oath to the court to tell the truth. Typically, the question is phrased like this: "Do you swear to tell the whole truth and nothing but the truth, so help you God?" Some states require the witness to place his right hand on the Bible and swear by the Bible to tell the truth. In other states, you can opt out of the Bible swearing by affirming to tell the truth. This version asks: "Do you affirm to tell the whole truth and nothing but the truth under the pains and penalties of perjury?" Promising to do either one places an obligation on a witness's conscience and makes him liable to perjury charges if he should lie on the stand.

Many others take similar oaths in court: prospective jurors, jurors, bailiffs, interpreters, and reporters. Children are not required to take the oath. They are told of the importance of telling the truth, but they don't have to swear to it on a Bible.

Where do I see it?

Mayella Violet Ewell (Collin Wilcox) is sworn in before her testimony in *To Kill a Mockingbird*.

How can I use it?

What if a witness doesn't tell the whole truth and nothing but the truth? This is not just a sin of omission or a little white lie. In court this is called perjury. Courts treat perjury as a very serious offense because the oath has been broken. The court has been lied to. The trial has been soiled by such lies and the outcome may be greatly affected. Perjury may be considered a misdemeanor or felony and the offender could serve jail time if prosecuted.

Witness swears in. *To Kill a Mockingbird*, Universal Pictures, 1962.

In creating your fictional trial, you might consider introducing a witness who perjures. Her motivation for doing so could be to prolong the trial, to create a mistrial, or to discredit another witness. In doing any of these, you have given the audience a new nugget about the case, you have made a character revelation, you have furthered the mystery of the plot, and you have added more tension and conflict to the story.

Witness Testimony

What is it?

A witness is a person called to testify in a trial who has some knowledge pertaining to the case that will be helpful to the defense or prosecution. Witness testimony may be expert, firsthand, hearsay, character, or reputation. Expert witnesses — such as CSIs, fingerprint specialists, and medical examiners — have a professional stake in the case. They are put on the stand to explain a crime scene, shed light on a piece of evidence, or expand on the manner and mode of how a victim was killed. Firsthand witnesses are people who actually saw the crime committed and are there to bear witness to what they observed and experienced. Character or reputation witnesses are people who have or had a relationship with the defendant or victim. They are called on to bear witness to the character of the defendant or victim.

Where do I see it?

Defense attorney Vinny Gambini (Joe Pesci) challenges a witness who said she saw the defendants leaving the Sac-O-Suds in *My Cousin Vinny*. His challenge turns the case in favor of his clients and gives him the confidence he needs to win the case.

How can I use it?

When writing a character who has to testify on the witness stand, keep these guidelines in mind as to what makes for good or bad testimony. Write according to character.

Good Court Testimony:

Making eye contact with the attorney

Answering confidently

Testifying only about what was seen, heard, smelled, tasted, or felt

Correcting any errors you start to make

Speaking in a clear tone and at a normal pace

Being confident and assured

Waiting for the attorney to ask the entire question before answering

Using proper address — your honor, judge, sir, Ms., Mr., Madam

Avoiding gum chewing, fidgeting, phone use, hands in pockets, wearing sunglasses

Bad Court Testimony:

Shifty eye contact, avoiding eye contact with the attorney

Starting sentences with "I believe ..." or "I'm not sure..."

Guessing or assuming what you saw, heard, smelled, tasted, or felt

Letting errors go and hoping no one catches them

Speaking quickly, softly, or muttering

Appearing overconfident

Interrupting the attorney before he has finished asking the question

Using improper addresses: yo, you, hey, listen, and first names

Jingling keys and coins, playing with your phone, chewing gum, wearing sunglasses, fidgeting

Woman testifies. *My Cousin Vinny*, 20th Century Fox, 1992.

■ *Exercise 1.*

Screen the opening scene of *The Shawshank Redemption*, when Andy Dufresne is on trial for the murders of his wife and her lover. Discuss the following questions based on what you just saw. What pieces of evidence does the defense attorney state were present? What do you consider circumstantial evidence in this case? What do you consider direct evidence? Physical evidence? What kind of gun was used? Was DNA evidence used? What DNA evidence would have been helpful to prove Andy's case? Based on what you saw and what you know about fingerprint deterioration, would investigators have found Andy's fingerprints on the bullets? Who else testified in Andy's case? Do you think it was a good idea for Andy to testify on his own behalf? Based on what we know about the evidence at the scene of the crime from this opening scene, do you think a defense attorney should have allowed Andy to testify? In this scene, why do you think we never hear from the prosecuting attorney?

■ *Exercise 2.*

Visit a public courtroom near you and sit in on a criminal jury trial for one day. Arrive early. Take notes of your surroundings, what you see, hear, the people around you. This is the perfect place to refine your people-watching skills. Who do you think are the family members? The press? Why do you think this? Once the trial gets started, take notes on the attorneys, judge, witnesses, and jury members. Are there any who stand out? What makes them interesting to you? Are there any you identify with? What do you identify with and why? What is the case about? What are the arguments presented from each side? What evidence is presented? How is it presented? Who are the witnesses and how well do they testify? Look at the jury members. Select a few and, based on what you observe about them, write a short character description about who they are, what they like and dislike, what they do for a living. What are they sacrificing while on jury duty? How do you think they will cast their vote in this case and why?

Crime writing is puzzle solving. It's using the left and right sides of the brain. It's crossword puzzle meeting sudoku, logic and pathos. It's an arena pregnant with possibilities and points of view.

At its core, great crime writing and great crime writers are simply searching for justice and meaning in our fallen world. We want to make sense of the endless filth that clogs our headlines, our streets, our courtrooms.

I posit that the great crime stories happen over the perversion of three main things: drugs, sex, and money. Behind them are all-consuming temptations for control, lust, and greed. These are arguably our greatest temptations as humans, and from them stem some of the greatest evils this world can know.

But our stories — real life and fictitious — do not have to end in the pit of darkness. Thankfully, we are all capable of redemption, even those with the blackest of hearts.

Temptation, sin, and redemption; Since the time of Adam and Eve, this trifecta of the human condition has been at the root of all great stories. There will always be temptation. As a result, there will always be crime. And thus, there will always be a need for justice and redemption.

Tell *these* stories, my friends.

Running on about Resources

Chewing the Fat with CSIs

ChoicePoint. Software system for background checks operated by LexisNexis. *http://www.lexisnexis.com/risk/solutions/employment-screening.aspx*

Criminalistics: An Introduction to Forensic Science by Richard Saferstein (seek out current edition). It's an expensive manual (more than $92 new on Amazon, but check out half.com for a used version or your local college bookstore). My forensics mentor, Dr. Janis Cavanaugh prefers this book above all others. It's academic and technical, but not impossible.

Dr. Janis Cavanaugh's Wonderful World of Forensic Science. Go to the site and click on links. There are sixty-nine links to professional forensic science sites. *http://www.janiscavanaugh.com/*

FBI Guide to Collection of Physical Evidence and Crime Scene Investigation. *http://www.fbi.gov*

Forensics R Us. If you are looking for professional, short-term training in crime-scene investigation and fingerprinting, you will want to check this out. There are dozens of links to many professional forensic science sites. *http://www.forensicsrus.com/index.html*

Forensics Demystified by Barry J. Fisher, McGraw-Hill, 2006. This book is the closest thing you'll get to a forensics for dummies. Written by L.A. and N.Y.C. crime lab specialists, it delves into technical detail on many of the same topics as does *Forensic Speak*. A great resource if you want to delve more deeply into a particular forensic topic.

Forensic Recovery of Human Remains: Archaeological Approaches by Tosha L. Dupras, John J. Schultz, Sandra M. Wheeler, and Lana J Williams. Taylor & Frances Group, LLC. 2006. Yes, it's academic and pricey, but a must-have if you're doing hard-core research in forensic anthropology.

Forensic Science Solutions, LLC. If you want an online class on criminal profiling, this is the spot. There is also a bookstore and resource page. *http://www.corpus-delicti.com*

Gizmos & Gadgets. On this site you'll find some wonderful instructions on how to use many of the CSI tools such as directions on how to use Hemastix, dust and lift prints from dark surfaces, and cast shoe impressions from ground covered in snow. *http://www.csigizmos.com/products/toolimpressionmaterial/csds.html*

HemaTrace Instructions. This document examines how to use HemaTrace, a presumptive test for human blood. *http://www.4n6shop.cz/static_pages_files/ file/Hematrace_Forensic%20Science_Silenieks.pdf*

National Institute of Justice, Electronic Crime Scene Investigation: A Guide for First Responders. The government standard for investigating electronic crime scenes. *http://www.ncjrs.gov/pdffiles1/nij/187736.pdf*

Soil Impression Casting with Dental Stone. Provides a nice how-to pictorial. *http://www.evidentcrimescene.com/cata/cast/dscasting.html*

Techniques of Crime Scene Investigation by Barry J. Fisher, CRC PR I Llc, 2003.

Torchered Minds: Case Histories of Notorious Serial Arsonists by Detective Ed Nordskog, Arson/Bomb Investigator, Los Angeles County Sheriff's Department, 2011. I attended an informative seminar Ed gave on arson cases and the profile of an arsonist. His credentials speak for themselves. There may be no better arson investigator on the West Coast than Ed. *http://www.torcheredminds.com*

World of Forensic Science, Gale Cengage Learning, 2005, two-volume book, a little pricey and academic, but worth the investment, especially for researchers.

Where to Purchase CSI Equipment, Forensic Books and Supplies
http://www.evidentcrimescene.com
http://www.forensicsource.com
http://www.lynnpeavey.com
http://www.medtechforensics.com
http://www.sirchie.com

Coroner Chat

AAFS –American Academy of Forensic Science. *http://www.aafs.org/*

Death Detective Dysfunction. This six-chapter report from ProPublica, PBS Frontline, and NPR studied the nation's coroner and medical examiner systems from 2,300 counties in the U.S. for one year. Published February 1, 2011. Links to the chapters can be found here: *http://www.npr.org/2011/02/01/133301436/ the-real-csi-death-detective-dysfunction*

Death in Paradise: An Illustrated History of the Los Angeles County Department of Coroner by Tony Blanche and Brad Schreiber. Running Press, 2001. Just like the title suggests, this is an excellent coffee-table book that provides historical insight into the L.A. Coroner's office and L.A.'s seedier history.

DMORT. This site by the U.S. Department of Health and Human Services explains disaster mortuary operational response team procedures and how to volunteer. *http://www.phe.gov/Preparedness/responders/ndms/teams/Pages/dmort.aspx*

Fictional Medical Examiners & Coroners. Let's hear it for Wikipedia for compiling a list of the top fictional medical examiners and coroners in novels, TV, and film in the past twenty years. *http://en.wikipedia.org/wiki/List_of_fictional_medical_examiners*

Firefighter Autopsy Protocol. The U.S. Fire Administration and FEMA created this document to educate firefighters about what to do with burn victims' bodies. *http://www.nifc.gov/fireInfo/fireInfo_documents/firefighter_autopsy_protocol.pdf*

Forensic Nexus. Forensic Nexus and Dr. Janis Cavanaugh's Wonderful World of Forensics may be the only sites you'll ever need. Forensic Nexus has links to more than 150 forensically related sites. *http://forensicnexus.com/organizations/*

Journal of Forensic Science. This journal is published by the American Academy of Forensic Sciences. Access to articles is limited to subscribers, but you can search and request full articles at your local university or medical library. *http://www.aafs. org/journal-forensic-sciences*

How Cadavers Make Your Car Safer. It's true. Car manufacturers have used human bodies in automobile testing. Warning: Some pictures on these sites are a touch disturbing.
http://jalopnik.com/5622667/how-a-cadaver-made-your-car-safer
http://www.wired.com/autopia/2010/08/how-a-cadaver-made-your-car-safer/

Forensic Science International Journal. You have to be a subscriber, but you can search for abstracts and then request the full article at your local university or medical library. http://www.fsijournal.org/

NAME – National Association of Medical Examiners. There are some colorful links under Medical Examiner/Coroner; my favorite is California Death Investigations, authored by John R. Hain, M.D. in Monterey. Medical examiner by day, meditation counselor by night. http://thename.org/

Post Mortem: Death Investigation in America, PBS Frontline, February 2011, 53:40 minutes. The program is a video version of the six-part print investigation, and it does a very good job of looking at the coroner versus medical examiner system and the flaws of our death investigation systems. http://www.pbs.org/wgbh/pages/frontline/post-mortem/

Spitz & Fisher's Medicolegal Investigation of Death, Guidelines for the Application of Pathology to Crime Investigation by Werner Spitz, Daniel Spitz, and Russell S. Fisher. The bible on death investigation for forensic pathologists and medical examiners. Be forewarned that it is graphic and highly technical.

Stiff: The Curious Lives of Cadavers by Mary Roach, 2004. The history of cadaver use for science and other odd undertakings.

The Black Dahlia Case, as told by the daughter of the forensic psychiatrist on the case. Ms. Jacque Daniels is getting up there in years, and I had the privilege to hear one of her last presentations at the Academy. And she definitely has an opinion on who killed the Black Dahlia. Don't worry, he's not out there anymore. He died in 1977. www.policepscyhiatrist.com

The Effect of Various Coverings on the Rate of Human Decomposition by Angela Madeleine Dautartas, University of Tennessee, Knoxville, Trace: Tennessee Research and Creative Exchange Graduate School. This is Dautartas' master's thesis from August, 2009, so be prepared. http://trace.tennessee.edu/cgi/viewcontent.cgi?article=1098&context=utk_gradthes

Toxicology Tête-à-Tête

Erowid. My toxicologist friend recommended this site to me. What a diamond in the rough. This is a comprehensive site about drugs and drug use. There are entries by drug users that go into detail about drug trips, use, and abuse. http://www.erowid.org/psychoactives/slang/slang.shtml

Encyclopedia of Earth. The section on toxicology is well-written and easy to follow for the lay person. http://www.eoearth.org/article/Toxicology

Forcon – Forensic Toxicology Services. Forcon is a consulting service. If you need to speak with a toxicologist and you don't have one in your contact list, here's an option. Disclaimer: I haven't personally used them. http://www.forcon.ca/index.html

The Poisoner's Handbook by Deborah Blum, Penguin Press, 2010. This gem of a book outlines the history of poisoning.

Black Tar Heroin, NPR report, February 16, 2010. Black tar heroin is on the rise because it's cheap and easy to make. Stay current and remain aware. http://www.npr.org/templates/story/story.php?storyId=123781346

Fingerprint Talk

Automated Fingerprint Identification Systems (AFIS) by Peter Komarinski, with Peter T. Higgins, Kathleen Higgins, and Lisa K. Fox, Elsevier Academic Press, 2005. My fingerprint instructor constructed her entire curriculum from this book, which has been in print for decades. The FBI developed this book to train fingerprint examiners, so it is an industry standard. Let me warn you: This book is *the* source, but your brain will overload if you try to understand it. Get a professional to guide you. It's still important and required to know how to hand-identify fingerprints, despite today's computer technology.

Historic Works on Fingerprints by Fauld, Hershel, Galton *http://www.mugu.com/galton/fingerprints/books/index.htm*

International Association of Identification. This is *the* professional organization for fingerprint examiners, the oldest and largest in the world. *http://www.theiai.org/*

INTERPOL – international police organization. *http://www.interpol.int/INTERPOL-expertise/Forensics/Fingerprints*

Michele Triplett's Fingerprint Terms. Wow! I discovered this site on my own. Later, it was recommended to me by one of L.A.'s top fingerprint specialists. *http://www.fprints.nwlean.net/index.htm*

The Reality of Fingerprinting: Not Like TV Crime Labs. *http://www.livescience.com/technology/080225-real-fingerprinting.html*

Quantitative-Qualitative Analysis of Friction Skin: An Introduction to Basic and Advanced Rideology (Practical Aspects of Criminal & Forensic Investigations) by David R. Ashbaugh. CRC Press, 1999. This is a textbook-quality resource, not cheap, but thorough.

SCAFO – Southern California Association of Fingerprint Officers. *http://www.scafo.org/*

The Science of Fingerprints: Classifications and Uses by the FBI, 1988. This is the FBI's official textbook on fingerprinting. Even though it's more than twenty years old, the FBI still uses it to train fingerprint examiners.

The Weekly Detail, a weekly emailed newsletter for latent print examiners written by latent print examiners discussing cases and updates in the fingerprinting field. Started on August 6, 2001. Anyone can sign up. *http://www.clpex.com/TheDetail.htm*

DNA Lingo

Ask a Geneticist. This highly informative article by Dr. Azita Alizadeh at the Department of Genetics, Stanford University School of Medicine explains what happens to DNA in chimerics, mosaics, and bone-marrow-transplant patients. *http://www.thetech.org/genetics/ask.php?id=208*

Electrophoresis videos, University of Michigan. *http://www.umd.umich.edu/labtv/modules/agarosegel/agarose.html*

DNA Evidence Can Be Fabricated. A *New York Times* article by Andrew Pollack, August,17, 2009 explains how scientists in Tel Aviv fabricated blood samples with real DNA that U.S. labs couldn't detect as fake. *http://www.nytimes.com/2009/08/18/science/18dna.html?_r=3*

Grim Sleeper Case. Read about the first successful use of familial DNA matching in solving a serial murder case in this *LA Times* article, July 10, 2010, by Maura Dolan, Joel Rubin, and Mitchell Landsberg. From this article you'll see a list of archived articles that provide additional background on the case. *http://articles.latimes.com/2010/jul/08/local/la-me-grim-sleeper-20100708*

Want more? Go to the Grim Sleeper website. *http://thegrimsleeper.com/*

How DNA Works video. Check out this cool video on author Stephen C. Meyer's home page that explains how DNA works. His book is called *Signature in the Cell: DNA and the Evidence for Intelligent Design. http://www.signatureinthecell.com*

Using DNA to Solve Crimes: Human Genome Project. The U.S. government's Human Genome Project website lists some unusual uses of DNA testing in solving death investigations of September 11, unknown tombs, and Nicolas Romanov, the murdered last czar of Russia, and even determining wine heritage. *http://www.ornl. gov/sci/techresources/Human_Genome/elsi/forensics.shtml*

Blood Spatter Speak

Blood Patterns: Tools of the Trade. Discovery Channel, F2: Forensic Factor. Ron Englert, a crime-scene reconstructionist, answers questions about what bloodstains can tell you about the crime. Some graphic images, but keep in mind they are reconstructed scenes with live people posing as dead ones. *http://www.discovery-channel.ca/Article.aspx?aid=13278*

Blood Spatter Experiment. David Katz's step-by-step, hands-on experiment helps you understand blood spatter angles. It even includes a formula for making your own blood. *http://www.chymist.com/BLOODSTAIN%20PATTERNS.pdf*

FBI Laboratory Services Bloodstain Terminology. This is the preferred standard list the FBI uses when discussing bloodstain patterns at crime scenes, so everyone is on the same page. This list should help broaden your understanding of blood spatter. *http://www.fbi.gov/about-us/lab/forensic-science-communications/fsc/july2009/ standards/2009_04_standards01.htm/*

Fly spatter. *http://hemospat.com/terminology/index.php?cat=misc&sub=fly-spots*

How Blood Pattern Analysis Works. Found under the website How Stuff Works, this six-part, easy-to-follow tutorial won't certify you as a blood spatter analyst, but will provide you with the basics. *http://science.howstuffworks.com/bloodstain-pattern-analysis.htm*

Gabbing about Guns

American Rifleman. This top-notch resource includes everything you want to know about guns, rifles, ammo, and accessories. It includes many informative videos. *http://www.americanrifleman.org*

American Handgunner. Everything you want to know about handguns will be found here, including a link called Cop Talk to help you authenticate police weapons in your writing. *http://www.americanhandgunner.com/*

ATF – Bureau of Alcohol, Tobacco, Firearms, and Explosives. *http://www.atf.gov/*

Best Guns Website. In this video from World According to Jim, Jim shows you his favorite gun websites and explains what to find and why they are good sites. There is also a list of the websites at this link. The video is 14:45 minutes long. *http://www.youtube.com/user/worldaccordingtojim*

Guns for Dummies by The Late Boy Scout. This six-part YouTube series explains gun basics. It's rather long and a little campy, but informative if you have the patience. *http://www.youtube.com/user/TheLateBoyScout*

How Ammo Is Made. A Hornady company video shows you how rifle ammo is made. *http://www.americanrifleman.org/videos/how-is-ammo-made/*

International Defensive Pistol Association. If you're into pistols or want to learn more about pistols, this is your site. *www.idpa.com*

NRA – National Rifle Association. Information on rifles, shooting, competitions, but also a news and political entity to keep you updated about gun rights. *http://www.nra.com*

The Shooter's Bible by Stoeger Publications. Touted as the world's best firearm reference book, Stoeger has been publishing the bible for eighty years. The 2012 bible was the 103rd edition. It contains every type of legal firearm and ammo that exists. If you had to purchase only one book on firearms, this is the one you need. A must-have for writers, researchers, and those who want to stay current on firearms.

U.S. Handgun Laws. This site has more than just laws. You can research gun news, gun safety, and women's issues regarding firearms (such as shooting when pregnant). It includes a map on the home page, on which you can click on any state and be taken to that state's handgun laws. *http://www.handgunlaw.us*

Courtroom Confabulation

The CSI Effect: Does It Really Exist? by Honorable Donald E. Shelton, National Institute of Justice, March 17, 2008. *http://www.ojp.usdoj.gov/nij/journals/259/csi-effect.htm*

The CSI Effect: Popular Fiction About Forensic Science Affects the Public's Expectations about Real Forensic Science, by N.J. Schweitzer and Michael J. Saks, *Jurimetrics*, Spring, 2007, 357–64.

The CSI Effect: The Truth About Forensic Science, Jeffrey Toobin, *New Yorker*, May 7, 2007. *http://www.newyorker.com/reporting/2007/05/07/070507fa_fact_toobin*

Federal Rules of Evidence. This site is hosted by the Federal Rules of Evidence Review and keeps you current with evidence cases in the U.S. *http://federalevidence.com/rules-of-evidence*

Formal Discovery: Gathering Evidence for Your Trial. Attorney Joseph Matthews lays out a clear explanation of how to gather evidence for a trial on Nolo Network. *http://www.nolo.com/legal-encyclopedia/formal-discovery-gathering-evidence-lawsuit-29764.html*

Miranda Rights. This site explains what Miranda rights are and the difference between admissible evidence and hearsay. *http://www.mirandarights.org/admissibleevidence.html*

NCIC – National Crime Information Center. On this site you can learn about the nineteen different crime files the FBI keeps, read about cases the FBI has cracked, and join the FBI's email update list. You will be sent crime safety tips, stories, scam warnings, and who's been added to the most-wanted list. *http://www.fbi.gov/about-us/cjis/ncic*

U.S. Department of Justice, United States Attorneys Kid's Page. Yes, it's written for kids, but adults can benefit, too. This site walks you through the trial process in nine easy steps with drawings and bolded terms. *http://www.justice.gov/usao/eousa/kidspage/step1.html*

Jen's Fun Forensic Finds

Forensics and Fiction: Clever, Intriguing, and Downright Odd Questions from Crime Writers by D. P. Lyle, M.D. Dr. Lyle answers a lot of unusual questions in this book. I think it's best used as a resource if you are brainstorming or want to jog your idea bank. Dr. Lyle seems like he would also be accessible if you have off-the-wall questions about how people suffer and die.

Forensics and the X-Files. A fan-based website devoted to the *X-Files* show that breaks down the show and forensic science basics. *http://www.x-fileslexicon.com*

L.A. Bizarro, The All-New Insider's Guide to the Obscure, The Absurd, and the Perverse in Los Angeles by Anthony Lovett and Matt Maranian, Chronicle Books, 2009. My husband was given this book as a Christmas gift from a coworker. We thought it was funny and cute until I actually started working my way through this gem. I found things like the Dapper Cadaver, prop shop. Who knows how often that'll come in handy?

USC Medical Library. Wow, wow, and wow. I'm a total library geek to begin with, but this place made me want to enroll in medical school. Located in South Los Angeles, the library is easy to navigate. All the back-issue forensic science journals are located on the lower basement floor. The reference librarians are stellar! One of them took the time to look up and print an article for me that I couldn't access because I'm not a student, alumna, or faculty.

UCLA Biomedical Library. Nestled in the streets of Westwood, California, this library has that government-building look and feel. The reference librarians here were also very helpful, but busier and not able to give me the same kind of individual attention as at USC. However, the librarian I spoke with was able to find my article quickly online, though I had to pay a small fee for this one.

The Black Hand by Chris Blatchford, Harper, 2008. This book is about the Mexican Mafia, its history, influence, and infiltration into the U.S. Blatchford is a news reporter who writes about gangs in Los Angeles.

The Home Scientist. A series of short videos literally from a scientist's home lab that show you how to process forensic fingerprinting or forensic presumptive drug testing. Nerdy, but informative. *http://www.youtube.com/thehomescientist*

The Paley Center for Media Library, Scholar's Room. Located in downtown Beverly Hills, this center is like the CDC (Center for Disease Control) of radio and television. Everything from the first radio waves to the present is here. I must give a shout-out to the most helpful researcher, Martin G. This man is literally a walking encyclopedia of television history. Someone should seriously download his brain into book form. I have to credit Martin for steering me in the right direction to look at old medical and detective shows and for giving me such a passionate history of their development. *http://www.paleycenter.org/*

Working Stiffs: Playing Dead on TV Can Keep a Career on Life Support by Amy Chozick, WSJ, February 9, 2011. Ever thought about acting but you feel kind of stiff in front of the camera? Not a problem. There are dead-body roles for you on the sets of crime shows. *http://online.wsj.com/article/SB10001424052748703439 5045761160926726122366.html?KEYWORDS=working+stiffs*

I'm always finding fun, new forensic gems. Stay updated with my newsletter. Sign up at *www.jenniferdornbush.com*.

Filmography

12 Angry Men, Orion-Nova Productions, United Artists, 1957

Anatomy of a Murder, Columbia Pictures, 1959

Body of Proof, Matthew Gross Entertainment, ABC, 2010–

Bones, Far Field Productions, 20th Century Fox, 2006

Breaking Bad, High Bridge Productions and Gran Via Productions, Sony and AMC, 2008

Call Northside 777, 20th Century Fox, 1948

Castle, Beacon Pictures ABC, 2009–

Chumscrubber, The, Newmarket Films, 2005

CSI, Jerry Bruckheimer TV, CBS, 2000–

Dexter, Showtime, 2006–

Fargo, MGM, 1996

Fugitive, The, Warner Bros., 1993

Grosse Pointe Blank, Buena Vista Pictures, 1997

Homicide: Life on the Street, NBC, 1993–99

Informant, The, Participant Media, Groundswell Productions, Warner Bros., 2009

Kojak, Universal TV, CBS, 1973–78

Law & Order: Criminal Intent, Wolf Films, NBC Universal, 2001

Leaves of Grass, Millennium Films and First Look Studios, 2009

Legally Blonde, Marc Platt Productions, MGM, 2001

Maria Full of Grace, HBO Films, 2008

Men in Black, Columbia Pictures, 1997

Monk, USA Network, Universal, 2002–09

Moonlighting, ABC Circle Films and Picturemaker Productions, ABC, 1985–89

My Cousin Vinny, 20th Century Fox, 1992

NCIS, Belasarius Productions, CBS, 2003–

Night Court, Starry Night Productions, Warner Bros., TV, NBC, 1984–92

Old School, Dreamworks SKG, 2003

Prestige, The, Touchstone and Warner Bros., 2006

Pushing Daisies, Jinks/Cohen Company and Living Dead Guy Productions, ABC, 2007–09

Quincy M.E., Glen A. Larson Productions, Universal NBC, 1976–83

Rear Window, Universal, 1954

Rope, MGM, 1948

Royal Tennenbaums, The, Touchstone Pictures, 2001

Runaway Jury, New Regency Pictures, 20th Century Fox, 2003

Shawshank Redemption, The, Castle Rock Entertainment, Columbia Pictures, 1994

Silkwood, 20th Century Fox, 1983

Six Feet Under, HBO, 2000–05

Snatch, SKA Films and Columbia Pictures, 2000

Splice, Dark Castle, Copperheart, and Gaumont Productions, Warner Bros., 2009

Stand By Me, Columbia Pictures, 1986

Sunshine Cleaning, Overture Films, 2008

To Kill a Mockingbird, Universal International Pictures, 1962

Traffic, USA Films and Universal, 2000

True Grit, Skydance Productions, Paramount, 2010

Veronica Mars, Rob Thomas Productions, UPN, Warner Bros., 2004–07

Weeds, Tilted Productions, Lions Gate, 2006–

For Additional Forensic Viewing

48 Hours Mystery

Autopsy Files, The

Autopsy Series

Biography

Blood Simple

Chuck

Client, The

Closer, The

Compulsion

Courtroom TV

Crime 360

Criminal Intent

Criminal Minds

Crossing Jordan

Death Detectives, The

DOA

Dr. G. Medical Examiner

Dragnet

Erin Brockovich

Firm, The

First 48, The

Forensic Files

Gangland

Gone in Sixty Seconds

Green Mile, The

Hawaii Five-O (original and recent)

Hill Street Blues

Hitchcock, Alfred

Holmes, Sherlock

In Session

Judge Judy

Judging Amy

L.A. Law

Lie to Me

Life

Lock Up

Medium

Naked City

No Country for Old Men

North Mission Road

NYPD 24/7

Plant Evidence, Courtroom TV (May 5, 1992)

Random Hearts

Reefer Madness

Rizzoli & Isles

Royal Pains

Silence of the Lambs

Sixth Sense

Tales of the Texas Rangers (radio)

Trace Evidence

TruTV

Two and a Half Men (CSI crossover episode)

Unnatural Death: Confessions of a Medical Examiner

Usual Suspects, The

Wire, The

Woman's Murder Club

X-Files, The

"Through the memory of death the mind keeps a vigil, it comes to an awareness, and egotistical thoughts and pride flee, cultivating in the soul a humble spirit without vain glory." — *St. Pahomios*

Index

·········

About the Author

Jennifer Dornbush was raised in northern Michigan, the oldest daughter of a medical examiner whose office was in their home. She literally grew up around the dead and, for twenty years, had a courtside view of the forensic world. She and her sisters often assisted on casework and were subject to endless dinnertime case reviews. Other than a few nightmares and therapy sessions, her childhood as a medical examiner's daughter has given Jennifer some very uncanny experiences, good for storytelling. To round out her knowledge of death investigation, Jennifer completed more than 360 hours of CSI training at the Forensic Science Academy and continues to expand her forensic savvy. Her half-hour TV pilot, *Home Bodies,* inspired by her life as a medical examiner's daughter, was awarded Humanitas' New Voices Award. Several of her TV and film scripts have placed at Austin, Nicholl's, and NBC's Writers on the Verge.

Contact Jennifer or sign up for her *Forensic Speak Newsletter* at: *http://www.jenniferdornbush.com*.

SAVE THE CAT! ®
THE LAST BOOK ON SCREENWRITING YOU'LL EVER NEED!

BLAKE SNYDER

BEST SELLER

He's made millions of dollars selling screenplays to Hollywood and now screenwriter Blake Snyder tells all. "Save the Cat!®" is just one of Snyder's many ironclad rules for making your ideas more marketable and your script more satisfying — and saleable, including:
- The four elements of every winning logline.
- The seven immutable laws of screenplay physics.
- The 10 genres and why they're important to your movie.
- Why your Hero must serve your idea.
- Mastering the Beats.
- Mastering the Board to create the Perfect Beast.
- How to get back on track with ironclad and proven rules for script repair.

This ultimate insider's guide reveals the secrets that none dare admit, told by a show biz veteran who's proven that you can sell your script if you can save the cat.

"Imagine what would happen in a town where more writers approached screenwriting the way Blake suggests? My weekend read would dramatically improve, both in sellable/producible content and in discovering new writers who understand the craft of storytelling and can be hired on assignment for ideas we already have in house."
> – From the Foreword by Sheila Hanahan Taylor, Vice President, Development at Zide/Perry Entertainment, whose films include *American Pie, Cats and Dogs, Final Destination*

"One of the most comprehensive and insightful how-to's out there. Save the Cat!® is a must-read for both the novice and the professional screenwriter."
> – Todd Black, Producer, *The Pursuit of Happyness, The Weather Man, S.W.A.T, Alex and Emma, Antwone Fisher*

"Want to know how to be a successful writer in Hollywood? The answers are here. Blake Snyder has written an insider's book that's informative — and funny, too."
> – David Hoberman, Producer, *The Shaggy Dog* (2005), *Raising Helen, Walking Tall, Bringing Down the House, Monk* (TV)

SAVE THE CAT!
The Last Book On Screenwriting You'll Ever Need!

BLAKE SNYDER

BLAKE SNYDER, besides selling million-dollar scripts to both Disney and Spielberg, was one of Hollywood's most successful spec screenwriters. Blake's vision continues on *www.blakesnyder.com*.

$19.95 | 216 PAGES | ORDER NUMBER 34RLS | ISBN: 9781932907001

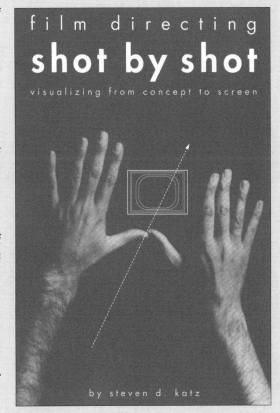

THE SCRIPT-SELLING GAME 2ND EDITION
A HOLLYWOOD INSIDER'S LOOK AT GETTING YOUR SCRIPT SOLD AND PRODUCED

KATHIE FONG YONEDA

The Script-Selling Game is about what they never taught you in film school. This is a look at screenwriting from the other side of the desk — from a buyer who wants to give writers the guidance and advice that will help them to not only elevate their craft but to also provide them with the down-in-the-trenches information of what is expected of them in the script selling marketplace.

It's like having a mentor in the business who answers your questions and provides you with not only valuable information, but real-life examples on how to maneuver your way through the Hollywood labyrinth. While the first edition focused mostly on film and television movies, the second edition includes a new chapter on animation and another on utilizing the Internet to market yourself and find new opportunities, plus an expansive section on submitting for television and cable.

"Kathie Fong Yoneda knows the business of show from every angle and she generously shares her truly comprehensive knowledge — her chapter on the Web and new media is what people need to know! She speaks with the authority of one who's been there, done that, and gone on to put it all down on paper. A true insider's view."

> — Ellen Sandler, former co-executive producer of *Everybody Loves Raymond* and author of *The TV Writer's Workbook*

"I've been writing screenplays for over 20 years. I thought I knew it all — until I read The Script-Selling Game. *The information in Kathie Fong Yoneda's fluid and fun book really enlightened me. It's an invaluable resource for any serious screenwriter."*

> — Michael Ajakwe Jr., Emmy-winning TV producer, *Talk Soup*; Executive Director of Los Angeles Web Series Festival (LAWEBFEST); and creator/writer/director of *Who... and Africabby* (AjakweTV.com)

KATHIE FONG YONEDA has worked in film and television for more than 30 years. She has held executive positions at Disney, Touchstone, Disney TV Animation, Paramount Pictures Television, and Island Pictures, specializing in development and story analysis of both live-action and animation projects. Kathie is an internationally known seminar leader on screenwriting and development and has conducted workshops in France, Germany, Austria, Spain, Ireland, Great Britain, Australia, Indonesia, Thailand, Singapore, and throughout the U.S. and Canada.

$19.95 | 248 PAGES | ORDER NUMBER 161RLS | ISBN: 9781932907919

24 HOURS | 1.800.833.5738 | WWW.MWP.COM

STORY LINE
FINDING GOLD IN YOUR LIFE STORY

JEN GRISANTI

Story Line: Finding Gold in Your Life Story is a practical and spiritual guide to drawing upon your own story and fictionalizing it into your writing. As a Story Consultant and former VP of Current Programs at CBS/Paramount, most of the author's work with writers has focused on creating standout scripts by elevating story. The secret to telling strong story is digging deep inside yourself and utilizing your own life experiences and emotions to connect with the audience. As a television executive, the author asked writers about their personal stories and found that many writers had powerful life experiences, yet had surprisingly never drawn upon these for the sake of their writing because these experiences seemed to hit a little too close to home. This book is about jumping over that hurdle. The goal is not to write a straight autobiographical story which rarely transfers well. Rather, the intention is to dig deep into your well of experience, examine what you have inside, and use it to strengthen your writing. By doing so, you will be able to sell your scripts, find representation, be hired, and win writing competitions.

"Jen Grisanti has spent her entire professional life around writers and writing. Her new book is nothing less than an instruction manual, written from her unique perspective as a creative executive, that seeks to teach neophyte writers how to access their own experiences as fuel for their television and motion picture scripts. It aspires to be for writers what 'the Method' is for actors."

> — Glenn Gordon Caron, writer/creator,
> *Moonlighting, Clean and Sober,*
> *Picture Perfect, Love Affair, Medium*

"Jen Grisanti gets to the heart of what makes us want to be storytellers in the first place — to share something of ourselves and touch the spirits of others in the process. Her book is a powerful and compassionate guide to discovering and developing stories that will enable us to connect — with an audience and with each other."

> — Diane Drake, writer, *What Women Want, Only You*

JEN GRISANTI is a story consultant, independent producer, and the writing instructor for NBC's Writers on the Verge. She was a television executive for 12 years at top studios. She started her career in television and rose through the ranks of Current Programs at Spelling Television Inc. where Aaron Spelling was her mentor for 12 years.

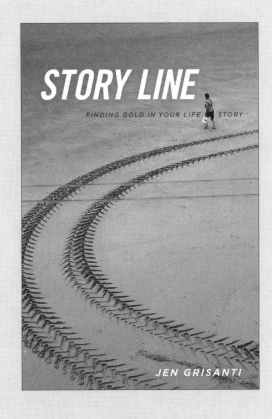

$26.95 | 250 PAGES | ORDER NUMBER 156RLS | ISBN: 9781932907896

24 HOURS | **1.800.833.5738** | **WWW.MWP.COM**

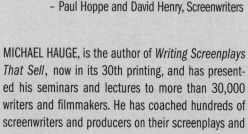

THE HOLLYWOOD STANDARD
2ND EDITION
THE COMPLETE AND AUTHORITATIVE GUIDE TO SCRIPT FORMAT AND STYLE

CHRISTOPHER RILEY

BEST SELLER

This is the book screenwriter Antwone Fisher (*Antwone Fisher*, *Tales from the Script*) insists his writing students at UCLA read. This book convinced John August (*Big Fish*, *Charlie and the Chocolate Factory*) to stop dispensing formatting advice on his popular writing website. His new advice: Consult *The Hollywood Standard*. The book working and aspiring writers keep beside their keyboards and rely on every day. Written by a professional screenwriter whose day job was running the vaunted script shop at Warner Bros., this book is used at USC's School of Cinema, UCLA, and the acclaimed Act One Writing Program in Hollywood, and in screenwriting programs around the world. It is the definitive guide to script format.

The Hollywood Standard describes in clear, vivid prose and hundreds of examples how to format every element of a screenplay or television script. A reference for everyone who writes for the screen, from the novice to the veteran, this is the dictionary of script format, with instructions for formatting everything from the simplest master scene heading to the most complex and challenging musical underwater dream sequence. This new edition includes a quick start guide, plus new chapters on avoiding a dozen deadly formatting mistakes, clarifying the difference between a spec script and production script, and mastering the vital art of proofreading. For the first time, readers will find instructions for formatting instant messages, text messages, email exchanges and caller ID.

"Aspiring writers sometimes wonder why people don't want to read their scripts. Sometimes it's not their story. Sometimes the format distracts. To write a screenplay, you need to learn the science. And this is the best, simplest, easiest to read book to teach you that science. It's the one I recommend to my students at UCLA."

— Antwone Fisher, from the foreword

CHRISTOPHER RILEY is a professional screenwriter working in Hollywood with his wife and writing partner, Kathleen Riley. Together they wrote the 1999 theatrical feature *After the Truth*, a multiple-award-winning German language courtroom thriller.

$24.95 | **208 PAGES** | **ORDER NUMBER 130RLS** | **ISBN: 9781932907636**

CINEMATIC STORYTELLING
THE 100 MOST POWERFUL FILM CONVENTIONS EVERY FILMMAKER MUST KNOW

JENNIFER VAN SIJL

BEST SELLER

How do directors use screen direction to suggest conflict? How do screenwriters exploit film space to show change? How does editing style determine emotional response?

Many first-time writers and directors do not ask these questions. They forego the huge creative resource of the film medium, defaulting to dialog to tell their screen story. Yet most movies are carried by sound and picture. The industry's most successful writers and directors have mastered the cinematic conventions specific to the medium. They have harnessed non-dialog techniques to create some of the most cinematic moments in movie history.

This book is intended to help writers and directors more fully exploit the medium's inherent storytelling devices. It contains 100 non-dialog techniques that have been used by the industry's top writers and directors. From *Metropolis* and *Citizen Kane* to *Dead Man* and *Kill Bill*, the book illustrates — through 500 frame grabs and 75 script excerpts — how the inherent storytelling devices specific to film were exploited.

You will learn:
· How non-dialog film techniques can advance story.
· How master screenwriters exploit cinematic conventions to create powerful scenarios.

"Cinematic Storytelling *scores a direct hit in terms of concise information and perfectly chosen visuals, and it also searches out... and finds... an emotional core that many books of this nature either miss or are afraid of.*"

— Kirsten Sheridan, Director,
Disco Pigs; Co-writer, *In America*

"*Here is a uniquely fresh, accessible, and truly original contribution to the field. Jennifer van Sijll takes her readers in a wholly new direction, integrating aspects of screenwriting with all the film crafts in a way I've never before seen. It is essential reading not only for screenwriters but also for filmmakers of every stripe.*"

— Prof. Richard Walter,
UCLA Screenwriting Chairman

JENNIFER VAN SIJLL has taught film production, film history, and screenwriting. She is currently on the faculty at San Francisco State's Department of Cinema.

$24.95 | 230 PAGES | ORDER NUMBER 35RLS | ISBN: 9781932907056

THE MYTH OF MWP

In a dark time, a light bringer came along, leading the curious and the frustrated to clarity and empowerment. It took the well-guarded secrets out of the hands of the few and made them available to all. It spread a spirit of openness and creative freedom, and built a storehouse of knowledge dedicated to the betterment of the arts.

The essence of the Michael Wiese Productions (MWP) is empowering people who have the burning desire to express themselves creatively. We help them realize their dreams by putting the tools in their hands. We demystify the sometimes secretive worlds of screenwriting, directing, acting, producing, film financing, and other media crafts.

By doing so, we hope to bring forth a realization of 'conscious media' which we define as being positively charged, emphasizing hope and affirming positive values like trust, cooperation, self-empowerment, freedom, and love. Grounded in the deep roots of myth, it aims to be healing both for those who make the art and those who encounter it. It hopes to be transformative for people, opening doors to new possibilities and pulling back veils to reveal hidden worlds.

MWP has built a storehouse of knowledge unequaled in the world, for no other publisher has so many titles on the media arts. Please visit www.mwp.com where you will find many free resources and a 25% discount on our books. Sign up and become part of the wider creative community!

Onward and upward,

Michael Wiese
Publisher/Filmmaker